MW01065886

The Jewish People and Jesus

Is It Time For Reconciliation? You Decide

Joseph A. Butta, Jr. with Steven E. Daskal

AuthorHouse™
1663 Liberty Drive
Bloomington, IN 47403
www.authorhouse.com
Phone: 1-800-839-8640

First published by AuthorHouse 8/19/2010

ISBN: 978-1-4520-3797-4 (e)
ISBN: 978-1-4520-3795-0 (sc)
ISBN: 978-1-4520-3796-7 (hc)

Library of Congress Control Number: 2010908509

Printed in the United States of America
Bloomington, Indiana
This book is printed on acid-free paper.

THE JEWISH PEOPLE AND JESUS
Is it time for reconciliation?
You decide

FOREWORD:

Hello Mishpochah. Perhaps you may be wondering why I used the Hebrew word meaning family. Although I am not Jewish, the Jewish people are often on my mind. Recently after reading the Torah it became apparent to me that we share something special. We share the Tenakh. No two faiths on earth share and revere the same Holy Scripture. I'm not trying to minimize our difference but what we share is nonetheless significant. With this realization I was inspired to write this work. In Our Father's Tenakh I have learned a great deal about you. He loves you and made many promises to you with the caveat that you obey and love him.

As with most families there are occasional problems. After settling in the Promised Land (Canaan) a famine came and your ancestors were welcomed in by their neighbors (Egyptians). As the years passed the government changed, the neighbor turned hostile, and decided to enslave your ancestors. Through this 400 year ordeal your descendents, the tribes of Jacob the patriarch, were bound together. Through this enslavement your ancestors became the people of Israel. Our Father convinced one of your brothers to go with him on a rescue mission and together they set your ancestors free. Despite this many of them were ungrateful and Our Father didn't permit any of them to realize his promise. So Our Father gave their offspring a land to conquer and call their own but He also told them not to trust the neighbors (Canaanites and others). This conquest freed the people of Israel from their slave mentality. They thought they knew better and often did not pay attention so Our Father kept disciplining them. He even sent his most trusted to them and they still didn't get it right. This had to be done to free them of paganism and establish the royal lineage of David. So when another neighbor (Assyria) came and kidnapped many of them Our Father let it happen because they were not acting like his children. Another part of the family (Judah) remained on their land for a while longer but they eventually failed in the same way so Our Father did not intervene and they also lost their land (Babylonian Captivity). Eventually these relatives were sorry for how they treated Our Father and each other. Another member of the neighborhood (Persia) went after the kidnappers (Babylonians) and rescued your ancestors. This member of the neighborhood (Persia) allowed your ancestors to return to the land that Our Father gave them. This allowed your ancestors to become the Jewish people. Things got back to relative normalcy until years later when this big bully (Rome) from outside the neighborhood was invited into the land by the current rulers (Hasmoneans, a dynasty descendent from the Maccabees who defeated the Greek Seleucids), and just took over. The reliance on the nations and not Our Father made the situation worse.

The result of this was that many of the relatives became disheartened. Years earlier Our Father prepared a plan to deal with this possibility. His plan included sending his heir to reinforce his message to the relatives in order to free them of the things that they did to offend Him. Being just, Our Father reasoned if His family freed themselves from the things that offend Him then He'd initiate His plan to free them from the bully (Rome). Our Father's heir spoke to the relatives. He healed many of them and showed them how they could do things that pleased Our Father. The Heir said that he was very close with Our Father and did everything that Our Father wanted. The Heir explained that your relatives had to change their heart and put their trust in Him. The leaders among your relatives claimed that the Heir had it all wrong. They were in fact pleasing Our Father and did not have to honor the one Our Father sent because they did not think that Our Father sent Him. Finally fearing that many of the relatives would start to trust the Heir and that this would upset the bully to the point that the relatives would suffer because of Him, they turned the Heir over to the bully stating that he was a threat to their way of life and a threat to the bully. In fact these leaders were appointed by the bully and didn't want anything to upset their station. The bully asked the relatives what they wanted. The relatives wanted the bully to get rid of Our Father's heir. As a result the bully brutalized the one that Our Father sent. Our Father was angry but gave your relatives some time to come to terms with what they allowed to happen.

Rather than do this, they eventually turned against the bully and tried to force the bully to leave them alone. Since they disrespected the Heir, Our Father decided to stay out of this fight. Your relatives lost their homes, their land and Our Father even allowed His house to be destroyed. Many of the relatives were forced out of the neighborhood into places where they were not welcome. To make matters worse some of these strangers who claimed to honor Our Father and his Heir treated many of the relatives terribly. This did not please Our Father. Those who claimed to honor the heir that Our Father sent became the oppressors of your ancestors. Then in time followers of your cousins (Ishmaelites) came up out of the Southside (Arabia) and claimed the land that Our Father gave to you as their own. They also brought the son's of Lot, Moab/ Ammon, the son's of Esau, Edom/Midian, and the son's of Ham, Egyptians and Berbers, into their new religion. After Our Father's anger calmed down He made plans to bring the relatives back to the property that He gave them. Our Father is faithful and He brought many of the relatives back. This has angered the south side cousins. They are so angry it's almost impossible to reason with many of them. In the meantime many of those who love Our Father and honor his Heir have developed empathy for His children (the Jews) and repented for misdeeds in the past (Christian anti-Semitism). Some of Our Father's natural born kids are not too happy that those who honor the Heir believe that they have been adopted by Him. What Our Father has made known to those that honor the Heir is that His family is still not whole. He wants those who believe they are adopted sons to help bring about a family reconciliation between the mishpochah and Our Father's Heir. Most of the mishpochah have reasons why they want no part of this reconciliation. Most of them cite writings made long ago by their teachers (Sages and Rabbis) that explained why the Heir, their elder brother, was wrong and did not represent Our Father's interests. Many of them placed as much trust and emphasis upon the teachers words as they do upon Our Father's words. For an outsider like myself there is a lingering question. How can we be sure that the writings of the teachers are accurate? If they were not accurate then perhaps reconciliation can occur, a reconciliation that will bring the whole family together both His first love and those who honor the heir and believe they are adopted sons of the Father. As a non Jewish person, but one who comes from a strong culture, I understand that one does not want to give up or change to something that is not familiar. Our Father alone is the changer of hearts.

This book will take aim at logic and common sense, the mind of both Our Father's first love (The Jewish People) and those who honor the Heir. The promise of this work is that we will think and reason together and at the end of this journey make our own informed decision for or against reconciliation. What I will pray for is that the Natural born sons agree that reconciliation can occur without compromising ones Jewishness. There is no case made here for introducing the Jewish people to Gentile Christianity as expressed in Catholicism or Protestantism. If it can be shown that the works of the teachers were in error as they relate to the Heir then perhaps Our Father can touch hearts to permit reconciliation between the Jewish People and Jesus. This act will end the estrangement between Jewish people and those who honor the Heir. Reconciliation means accepting Jesus (Hebrew Yeshua) as the promised one of God our Father without forsaking Jewishness.

What I have done in this work is take the Jewish point of view as stated in David Klinghoffer's book "Why the Jews rejected Jesus" and restated these ancient arguments against reconciliation. I argue for reconciliation then leave the reader to decide. Undoubtedly some who read the contents of this book may get angry and not be able to accept reconciliation. For those of you who cannot or will not agree to reconciliation and believe that God has not revealed anything concerning the promised messiah since Malachi concluded his book of prophesy 2400 years ago consider this. The messiahs that many in Judaism accept, messiah ben Joseph and messiah ben David are not divine. From the Orthodox Jewish perspective messiah ben Joseph and messiah ben David are altogether human. If this is so consider the following: Mic. 5:1 "Bethlehem...out of thee shall ONE come forth unto me that is to be RULER in Israel; whose goings forth are from of old, from everlasting." Zech.9:9 "Rejoice daughter of Zion...daughter of Jerusalem; behold your KING comes to you riding upon an ass and upon a colt the foal of an ass." Zech.14:9 "And the LORD will become KING over all the earth; on that day the Lord will be one and his name one." The prophets state that the ruler in Israel will be born in Bethlehem. His origin is from the beginning of time itself. The King of Zion/Jerusalem will be seen riding upon an ass/the foal of an ass. Finally the Lord will become King over all the earth. Yeshua was born in Bethlehem; He rode into Jerusalem on an ass/the foal of an ass. Yeshua claimed to be the Lord. How then can the messiah not be divine? Gen.11: 6-7 "And the Lord said, Behold they are one people and they have all one language and this is only the beginning of what they will do; and nothing that they propose to do will now be impossible for them. Come, let US go down; and THEY confused their language that they may not understand one another's speech." When God states 'Let us go down' who is God speaking to? The messiah to come must be born in Bethlehem. In the days of Yeshua, Bethlehem, the city of David was a Jewish town. Today Bethlehem is a Palestinian town and part of the West Bank. One would think that Jewish people would flock to live there, they don't. The probability of a Jewish Messiah being born in Bethlehem for the past 40 years or in the foreseeable future is problematic. You must also have proof of his linage. A descendent of the Tribe of Judah, the house of David, through his son Solomon yet excluding Solomon's descendent Jeconiah and his descendents. This Messiah must be holy. This does not bode well for some Revisionist, Reform, and Conservative Jewish people who have or are in the process of permitting homosexual marriage or will allow gay rabbis. Many of the statements made in this book relate to how the Jewish people love the Law. Lev. 18:1,22 "And the Lord spoke unto Moses and saying, speak unto the children of Israel and say to them you shall not lie with a man as with a woman it is an abomination." This is certainly part of the Law yet many Jewish people are choosing to ignore what Yahveh calls an abomination. He must also climb through the political process in Israel. He's not going to just show up and declare himself. If he did how would the Israelis determine if he is the one? Many would think that this person would be mashuginah. He must prove himself not only to the people of Israel but to the world. This non divine Messiah must be placed in the position to deal with the political realities of the day. This includes the rising tide of Radical Islam and a hostile Muslim world that practices "Struggle" Jihad i.e. holy war against the enemies of Islam. The Prophet of Islam destroyed the Jewish communities of Arabia in his day. Millions of his followers will strive to emulate his example. He'll have to deal with the secular nature and ingrained anti-Semitism of Europe. Contemporary Europe increasingly devalues its Judeo-Christian past. He will have to deal with Russia; while this human Messiah must reach out to Hindu India. Millions in this country don't know the God of Abraham. Then there is the Peoples Republic of China that comprises over one billion souls. Can this human messiah from little Israel convince Communist China to make pilgrimage to Jerusalem and worship the Lord? He must fulfill scripture and prove to 2 billion Christians that Yeshua got it wrong and that his eye witness followers who died for their testimony to Yeshua were all liars. According to Isaiah 11 the Messiah will come from Jesse, father of David the King. He will dish out justice upon the earth. This human Messiah will also be able to change the behavioral patterns of animals. See Verses (6-9). How is this possible? Verse 10 "A root of Jesse will stand for an ensign of the peoples. The nations shall seek him." Verse 11 states what the Lord shall do. Verse 12 He (the Lord) shall set up an ensign for the Nations. Notice we have the root of Jesse and the Lord doing the same thing. Could it be that they are one and the same? What you must ask yourself is how can a totally human messiah do all these things? He must change the heart of the Muslim world i.e. some of these people no doubt will be trying to kill him, Change the heart of the Secularist in Europe and America, Deal with Russia, Bring the Atheist Chinese into the fold, convince the Hindu's not to be polytheists, and disprove Yeshua to biblical Christians. A human messiah will fail on all of these accounts. The Messiah to come was already born in Bethlehem over 2000 years ago. When he returns, there will be no doubt who he is; for according to Dan 7 he shall descend from heaven with great power and glory. The entire world will witness this. Those who resist will risk war with God. All those who witness the event, Jews and non-Jews, will realize that the Lord has just tangibly entered into the affairs of men. This appearing will cause conflict and then peace. This peace will be so complete that even the animals will obey him and their kingdom and the kingdom of men will finally be in harmony. God be with you my Jewish brothers and non Jewish readers to help you reconcile and accept the Holy One of Israel who gave his life for us and who will return to be with his family both Jew and non-Jew. Brothers and sisters may we find unity with the God of Abraham, his Messiah who gave his life for us yet brings inner peace, and the Holy Spirit who when invited into our lives changes our hearts. Amen

Take each issue and work it individually and make up your own mind to your satisfaction. Try to enjoy yet be challenged by this labor of love. May the God of Abraham Isaac and Jacob, Yahveh Elohim, guide us and bless us on this journey together.

CONTENTS

INTRODUCTION

What I will attempt to do in this book is accurately portray traditional Jewish objections to reading the New Covenant and accepting it at face value. These objections or arguments against the New Covenant will follow the word "Objection". In my reply I will attempt to answer the traditional Jewish objection. My reply will follow the word "Response". After this response I will attempt to join or lead into the next objection. This will occur after the word "Segue". I will do my best to accurately portray traditional Jewish objections with respectful responses that will lead to the next objection and response. The point is that traditional Jewish objections to the New Covenant scriptures have been based on the words of Jewish sages. These opinions are found within the full body of Jewish tradition or the Oral Torah/Talmud. If it can be shown that the opinions of the sages in regard to interpreting the written Torah are less than fully accurate, then one who seeks truth must investigate the collection of first century documents known as the New Covenant. Both traditional Jewish people and believers in Yeshua accept the Tenakh/ Old Covenant as divinely inspired of God. We differ in terms of the interpretation of the Tenakh/Old Covenant. Interpretation of the Tenakh is determined by the Oral Torah/Talmud for most Jews and the New Covenant Scriptures for Christians. The question then becomes which source accurately interprets the words of Moses, David, and the Prophets in relation to the blessed hope of Israel—the Messiah? That's where you come in. You decide.

SECTION 1:

THE JEWISH PEOPLE, THEIR SAGES, AND THE PROPHETS

Chapter 1

Modern Jewish Opinion Concerning Reconciliation

OBJECTION: Jesus is the Christian Messiah (1)

RESPONSE: This term is redundant. It also insinuates that people who became followers of Yeshua were looking for a Messiah like Yeshua. The Messiah that first century Jews were looking for was the liberator/warrior King who would free the Jews of foreign bondage. The messiah that the Jewish believers in Yeshua accepted was a spiritual liberator who was to them not only the messiah of Israel but the redeemer of the world. These Jewish believers in Yeshua preached the story of the Jew Yeshua to non-Jews. In doing so they spoke of His impact on people's lives which to them were truths that Jewish believers and Gentiles could position against Greek stoicism and Roman paganism. Following Yeshua's example resulted in concrete benefits for the Gentile community. Spiritually these early believers could understand how the Yeshua story reconciled them with God. Also in practice it worked; therefore, people became believers.

SEGUE: The influence of Yeshua in history had an impact on the establishment of Hospitals, Universities, Literacy for all, Free enterprise, Separation of political powers in government, Liberty, Abolition of slavery, Science, Discovery of a new world, Elevation of women, Charity, High Standards of justice, Elevation of the common man, Condemnation of Adultery and homosexuality,

Regard for human life, Civilizing primitive cultures, codifying languages, Inspiration for art and music, and the transformation of countless people from liabilities into assets. Did this have a positive impact on the formation of the United States? (2)

OBJECTION: <u>Because the Jewish people rejected Jesus, the U.S. was able to develop into the most Christian, tolerant, and good-hearted country in history.</u> (3)

RESPONSE: From the Christian perspective the Messiah had to be rejected by His own people first before He could return to those who rejected Him as their Messiah King. The Jewish rejection of Yeshua, coupled with large scale Gentile acceptance, led people in the more biblically literate nascent United States to develop uniquely among the nations because the words of Yeshua and his followers were read and practiced. From a Christian perspective it made no sense for God to bless the United States as a nation knowing that the majority of its citizens followed Yeshua, a deceiver, and the Apostles who were willing accomplices to this misrepresentation of truth. To believe the stated objection one must believe that Christians follow a fraud yet despite this; a good outcome has occurred. From another perspective had the Jews accepted Yeshua as Messiah and the Romans still put him to death, like bar Kochbah, (4) then Yeshua would have been proven false. Since the Judeans rejected Yeshua; He could not establish a Kingdom in violation of their will or violate the scriptures. From the Jewish perspective Yeshua did not bring eternal peace therefore He could not be the Holy One. From a Christian biblical perspective the Messiah had to be rejected by the Jewish people at that time. This rejection, foretold by the prophets and according to God's divine purpose, allows the Gentiles to accept the God of Abraham, Isaac and Jacob.

SEGUE: We have seen that reading and practicing the teachings of Yeshua have helped Gentile nations, especially the United States, develop into Just nations. The other so called "Christianized nations" who have persecuted the Jews and not followed the teachings of Yeshua have not developed to their potential. Since this is so, what other benefits did his teachings have for Gentiles?

OBJECTION: <u>The Christian faith helps Gentiles have a relationship with God</u>. (5)

RESPONSE: How is it possible for Christians to know the God of Israel and His will for the lives of Gentiles through someone who was a fraud? His followers would have also known that they were deceivers. The accounts of Yeshua resurrected were either true or not true. If their account of him was known deceit how then did Christians develop a relationship with the one true God?

SEGUE: Since the Christian faith has helped Gentile Christians to have a relationship with God why then does it seem that these Christians portray historical Jews in less then favorable light?

OBJECTION: <u>It makes no sense why Mel Gibson vilified Jews in his film Passion of the Christ.</u> (6)

RESPONSE: The *Passion of the Christ* was just that the story of the 12 hours leading up to Yeshua's execution. It pre-supposes that people are familiar with the story.

In this light the film was made for believers and those searching for direction in their life. In Matt.21:12-13 Yeshua drives out the money lenders in the Temple. This makes the Scribes and Pharisees look bad and disrupts Temple commerce. In Matt.21:14-16 Chief Priests and Scribes become indignant after Yeshua heals people in the Temple especially after other Jews were referring to Yeshua as Hosanna Son of David. In Matt.21:23-46 Yeshua outwits the Chief Priests and Pharisees while quoting from Ps.118: 22-23 concerning their rejection of him. Yeshua did not expect to be accepted by them. This fulfilled the scripture that he quoted to them. In Matt.22 Yeshua informs the Judean leaders concerning the true intent of the scripture. This made them look bad in front of others. In Matt. 23 Yeshua seals their wrath against him by describing their hypocrisy. Yeshua predicts Jerusalem's demise and tells the Jews that they won't see him again until they say Baruch ha ba B'shem Adonai i.e. "Blessed is he who comes in the name of the Lord". (7) Until this happens among the Jewish people there will be no Messiah. When one is familiar with the story the telling of it makes obvious sense.

SEGUE: It is not inherently wrong to portray some Jewish Leaders in less than a favorable light if historically that depiction is accurate. The Tenakh portrays numerous occasions when some Jews behaved in ways that were not pleasing to God. (8)

OBJECTION: <u>If enough Jews should depart from the true religion, Judaism, the whole people would suffer chastisement: violence and exile from the land of Israel</u>. (9)

RESPONSE: In light of this statement and considering the events of 721 B.C.E., the Kingdom of Israel was exiled from the land. In 586 B.C.E., the Babylonians exiled the Kingdom of Judah from their land. How are we to interpret the events of 70 C.E. when the Romans destroyed Jerusalem and the Temple? In the events prior to 70 C.E. Yeshua was not an issue. The sons and daughters of Jacob were behaving like the pagan nations. Using this logic the Jewish people by 70 C.E. must have departed from true religion. Israel had rejected Yeshua. If Yeshua was the Messiah a case can be made that Israel abandoned true religion or the fulfillment of their faith by rejecting him. Today most Jews fall outside of orthodoxy. Should Jews who are atheists, agnostics, new agers, Marxists, and Buddhists be more of a concern to Jewry than Jews who have accepted Yeshua as the Messiah and strive to live their lives according to the Bible?

SEGUE: The point here is that the Jewish people suffered chastisement, violence, and exile after the Judeans rejected Yeshua. How do these events, the Jewish rejection of Yeshua, coincide with what Jewish people believe is true concerning the Messiah?

OBJECTION: The ingathering of Jews from the Diaspora came before the reign of Messiah. This precedes the establishment of the New Covenant (renewed commitment to Torah observance) spoken of in Jer.31. The New Temple would precede recognition of God by the non-Jews: (10)

RESPONSE: The ingathering could never have applied to Yeshua's day. Although many Jews did live outside the confines of Israel, Jewish people were firmly established in Judea and Samaria. Another great Diaspora was to be initiated in 70 C.E. and be completed by 135 C.E. The ingathering has happened in our day, so by this rendering we are getting close. Yeshua claimed to establish a New Covenant. This has been accepted by over 2 billion including 200,000 Jewish believers (11). Those who accept His teaching worship the Hebrew God. Stating that the New Temple precedes non-Jews recognizing God is simply not true. One of the previous Objections stated that Christian faith helps Gentiles have a relationship with God. Furthermore if this is true why do the Jews of Israel continue to deny permission for the Temple to be rebuilt? Don't they believe that this is the final ingathering? (12)

SEGUE: What we have established so far is that Jewish people were already in Judea and Samaria like they are today in modern day Israel. The difference was of course the Roman occupation. In contemporary times the Arabs control part of the land that encompassed ancient Israel. What we can say is that most Jews live outside of Israel and that 2 billion people claim allegiance to a faith that worships the God of the Hebrews. If we know this to be true, what then is the central issue why Jewish people oppose reading the New Covenant and accepting it at face value?

OBJECTION: Jewish scholars do not find any substantial points of disagreement between Jesus and his contemporaries. What Jesus rejected was the oral Torah that explains the written Torah (13)

RESPONSE: In Mark 7: 6-13 it is clear from the New Covenant text that Yeshua's message concerned the intent of the heart. Volumes of commentary concerning the books of Moses meant nothing if they contradicted the intent of the written word or if the explanation did not take into account what Yeshua called the two Great Commandments. In Matt.22: 36-40 the commandments that Yeshua described can be found in Deut.6:5 and Lev.19:18. The issue then rests on the Torah being a cryptic document that can only be revealed by a key that unlocked this code. In our day we see a code being unlocked in terms of the Bible codes, but commentary on the written word is not lifted to the level of the written word of God unless the written word acknowledges that the commentary, oral tradition, must be adhered to and encompasses the authority of the written word of God. Moses does not speak of this oral tradition being valued as the revelation that he received from God. It should be noted that the Sadducees also rejected the authority of the Oral Law. The wrath of the Pharisees came against Yeshua because he accused the Pharisees of being "blind guides" who placed unreasonable burdens on the people and did nothing to lift this burden. The standard therefore is weighed against the essence of the law found in Deut.6:5 and Lev.19:18. You shall love Yahveh your God with all your heart, with all your soul, and with all your might. You shall love your neighbor as you love yourself.

SEGUE: Must a person faithfully observe the words of the Oral Torah, Jewish tradition, in order to observe the intent of Deut.6:5 and Lev.19:18? Could the words of God through Moses stand on their own merit without the commentary of the Rabbi's? If not, should the words of these Sages be lifted to speak with the authority of Moses since the written Torah does not state that it can only be interpreted via an Oral Torah that was revealed at Sinai as well? What did God mean when he proclaimed that his commandments must be obeyed?

OBJECTION: It is a fact that the practice of the commandments is a discipline unsuited to the requirements of a mass religion. (14)

RESPONSE: In Isa.42 God speaks of bringing his justice to the Nations (Gentiles). If the practice of the commandments is unsuitable to the requirements of a mass religion what then is God's intention concerning the Gentiles? How was bringing God's justice to the Gentiles supposed to happen under the old formula? The truth is it could not happen under the old formula, the Mosaic Law interpreted by the Oral Law or tradition. Since it could not happen under the old formula, but has happened through the teaching of Yeshua communicated to the Gentiles by St. Paul one must consider that God's justice has been communicated to the Gentiles through the Jewish followers of Yeshua.

SEGUE: Since it is established that Yeshua's teaching and example allowed non-Jews to understand their salvation history, is it possible that Jewish people hold other failed messiah's in higher esteem than Yeshua? We cannot call Yeshua's mission failed since he promised to return and since his teaching inspired a worldwide movement that has been with us 2000 years. Failed Jewish messiah's did not promise to return and did not inspire a major world faith.

OBJECTION: Simeon Bar Kochbah, hailed as the greatest sage of the day by Rabbi Akiva, was a failed messiah killed by the Romans at the siege of Beitar. He secured Jerusalem for two years and started Temple construction...Akiva and other Rabbi's were prepared to follow him. Bar Kockbah got things done. He led an uprising...until the presumptive messiah's death. Akiva had been overhasty. (15)

RESPONSE: In the Jewish mind Bar Kochbah commands a higher standing than the Nazarene Yeshua. Yet the Rabbi's of Bar Kochbah's day got it wrong. Rabbi Akiva was not a prophet. He hailed Simon Bar Kochbah as the greatest sage of his day. Rabbi Akiva thought Bar Kochbah to be the messiah. They were both wrong. After Bar Kochbah's death, how many Jews continued to follow him? Is it possible if this rabbi got it wrong concerning Bar Kochbah that he and other rabbis could also be wrong concerning the suffering servant of Isa.53?

SEGUE: If a rabbi and others got it wrong concerning Bar Kochbah could they also be incorrect concerning the perception that Jews living under an Islamic administration had it better. History has already taught us that Jews suffered greatly at the hands of professing Christians who did not live their lives according to the teachings of Yeshua.

OBJECTION: In 755 the Umayyad dynasty was established in Spain. It created a haven for Jews on the Iberian Peninsula. These "good times" lasted until 1013. (16)

RESPONSE: Although this is true one must not think that Jewish Muslim relations before this period were not without Jewish suffering.

624: Tabari VII 87; Bukhari V5B59N362; Ishaq 364 -The Banu Qaynuqa surrendered, they were exiled from Medina and sent into the desert. (17)

626: Ishaq VII 159; Ishaq 438 - Muhammad besieged the Banu Nadir Jews for 15 days. In return for their lives the Jews relinquished their possessions and property to Muhammad and were expelled from their land. Muhammad then declared and Allah promised that all of the Jews would be condemned. (18)

627: Tabari VIII 6-40; Ishaq 450-480- At the Battle of the Ditch, where the Meccans were defeated at Medina, Allah commanded Muhammad to march against the Qurayza Jews. After a 25 day siege Muhammad commanded the Jews to submit to Sa'd Mu'adh's judgment. They agreed in order to end the siege. After death was decreed, Muhammad ordered all males over puberty beheaded. 900 Jewish male captives were decapitated in the presence of Muhammad and the Jewish victim's mothers, sisters, wives, aunts, and children. The Prophet then took Rayhana, who just witnessed the death of her Father & Brothers, for Himself. She became his concubine. (19)

629: Ishaq 510-515; Tab VIII 116-123- Muhammad laid siege to Khaybar and surrounding towns for 19 days. All the men were executed. Their women were given to the Muslims and the children were sold into slavery. (20)

Tab VIII 129,130- After hearing the fate of the Khaybar Jews the Fadak Jews agree to give Muhammad ½ of all they produced. Umar would later expel them from Arabia. (21)

634: 4000 Jews & Christians massacred from Gaza to Caesarea.

643: Jews & Christians at Tripoli must forfeit their women and children; The population of Carthage was slaughtered.

853-859: Caliph Mutawakkil ordered all new churches in Egypt destroyed. Synagogues destroyed throughout Mesopotamia.

892: 40,000 Jews confirmed expelled from Caesarea during earlier Jihad

With the demise of the Umayyad dynasty and the eventual arrival of the Almohads Jewish suffering under Islam would intensify through the reconquista of Christian Spain.

1010 – 1013: Purge of Jews in Cordoba, Spain.

1014: Synagogues ordered destroyed in Egypt and Syria.

1033: 6000 Jews in Fez, Morocco executed.

1065: Jews forced to convert or die in Yemen.

1066: 3000 Jews in Granada slaughtered; most churches in Spain destroyed.

1077: Seljuk Emir Atsiz bin Uwaq murders 3000 Jews/ Christians in Jerusalem

1148: Nur-ed-Din orders every Christian killed at Aleppo, Syria; Spanish Jews threatened with Conversion or deportation.

1159: Jews & Christians in Tunis were given a choice between Islam or death.

1275: Jews forced to convert or die in Morocco.

1291, 1338: Jews forcibly converted at Tabriz.

1293-94;1301-2: Synagogues destroyed in Egypt and Syria.

1333, 44: Jews forced to convert or die in Baghdad.

1465: Muslim mobs at Fez kill thousands of Jews leaving 11 alive. (22)

SEGUE: Now that we've seen that Jewish existence in the lands that Muslims conquered was not preferable to lands where the majority were Christians an important distinction must be made. Muhammad and his followers did violence to Jews within two years of living among them. Yeshua and his followers did no violence to Jews nor taught others to do violence to the Jewish People. It is true that professing Christians did violence to Jewish people. We don't see large scale examples of this until the latter part of the 12th century in Europe. However, discrimination and hostility towards the Jews in the land of professing Christians goes back to the 6th century. When it was done it was always done in total disregard of Yeshua's teaching and the preaching of the evangelists and disciples of the early church. With this being established how do biblical Christians view God's relationship with the Jewish people?

OBJECTION: Christians deny the covenant with Israel and the commandments from Sinai. (23)

RESPONSE: Biblical Christians do not deny the covenant with Israel as they understand it. They would agree that God entered into an agreement with the Jewish people who are His first love. However, they would disagree that this covenant leads to near universal salvation among the Jewish people. Christianity states that a New Covenant has been established which is universal and includes the people of the original covenant. Biblical Christians do not deny the commandments from Sinai. The commandments to Christians include those things commanded in Ex.20 and Deut.5. Christians do not consider the stipulations found in the Oral Torah, tradition, as commandments from God. They are viewed as the opinions of Rabbi's. The adopted Sons, as Biblical Christians see themselves, do not have to abide by all the ritual and ceremony. Our Father has excused us from this stating that we do not have to become like his first love Israel, convert to Judaism first, in order to come to Him and be his adopted children. Biblical Christians believe that Jew and Gentile alike accept the provisions for salvation through the death and resurrection of the Messiah. This also includes loving God with all our power and loving our neighbors as ourselves. If we accept God's grace through faith and love and help others we are doing his will. (24)

SEGUE: Since Christians do not deny the commandments and God's covenant with his people how then can people be reconciled to God? How can both Jew and non-Jew know that there is atonement for their sin?

OBJECTION: The Jews ask how the crucifixion could be atonement for the sin of mankind. The sacrifice of God can be called infinite but God cannot die. If the sacrifice was of God-Man then it was not infinite, thus the purpose of the event was not met. Hasdai Crescas opined "Even if we posit that God can become incarnate, this redemption is impossible." This is so because disease is cured by the opposite, that is sin with commandments, rebellion with worship. The curing of disrespect with a great disrespect is curing rebellion with rebellion and sin with sin." (25)

RESPONSE: Gen.1:1-2 "In the beginning God created... and the spirit of God moved upon the face of the waters." What we learn is that in the beginning God was. God was what? John 4: 24 "God is spirit" Can there be any dispute in this? This spirit created the physical world where we reside. Notice in Genesis there is a distinction between God who is spirit and the Spirit of God that moves upon the face of the waters. John 1:1-4; In the beginning was the Word and the Word was with God and the Word was God. He was in the beginning with God; all things were made through him and without him was not anything made that was made." It is clear that God made all things. Since God made all things; God can send his being to take human form. A God-man cannot die for the sins of God but can die for the sins of men. Yeshua came to die for the sons of men therefore as God and man he bought redemption for mankind. Matt.27:50 "Yeshua cried again with a loud voice and yielded up his spirit." Luke 23:46 Then Yeshua crying with a loud voice and said, "Father into they hands I commit my Spirit." And having said this he breathed his last. John 19:30 Yeshua said, "It is finished." He then bowed his head and gave up his spirit. The Spirit that is God left him at death. So the physical body died, but this same tortured body revived three days latter when this same Spirit re-entered his physical body. As for sin it is not cured through the commandments. We know what sin is through the commandments. Lev.17:11 "For the life of the flesh is in the blood and I have given it to you upon the alter to make atonement for your souls for it is the blood that makes atonement by reason of the life." So we know that the shedding of blood and giving up of life atones for sin. As for rebellion see Ps.95: 7-11. For 40 years the generation that departed Egypt witnessed God's miracles but continued in their rebellion. Worship didn't cure their rebellion because rebellion is a problem of the heart. The heart must be changed. People can worship and still maintain a hardened heart. In Heb.3:13-14 we see that the cure for rebellion is the exhortation of those in Yeshua giving encouragement to one another. Although being our brother's keeper cannot bring salvation it can sustain and encourage those in need of God's saving grace. When the heart is changed then rebellion dies and God can be worshipped in spirit and truth according to John 4:24. When one views human existence as inherently sinful i.e. falling short of God's Holiness as described in the Tenakh, one comes to understand the need for accepting God's biblical provisions for atonement through faith in Messiah.

SEGUE: We just read how it was possible for God to become man and die for the iniquity of his creation. We've also seen scripturally what cures sin and rebellion. Is it therefore possible that some Jewish people saw scriptural fulfillment in another failed messiah?

OBJECTION: <u>Sabbatai Zvi: His apostasy was a mystery; the book of Psalms was found full of allusions to Zvi;</u>

Sabbatians stressed Isaiah 53 and stated that the Bible and Zohar foretold the details of Zvi's life and suffering; a Trinitarian doctrine that included the Holy Ancient One, Holy King, and Shechinah; Sabbatians concluded that their Messiah was not merely a human being, but a divine incarnation. (26)

RESPONSE: Yeshua never departed from Judaism. Zvi became a Muslim. The other allusions to Psalms, Isaiah, other parts of the Bible and incarnation have been proven false. Where was it foretold that the Messiah would be born in Anatolia? During his life he wasn't rejected by his people but he did leave the religion of his people. It was not foretold that the Jewish Messiah would accept the teachings of an Arab Prophet. In fact he converted to Islam to avoid suffering and death. He sold out his own people who placed their faith in him. There are little or no comparisons between Zvi and Yeshua.

SEGUE: Contemporary Jewish people acknowledge that both Bar Kockbah and Zvi failed as messiahs. What other things do Jewish people acknowledge or agree to? In fact isn't there another issue that defines the Jewishness of most Jewish people?

OBJECTION: Rabbi Abraham Joshua Heschel called for a Jewish alliance with Christians against secularism. Then 911 occurred. The trend for Jews is toward increased acceptance of Christianity, a friend of Jews, though resistance to Jesus remains as strong as ever...The only thing that Jews agree on today is that Jesus was not the Messiah. (27)

RESPONSE: Only the evidence of sin, a violation of God's commandments, could disqualify Yeshua from being the Messiah and Son of God. Did Yeshua tell people to put other gods before God? Yeshua's relationship to his heavenly Father was subordinate John12:49-50. Therefore he didn't place himself above his Father. Yeshua claimed to be the Son of the Father. This is only a sin if it is not true. Four first century documents known as Gospels state that it is true. Yeshua did not bow down to a graven image or tell others to do so. He did not take the name of the Lord in vain. He used that name for prayer and instruction. He observed the Sabbath day faithfully but not according to Jewish oral tradition. Breaking the tradition of men does not equate to sin. One must break the Lord's commandments. He honored his heavenly Father by stating to do his will, his earthly Father and his mother. He did not murder anyone nor commit any sexual sin. There is no evidence that he stole from anyone or lied about anyone. There is no evidence that he coveted others possessions or another woman? Only the evidence of sin can disqualify him. Over 200,000 Jews today have reconciled their faith to include Yeshua within a Jewish worship setting yet are also able to bridge the gap to Christian churches. (28)

SEGUE: Since modern Jewish people have difficulty finding evidence of Yeshua committing a sin in the New Covenant the main reason that he is rejected is because they are told that they will no longer be Jews if they accept him. Unlike Islam where Muslims can be killed if they become Christians Jewish people know they will have to count the cost if they reconcile their faith to include Yeshua. A decision for Yeshua could cost Jewish people family relationships and inheritance considerations. So generally is Judaism tolerant towards

Jews who chose to make Yeshua part of their faith experience?

OBJECTION: Judaism's Chief virtue is tolerance. This tolerance translates into Judaism not proselytizing. Christianity is less tolerant because it is a proselytizing faith. To the extent a Christian was not tolerant in this way it revealed a weakness in his religious thinking. (29)

RESPONSE: Judaism is not a more tolerant faith because it doesn't proselytize. Jewish people generally have little interest in non-Jews joining their ranks. The Israelites were originally tribal being members of 12 tribes. Those tribes could claim as their descendents Abraham, Isaac, and Jacob. So Jews not only had the same faith but the same blood line. Christianity is less tolerant because it wants all people to accept Yeshua? I am not speaking about coerced proclamations of faith or anything that violate ones ability to make up their own mind, but to say that Christianity is less tolerant because it is a proselytizing faith would only be valid if the person responding to the invitation were not free to decide for themselves or feared retribution by the party offering the invitation.

SEGUE: Since Judaism is the truth why not want to share this truth with the world? Not being willing to do this makes the holder of the truth more tolerant? In Matt.28:18-20 Yeshua said, "All authority in heaven and on earth has been given to me. Go therefore and make disciples of all nations baptizing them in the name of the Father and Son and the Holy Spirit teaching them to observe all that I have commanded you and lo I am with you always to the close of the age." Here the Jew Yeshua tells his followers to make disciples of all nations...and teach them to observe all that I have commanded you. How can this equate to being less tolerant? It is only less tolerant if all paths lead to God and salvation. This is not the belief of Christians or Jews. Therefore; the faith of Yeshua seeks to be inclusive with all peoples who accept the Lord. How can this faith be reconciled with a Judaism that still awaits its Messiah?

OBJECTION: <u>Judaism is a messianic faith assigning great significance to faith in a coming messiah, but premature messianism - believing the messiah had already come despite evidence before your eyes that the world remains as before-was poison</u>. (30)

RESPONSE: If this is true have Messianic Jews or Jews for Yeshua behaved like Sabbatians? Have they left Judaism meaning its practices? Have these Jews thrown the law and Judaism to the wind? This is not to say that they adhere to Orthodox legalism. How do they practice their religion? Are they a loving people? Do they have joy? All they have done is add Yeshua. Where is the poison? It is only poison if it is not true and harmful. They remain in the synagogue. As far as the world See Mark 13, Luke 21, and Matt 24. Yeshua stated that world affairs would get much worse. He never pretended that the world would suddenly be transformed. The times of the Gentiles had to be fulfilled first. See Luke 21:24. The burden is on those who don't believe to prove that Yeshua sinned. Only this can prove that he was not the messiah. Based on this it would be wise to reexamine Jewish interpretation based on commentary from Jewish oral tradition.

SEGUE: What is poisonous about accepting the Jew Yeshua within the confines of Judaism for Jewish people? Faith in Yeshua has no basis without Judaism. The religious practices of Yeshua were all within the confines of Judaism. Since this is true why must Judaism and Christianity be an "either/or" proposition?

OBJECTION: It seemed to pre-modern Jews and Christians that it could not be true that both Jesus and Judaism were aligned with God's intentions. One had to accept or reject the Christian claim for Jesus. If Christ was from God, then it made little sense to continue practicing Judaism. (31)

RESPONSE: Actually in this instance both pre-modern Christians and Jews were incorrect. In the book of Acts the Jewish believers in Yeshua concluded that gentiles did not have to become Jews first to come to Christ. Since this argument was made it follows that Jews who come to Yeshua do not have to join a Gentile church or stop being Jewish. Although following Rabbinical Judaism and being a follower of Yeshua are mutually exclusive, a sincere belief in Messiah would compel one to continually search the Tenakh and New Covenant. Actually Jews and Christians can both give each other something of great value. The Christians can give Yeshua to the Jews and the Jews can give the Church more Jewishness. In other words make the Church more Jewish. Both Jews and gentile Christians have much to gain. A church that is more Jewish will be more inviting to Jews and Synagogues that proclaim Yeshua will be most welcoming to Christians. (32)

SEGUE: Jews and Christians can undoubtedly give each other much. In fact can be a blessing to each other. With this new awareness does it still follow that Jews and Christians must remain mutually exclusive? The roots of Christianity are in Judaism however the Judaism of the Rabbi's draws nothing from Christianity. What can be called mutual sharing has occurred through the Messianic movement. Is it possible that together Jews and Christians could give the greatest blessing to humanity?

OBJECTION: <u>The Jewish rejection of Jesus gave the world its blessing.</u> (33)

RESPONSE: The presumption is that Christianity would have remained a Jewish sect. What is not considered is that the Jewish sect of Christianity would have still fulfilled Yeshua's great commission concerning making disciples of all men. The Jewish sect of Christianity would have also de-emphasized the Jewish oral tradition. With the oral tradition de-emphasized forward thinkers like Paul and others would have still challenged the Gentiles with the message of Christ. Another way to view this is how has the Jewish rejection of Yeshua benefited the Jews? If the Jews would have stayed within the Synagogue they still would have married other Jews and not lost their identity. From the Christian point of view the Jewish rejection of Yeshua was foretold in the Tenakh and by Yeshua himself. The scripture was thus fulfilled and Yeshua was proven correct. (34)

SEGUE: If our presumptions have been wrong what then can we say concerning the Jewish people, Yeshua, Judaism, and Christianity?

OBJECTION: <u>The Jews rejected the Christian claim for Jesus in large part because if God wanted them to see</u>

the true Messiah in Jesus, if in fact their eternal salvation was dependent on their making this identification then he would have made it much clearer far less open to doubt. (35)

RESPONSE: Luke18:31-34 "Behold we are going up to Jerusalem and all things that have been written by the prophets concerning the Son of Man will be accomplished. For he will be betrayed to the chief priests and the scribes and they will condemn him to death and will deliver him to the gentiles and they will mock him and spit upon him and scourge him and after they have scourged him they will put him to death and on the third day he will rise again." The messianic prophesies go back to Abraham in oral form and to Moses in written form. This goes back at least 3400 years to Moses time. All this time has passed and can it still be possible that there is no messiah? The issue isn't what the Jewish people believe God would have wanted. The assumption from the Jewish point of view is that they would know. Yeshua predicts his rejection. Luke 22:37 "For I tell you that this which is written must be fulfilled in me; and he was reckoned with transgressors; for what is written about me has its fulfillment. The sin of the Jewish nation from that time to the destruction of Jerusalem and the temple is what prevented them from seeing their promised one. What sin? Since Israel was under Roman domination, Jewish positions of authority had to be either appointed or approved by the Romans. The Romans wanted to ensure that the people paid their taxes and remained quiet. It was this leadership, fearing that Yeshua was stirring up the crowd concerning Temple protocol that rejected Yeshua. In doing so they passed this rejection to the Jews for generations to come.

SEGUE: The attempt in this first chapter was to respond to general Jewish objections to reconciliation. With this section now behind us let's examine what the great sages of Judaism have stated through the ages.

Chapter 1 Notes

1. Klinghoffer, Why the Jews rejected Jesus, P.1
2. Kennedy, What if Jesus had never been born, PP. 3-4
3. Klinghoffer, P.8
4. Ibid., P.121
5. Ibid., PP.9-10
6. Ibid., P.11
7. Matt.23:39
8. IIChron.36:5-7
9. Klinghoffer, P.30
10. Ibid., P.36
11. I learned this from Author Joel Rosenberg
12. Klinghoffer, PP.9-10
13. Ibid., P.55
14. Ibid., P.99
15. Ibid., PP.120-121
16. Ibid., P.153
17. Spencer, The Truth about Muhammad, PP.111-113
18. Ibid., PP.121-122
19. Ibid., PP.128-133
20. Ibid., PP.139-140

21. Peters, Muhammad and the origins of Islam, PP.228-229
22. Warraq, Why I am not a Muslim PP.225-240
23. Klinghoffer, P.175
24. Gal. 4: 1-7
25. Klinghoffer, P.176
26. Ibid, PP.194-195
27. Ibid, PP.192-193
28. See Note 11
29. Klinghoffer, PP.197-198
30. Ibid, P.196
31. Ibid, P.200
32. Acts 15:12-21; Amos 9:11-12
33. Klinghoffer, P.201
34. Ps.118:22-23; Isa. 53:3; Matt. 20:17-19; Mark 10:32-34; Luke 9: 22, 44-45; 17:25
35. Klinghoffer, P.210

Chapter 2

Josephus, Maimonides, and Nachmanides Concerning Reconciliation

OBJECTION: Josephus eyewitness account of the Pharisees is hard to reconcile with that of the New Covenant. (1)

RESPONSE: Flavius Josephus was born in 37 C.E. seven years after the death of Yeshua. Josephus had the benefit of viewing the Pharisees through a Jewish and Roman lens. He never observed Yeshua because he was born 7 years too late. Since this is true, Josephus could not have observed the dynamic that resulted from the discussions that occurred between the Pharisees and Yeshua as described in Matt.21, 22, and 23. In these texts the Pharisees are often dressed down in public by Yeshua. This often occurred in public before their co-religionists the Sadducees and Scribes. The Pharisees stressed the traditions of the elders when interpreting the scriptures and believed in the resurrection of the dead. The Sadducees denied the resurrection of the dead, but placed less emphasis on the interpretations of the Rabbis. The Scribes were Levites who were responsible for copying the scriptures and routine Temple administration. By being embarrassed in public it made perfect sense that they would try to trip up Yeshua by presenting him with real and hypothetical situations. Therefore it is understandable that the Pharisees as described by the New Covenant authors and Josephus would differ. In this light their divergence makes sense. (2)

SEGUE: Being a historian who was Jewish, yet accepted by the Romans, Josephus would have been comfortable speaking with the Christian sect in Judea. He wrote about the Jews of his day but how did he describe Yeshua who he never met or heard?

OBJECTION: "Now there was about this time Jesus a wise man, if it be lawful to call him a man, for he was a doer of wonderful works, a teacher of such men that as receive the truth with pleasure. He drew over to him both many of the Jews and gentiles. He was Christ (Messiah/Anointed); and when Pilate at the suggestion of the principal men among us had condemned him to the cross those that loved him at first did not forsake him, for he appeared to them alive again the third day, as the divine prophets had foretold these and 10,000 other wonderful things concerning him; and the tribe of Christians, so named from him are not extinct at this day." It seems that the Paragraph is not entirely from the hand of Josephus, but rather a later Christian insertion: (3)

RESPONSE: *The Jewish War,* Josephus first work was completed 75 C.E. His second work *Jewish Antiquities* was completed in the year 93 C.E. By then Josephus was aware of Jewish rejection of Yeshua, the Gospels of Mark and Matthew, written by Jews, and the destruction of Jerusalem. His statements about Yeshua are to the point. How would Josephus' works be accepted or be deemed credible by hitting the Jewish people over the head with Yeshua? Yeshua had already been rejected. By this time Josephus was aware of the Gospel accounts. Why should he go into detail about Yeshua when others had already done so? Being aware of the Christian accounts he was also aware that those accounts included predictions of Jerusalem's destruction before it occurred. He acknowledged Yeshua in light of Dan. 9:24-27. As far as being a later Christian insertion one would have to believe that no Jew had an original copy and no one in the Jewish world caught this obvious embellishment. Where are their accounts? The Christians did this to a Jewish work without the Jews of that time or future generations discovering it? What we do know is that Tacitus the Roman historian mentions Yeshua and Pontius Pilate in 110 C.E. in his Annals lib. XV. Cap 44. Josephus record existed at that time. In *Origen, the Comment in Matth*. written in 230 C.E., Josephus is again quoted as calling Yeshua the Christ. (4)

SEGUE: There is no proof that Josephus words concerning Yeshua were a Christian embellishment. As a historian it seems that he found the Christians more credible than the Jewish authorities he spoke to about the matter. Did Josephus mention other followers of Christ?

OBJECTION: <u>Christians are absent from the four party descriptions of Jewish groups according to Josephus</u>: (5)

RESPONSE: In John12:19 the Pharisees' statement that the world has gone after him occurs before the Crucifixion. The statement has more to do with Yeshua's popularity vice the Pharisees. After the Crucifixion the dynamics changed. His death should have been the end of the movement. We all know that is not true. The

Jewish followers of Yeshua began to preach boldly about Yeshua. Eventually they were persecuted -- some even executed -- and they were cast out of the synagogues. How then could they be considered part of Judaism? By 75 C.E. the Yeshua movement was gaining momentum among the Gentiles. Josephus speaks very favorably of John the Baptist. He was a person of virtue and piety and was executed by Herod. Josephus then describes the condemnation of James, brother of Yeshua. People were so upset with the decision that they did not want other members of the Christian sect to be dealt with like this. (6)

SEGUE: One cannot grab anything negative about Yeshua or his followers from the words of the Jewish historian Flavius Josephus. Will we be able to say the same concerning other non-Prophetical sources in Judaism?

OBJECTION: Maimonides stated, *"Jesus imagined he was the Messiah, Ancient sages meted out a fitting punishment to him": (7)*

RESPONSE: If Yeshua received a fitting punishment did Bar Kochbah receive a fitting punishment? How about Sabbatai Zvi or the Lubavitcher Rebbi Schneerson? Although some Lubavitchers still insist that their Rebbi is the messiah, what impact did the Rebbi, Bar Kochbah and Sabbatai Zvi have on the world when positioned with Yeshua?

SEGUE: Rabbi Moses ben Maimon, Maimonides, lived in the 12th century, more than a millennium after Yeshua's time. From his remarks it seems as though he believed Yeshua was delusional. Based on what he thought Yeshua imagined i.e. made it up in his mind. Maimonides believed Yeshua received justice from his Jewish ancestors. Yeshua was either the Son of God Messiah of Israel, a good Jew who was deliberately misrepresented by followers who died for their faith in him, a deliberate deceiver or delusional. What we know about Yeshua comes from four 1st century documents and a first century Jewish historian. Maimonides opinions are probably based on Talmudic refutations dating back to Gamaliel and Rashi. Did Maimonides have other opinions that were based on fact?

OBJECTION: Maimonides accepts as historically accurate the version of the Crucifixion given in the Talmud. These verses state "On the eve of Passover they hung Yeshu ha'Notzri for he performed magic, enticed, and led astray Israel i.e. influenced others to worship alien gods." (8)

RESPONSE: Basically the gospel accounts, Maimonides, and the Talmud agree concerning the event of Yeshua's crucifixion. Jewish oral tradition makes the case that Yeshua was crucified because he performed tricks in order to entice and lead astray the people of Israel to worship alien gods. The Orthodox Jewish point of view interprets actions, even acts of healing on the Sabbath as intolerable. The idea of God becoming man and God having a triune nature were rejected. All of Yeshua's miracles dealt with healing, saving people or displaying His Lordship over nature. There were no gratuitous miracles. Someone was always made better when the supernatural occurred. Maimonides wrongly assumes that the Jewish People at that time were right standing. He learned this by studying the views of the Pharisees and Essenes who believed that they were the righteous of Israel and thus "suffering servants". According to Lev. 26 and Deut. 28 the Jewish people were not pleasing God. The proof was the Roman occupation. Yeshua quotes from Isa. 61:1-2 and he spoke about bringing liberty to the oppressed. This meant that the Jewish people needed to remove their sin before their physical captivity would end. The Jewish leadership chose to reject him and hand him over to their occupiers. What alien gods did Yeshua want the people of Israel to worship? Yeshua prayed to his Father the God of Israel. He always placed himself in a subordinate position to God the Father while affirming that he was sent by God. He said those who worshiped his Father and accepted him would receive the gift of the Ruach ha 'Kodesh, the Holy Spirit. (9)

SEGUE: The charges were that Yeshua faked miracles, really didn't heal anyone, and through a smooth tongue led Israel astray. For the Sanhedrin to involve the Romans this was a big deal and word of this would have swept through all of Judea and up into the Galilee. Maimonides is again incorrect. The Judeans handed Yeshua over to the Romans. The Romans did not crucify people for performing magic, leading the people of Israel astray religiously and encouraging the Judeans to worship alien gods. What other things did Maimonides/ Talmud say concerning Yeshua's crucifixion?

OBJECTION: <u>The Jewish authorities either killed him themselves (See previous) or conspired with the Romans to do so. According to Maimonides, "Finally he was overpowered and put a stop to by us when he fell into our hands and his fate is well known</u>." (10)

RESPONSE: John 19:18-19 "There they crucified him and with him two others with Yeshua between them." John 21:24 "This is the disciple who is bearing witness to these things. He has written these things and we know that his testimony is true." In addition, the crucifixion of Yeshua by the Romans is asserted by Tacitus, Flavius Josephus, Justin Martyr, Lucian The Greek, Syrian Mara bar Serapian, Phlegon, Pliny the Younger, Suetonius, Thallus via Julius Africanus, and Christian Scholar Tertullian who allegedly was aware of a report from Pontius Pilate to Emperor Tiberius concerning the Crucifixion of Yeshua. The Jews did not crucify people, the Romans did. Under Roman administration, The Jews would not have done this without Roman sanction. Moses Maimonides version of Yeshua's demise is again inaccurate. (11)

SEGUE: What we see by Maimonides' words and other opinions in the Talmud is that medieval Jewry was laying claim to destroying Yeshua. Clearly Maimonides and the Talmud are convinced that their forefathers did a good thing. He says nothing regarding the Jewish leadership of Yeshua's day. The fact that they were either appointees or approved by Rome matters little to Maimonides. What Maimonides did understand or at least empathize with was that the Jews of Yeshua's day like himself were subjects of Gentile rulers. The Sadducees in particular did not want to accept one who would bring the wrath of Rome against them. Can we then say that all anti-Semitic feelings towards Jews through the ages were solely developed by the Church or that medieval Jews certainly accepted that their forefathers were complicit in the brutalization of Yeshua? It does appear that the institutional church during Maimonides time forgot Yeshua's words from Luke 23:34 "Father forgive them for they know not what they do". What does Maimonides say about other Christian dogmas?

OBJECTION: Maimonides "Those who believe that God is one and that he has many attributes, declare the unity with their lips and assume plurality in their thoughts. This is like the doctrine of the Christians who say that he is one and He is three and that the three are one". (12)

RESPONSE: The building block of society is the family. God created it and God ordained it. Where did God get the idea for the family whereby one family can be made up of many members? Why is the uni-plural word Elohim used for God? There is one God "Elohim" with multiple parts. The head is Yahveh also known as the Father. Another member of the body is the mouth piece the Logos (Word) of Yahveh/God, also known as the Anointed. After his incarnation he was known as Yeshua, Yahveh's salvation, the Son of God. There is the Holy Spirit also God who interacts with humans to draw them closer to the Father and Son. There is one God i.e. yet like a body has more than one attribute. (13)

SEGUE: Thinking of God as one body is based on scriptural exegesis and helps explain the Godhead and why human beings are constructed as they are. Within the Godhead, the Father and Holy Spirit are not the brunt of discord between Jews and Christians. It always comes back to Yeshua. Since Yeshua is the continual issue what other opinions did Maimonides have concerning him?

OBJECTION: In the Mishneh Torah Maimonides stated: All matters relating to Jesus of Nazareth only serve to clear the way for King Messiah Zeph.3: 9. Thus the Messianic hope, Torah, and commandments have become familiar topics by those uncircumcised of heart and flesh, Hence when King Messiah will appear and succeed and be exalted they will recant and realize that they have inherited lies from their fathers that their prophets and forebears led them astray. (14)

RESPONSE: What this means is that the fraud Yeshua was used by God to clear the way for a king messiah and through this inspiration the fraud inspired in his followers the messianic hope. Because of him, the Torah and Commandments are also known among the nations. The remainder states that the true Messiah must be successful and be exalted by the Jewish people. In other words, do the Jewish people decide who will be the true messiah? I thought God determined who would be the true messiah. Finally the Christians have been led astray by the fraud Yeshua who harmed no one and spoke of God's love. Christians were led astray by a selfless Yeshua. Yeshua's claim to be the Son of God is only incorrect if not true. Maimonides could not see the 21st century. There is no human being who will change the Hearts of the Islamic world, North Koreans, Chinese and others in order to have a lasting peace. The only entity to bring 1000 years of peace to this world is God who will walk the earth and rule the affairs of men. (15)

SEGUE: Maimonides experienced a dilemma. He could not consider that Yeshua was the messiah because that would mean that he was wrong. So the challenge became describing how he could be right given reality as he understood it. In his reality and in the reality of Jewish people who trust his words, the flawed Yeshua made Gentiles familiar with Judaic concepts. Maimonides failed to explain how the "only human" messiah will attain global success. Christians have no such problem explaining how Yeshua will command the attention of Israel and the nations. To many Jewish people the messiah to come will be a type of Moses who is highly exalted in Judaism. How does Maimonides opine concerning Moses and Mosaic Law?

OBJECTION: <u>According to Maimonides "Moses our teacher was commanded by the Almighty to compel all inhabitants of the world to accept the commandments that were enjoined upon the children of Noah the seven categories of basic ethical rules obligatory for all mankind. If one does not accept these laws, he should be executed.</u> (16)

RESPONSE: Moses mission according to the Torah was to lead the Israelites out of Egypt and into the Promised Land. His mission did not include compelling all the inhabitants of the world to accept the commandments etc... Moses couldn't get the Israelites to keep the Commandments and was busy persuading God not to destroy all of them. As far as Maimonides execution comment. He must have witnessed too much Islamic justice in Muslim Spain, a land that he was forced to flee because of persecution. It seems to have influenced his view of God in the affairs of men. (17)

SEGUE: The part of this chapter including Maimonides opinions concludes with his opinion that non-Jews should be devoid of choice concerning the Mosaic law and that those who resist this should visit the gallows.

This statement by Maimonides is odd since medieval Judaism permitted expulsion not capital punishment. Most biblical Christians and Rabbinical Jews would concur that disagreements and discourse concerning religious issues should occur with ink and paper, from mouth to ear and by practicing what is preached. In trusting Talmudic tradition vice the gospel accounts, what kind of person did Maimonides think Yeshua was?

OBJECTION: Rabbi Eliezer originator of the Talmudic tradition of Jesus received this tradition from Yochanan ben Zakkai who died 80 C.E. It is believed he may have encountered Jesus. Moses Maimonides is in accord in the Mishneh Torah. In the censored 11th chapter "Hilchot Melachim" Jesus is revealed as a former student of Torah who went seriously off the rails and became a spiritual danger to the people of Israel. (18)

RESPONSE: The question becomes could the Jewish point of view be incorrect. The books of Exodus and Numbers displayed, had it not been for Moses intercession, that Yahveh was ready to consume his own people in a conflagration. Why? Because they kept getting it wrong. In Deuteronomy Yahveh tells Moses that the entire generation save a few will die in the desert and not pass into the Promised Land. The time of testing for Israel was 40 years. After 40 years the generation that was led out of Egypt was dead. In 30 C.E. the Sanhedrin including the Pharisees, Scribes and Sadducees reject Yeshua. If he were off the rails then certainly they did a good thing. If they made a bad decision then they rejected their Messiah, the Son of God. In Yahveh's patient manner a period of 40 years passed. Then in the year 70 C.E. Jerusalem and the Temple were destroyed and there would not be a nation state of Israel until 1948. Since many of the Prophets were also treated badly; is it out of the realm of possibility that the Jewish people would also miss the boat with their Messiah? If one can't accept this then why was Jerusalem and the Temple destroyed and why did the Jewish people suffer this long Diaspora? In Judaism segments see the events described above in terms of general faithlessness among the people, a means of purging heresy and corruption from the people of Israel, or a righteous Israel suffering for the sins of mankind. (19)

SEGUE: Rather than say things about Yeshua being a spiritual danger to the Jews, it would have been more convincing to argue that Yeshua sinned. Only the establishment of sin in the life of Yeshua eliminates his claim as God's Messiah. Perhaps others will try to make this connection.

OBJECTION: <u>Jesus' Mother Mary was a hairdresser who was married but conceived Jesus by a man named Pandira therefore he was referred to in the Talmud as Ben Pandira, the Son of Pandira. Mary was of the royal bloodline, but played the Harlot with carpenters. Pandira was her Paramour who was the carpenter not Joseph. According to Maimonides Jesus was the disciple of Joshua ben Perachya.</u> (20)

RESPONSE: According to the Talmud, Mary was a loose woman, a whore. This comes from either Rabbi Eliezer or his teacher Yochanan ben Zakkai who died before 80 C.E. Matthew was Yeshua's disciple. In Acts 1:13-14, Matthew is together with Mary praying with her other son's, Yeshua's brothers. This is not consistent with Mary being a whore. What we know from this is that

Matthew knew her. If the originators of the "Talmud Mary story" knew this "dirt" wouldn't her life style have been known by others? Yet Matthew who knew her wrote Matt.1:18-23 which states that Joseph was a nice man and that an Angel told him about Mary and that he wasn't to touch her until after Yeshua was born to fulfill Isa.7:14. Would a woman of the world have waited 9 months to have sex? Why did she marry Joseph a decent guy if she liked other men? In Luke 1: 28-30 the angel Gabriel states that Mary has found favor with God. In verses 46-55 Mary quotes from 1Sam.2:1-10. How many whores rattle off 10 verses from the Tenakh? If she was a whore how could this scandal have been kept quiet? If the Gospel writers knew it they would have also known that the entire Yeshua story was a sham. As far as Yeshua being the disciple of Joshua ben Perachya, Maimonides got it wrong. Joshua ben Perachya lived 100 years before Yeshua's birth. Since this part of the story is off by 100 years it is also probable that Mary the whore paramour of Ben Pandira is also misplaced and refers to a different Mary. For the Talmudic Mary is not consistent with other writings about her. (21)

SEGUE: The source for this fable is not even placed in the correct time period. When these events are all taken together this should lessen the credibility of Maimonides concerning the life of Yeshua. To some among the people of Israel they must decide if they can resurrect the credibility of Maimonides concerning Yeshua or if there are other sages who can make a more compelling point. Others with God's grace may begin to consider the words of Yeshua more closely.

OBJECTION: Nachmanides asserts the earth would turn peaceful when the Messiah comes. He accused Christians of being the biggest shedders of blood. Joseph Kimchi, 12th century sage stated Jesus accomplished nothing that can be seen. His son David wrote that 'The only place that Yeshua was lifted up and exalted was on the tree on which they hung him.' (22)

RESPONSE: In Luke 2:3-35 Simeon predicts Yeshua was destined for the fall and rise of many in Israel and for a sign that shall be spoken against. He would be a light to the gentiles and glory to your people Israel. Most Jews could not accept this and would come against his sign (cross), a light to the gentiles (for sure; Mic. 5:1-2) and glory to Israel not yet (Dan.7:13-14). In John 5:41-47 Yeshua states that he came in his Fathers name and he was not received, but another who comes in their own name will be accepted. Those who reject him will be accused by Moses because Moses wrote of him, but they don't believe his words. Matt. 8:11 Yeshua states that many will come from east and west and feast with Abraham Isaac and Jacob i.e. Gentiles will come to the knowledge of God through the ministry of Yeshua. John 8:46 "Which of you can convict me of sin? Mark 9:30 "The Son of Man is to be betrayed into the hands of men and they will kill him and having been killed he will rise again on the third day." Luke11: 47-48 "Woe to you for you built the tombs of the Prophets whereas your fathers killed them." Matt.19:28 "Truly I say you, in the world to come when the Son of Man shall sit on the throne of his glory, you shall also sit on 12 thrones judging the 12 tribes of Israel." Yeshua stated from the beginning that he would be rejected by his people but other people would believe in him. This has happened. He predicted that he would be killed, rise from the dead and sometime in the future sit on his throne.

Yeshua was rejected and killed just like other Prophets. The notion that the Jews will instinctively know their Messiah when he appears is mistaken. They will know him through the events of his first appearing. (23)

SEGUE: The assumption of those in the Jewish oral tradition is that Yeshua expected to be accepted and when he died his violent death this proved him to be false. The problem is that Yeshua predicted that he would be rejected by his own people throughout his ministry. His persecution was not unlike the Prophets that came before him. To be fair to Nachmanides perceptions, those professing Yeshua in gentile leadership positions were not only warring between themselves, but caused great suffering among God's chosen. From the point of view of those who were suffering, Christianity appeared to be a religion of blood and conquest. (24)

OBJECTION: Nachmanides stated nowhere does Isaiah 53 ever convey a belief that the Messiah scion of King David as distinct from his forerunner Messiah from the stock of Joseph would die. This allegorically depicted servant might be "like a sheep led to the slaughter" ready to die for the cause of the Lord, was different from actually being slaughtered. The Talmud stated that the Davidic Messiah, seeing how the Messiah son of Joseph has suffered will ask God for life and God will grant it. Isaiah reflected that the servant would live, have children, and enjoy success in battle. Nachmanides stated that whether the passage is to be taken literally or not referring to an individual or a collective Israel, there is no crucified Messiah in it. (25)

RESPONSE: Nachmanides speaks of a forerunner Messiah to the Messiah scion of David. In Mal.4:5 and in the Tenakh Mal. 3:23 "Behold I will send you Elijah the Prophet before the coming of the great and dreadful day of the Lord." In the Gospel according to Matthew "The disciples asked, why do the scribes say that first Elijah must come? Yeshua replied, "Elijah does come and he is to restore all things; but I tell you that Elijah has already come and they did not know him but did to him whatever they pleased So also the Son of Man will suffer at their hands. Then the disciples understood that he was speaking of John the Baptist." The Tenakh speaks of Elijah as the forerunner not a son of Joseph the messiah. There is only one true Messiah not multiple Messiah's. Nachmanides is wrong on other counts as well. The Book of the Prophet Isaiah states; "he was cut off out of the land of the living stricken for the transgression of my people. They made his grave with the wicked with a rich man in his death." The servant in this passage is killed. Yes the servant would live again. His offspring are those who believe in him and have promises of eternal life where they will become sons of God. See Prov.3: 11-12, Gal. 4:4-7, and Heb.12:7-8. (26)

SEGUE: Nachmanides developed his version of the Messiah and forerunner Messiah. Rather than strict adherence to the Tenakh it's more a development of his own machinations. To believe Nachmanides version one must develop a timeline whereby the Davidic Messiah will witness the suffering of the Messiah son of Joseph. According to this account God will answer the prayer of the Davidic Messiah. The Messiah son of Joseph will then procreate and be successful in war. I thought the Davidic Messiah is the Messiah successful in warfare? After all of this Nachmanides admits that this rendering may not be literal. What he concludes is what others also assert. They refuse to accept Yeshua.

OBJECTIONS: Nachmanides explained that since his ancestors living in the first century had rejected the claim made on Jesus behalf, it was enough to seal the case for him. They knew Jesus; they knew Paul. They knew what the prophets had to say. They knew what the rabbinic traditions indicated. With all this in mind they concluded that Jesus was not the Messiah. (27)

RESPONSE: Facts: The Jewish Prophets were treated no better than Yeshua. Does this mean that they were not prophets? Jewish people interpret the words of the Prophets through the lens of the Jewish Oral tradition that was not penned by the Prophets but by elders who did not speak 'Thus says the Lord'. If the oral tradition is in error Jewish thought concerning Yeshua is also in error. For it is this tradition that shapes Jewish thought. What they knew was that Yeshua told them things they did not want to hear. The question that Jewish people must answer is the following; why did all of Yeshua's Apostles preach Yeshua crucified and resurrected until the day they died? Their preaching and the preaching of St. Paul in the face of certain persecution and death led to Yahveh and Yeshua becoming a light to the Gentiles. (28)

SEGUE: Nachmanides admits that he rejects Yeshua based on what his ancestors decided. They may have known of Yeshua but they did not know him like the Apostles knew him. How did the Apostles and Paul live their lives after Yeshua was crucified? Up to 60 plus years after the events of 30 C.E. the last of them, the Apostle John, kept his faith in Yeshua. To the Jewish people of that time as with many today they may hesitate to examine the issue more closely. However, this issue deserves their attention. (29)

Chapter 2 Notes

1. Josephus, Jewish Antiquities, Book 18 Chapter 1:2- 4; Klinghoffer, PP.20-21
2. Ibid, Jewish Wars, Forward; Matt. 21:14-46; 22:1-46; 23:1-39
3. Ibid, Jewish Antiquities, Book 18 Chapter 3:3
4. Ibid, Jewish Wars Preface; Jewish Antiquities, Appendix: Dissertation I
5. Ibid, Jewish Antiquities, Book 18 Chapter 1:2-5; Klinghoffer, P.46
6. Ibid, Jewish Antiquities, Book18 Chapter 5:2; Book 20 Chapter 9:1
7. Klinghoffer, P.3
8. B.Sanhedrin43a, 107b, Sotah 47a, and M. Sanhedrin 6:4; Klinghoffer, P.73
9. Luke 4:18-19
10. Twersky, A Maimonides Reader, Epistle to Yemen P.441; Klinghoffer, P.161
11. Bruce, The New Covenant Documents: Are they reliable? Chapter 10; Chevallier, The Apologies of Justin Martyr and Tertullian; Chapter 21
12. Maimonides, Guide of the Perplexed, P.67; Klinghoffer, P.174
13. Gen.1:1-2, 26; 3:22; Ps. 110: 1; Isa. 48:16-17
14. Twersky, A Maimonides Reader, PP.226-227; Klinghoffer, P.179
15. Zech. 14: 3-4, 9, 16-17
16. Maimonides, Mishneh Torah, 'Hilchot Melachim' 8:10, 9:1; Klinghoffer, P.198

17. Num.14:11-23
18. Herford, *Christianity in Talmud and Midrash,* P.352; Klinghoffer, PP.141-2
19. Ex.31:9-14; Num.14:11-20; Deut. 1:34-37
20. B Shabbat 104b; B Sanhedrin 106a; Herford, PP.37ff; Klinghoffer, P.142
21. Klinghoffer, Why the Jews Rejected Jesus, P.142
22. Isa.2:4; Maccoby, op.cit. P.121; Talmage, op.cit, PP.30-31; Klinghoffer, P.161
23. Zech. 12:10.
24. See Chapter 1 notes # 34
25. B. Sukkak 52a; Klinghoffer, PP.169-170
26. Matt.17: 10-13; Isa. 53: 8-9
27. Klinghoffer, Why the Jews Rejected Jesus, P.171
28. IIChron.36:15-16; Matt.23:29-36
29. Chevallier, The Apologies of Justin Martyr and Tertullian, 50, 13 (PL.1, 534); (CChr. 1, 171); Flannery, Vatican Council II, P.818

Chapter 3

The Talmud Weighs In On Reconciliation

OBJECTION: the Talmud and Gospels agree on various points. John 19:31; Matt 26:64; Mark 14:62 speak of the blasphemy charge against Jesus. (1)

RESPONSE: The real point is missed here. Yeshua had forgiven sins and declared that He and the Father were one. This is why in latter Jewish works like the "Toledot Yeshu" it states that Yeshua performed wonders by abusing the Power of God's Name (YHVH or Yahveh) although Yeshua was named Yahveh's Salvation. In his book "Why the Jews rejected Jesus" author David Klinghoffer realized that the account of these events in the Toledot Yeshu were exaggerated. The text described how Yeshua wrote the letters of God's name on parchment and hid this inside a wound. When he forgot the code he reopened the cut to obtain the letters. (2)

SEGUE: What we just experienced was a 5th to 6th century work trying to discredit what three of the four first century Gospels state concerning Yeshua and the charge of blasphemy. Since many Jews can't or won't accept the first century accounts of Yeshua some others came up with alternate explanations hundreds of years later. For many Jews, during the time period cited above, the theory of two messiahs gave the best explanation.

OBJECTION: The Talmud states that Moshiakh ben Yosef the forerunner of Moshiakh ben David will die while Moshiakh ben David will live: (3)

RESPONSE: The Talmud comes up with the concept of two messiahs to explain the pierced messiah. The dilemma of Micah 5:1-2 and Dan.7:13-14 are not addressed. The rabbis practically make the point for Christians in that the legal Father of Yeshua was Yosef Matt 1:16-17. Coincidentally the father of Yeshua's legal guardian was also Jacob as the rabbis assert. Two messiahs are also problematic for another reason. If the rabbis were referring to an actual descendent of Joseph son of Jacob, the Patriarch, it would be most difficult to identify a messiah in modern times belonging to the tribes of Joseph, specifically Manasseh or Ephraim, since those tribes never returned, lest we consider the plight of the Samaritans, because of the Assyrian destruction of the Northern Kingdom of Israel in 721 B.C.E. If this is not the case the rabbis could be speaking of a descendent of David who has a father named Joseph. Messiah ben David (Moshiakh ben David) must be born in Bethlehem. He must be a son of David who was a descendent of Jacob's son Judah. Messiah ben David must be a descendent of David's family, and be born in David's city Bethlehem. Since the rabbis say that Messiah ben Joseph (Moshiakh ben Yosef) will die then he must be born in Bethlehem. This seems to indicate that Moshiakh ben Yosef cannot be a descendent of Joseph son of the Patriarch since he could not be born in David's city. This must be so because Messiah ben Joseph must die. Messiah ben David will not die. He must come on the clouds with great glory as described in Dan.7:13-14. How can he be "ben David" if he comes from heaven? Messiah ben David can only be son of David if he is born in

Bethlehem and fulfills Dan.7:13-14. This could only be true if Messiah Ben Yosef and Messiah ben David were one in the same person separated by different events and millennia of time. Messiah ben David must be born in David's city. The Messiah described in Dan.7:13-14 is Messiah ben David. He is Yeshua, Yahveh's Salvation, and Lord. (4)

SEGUE: The two messiah rabbinical theory cannot fulfill the Prophesy of Dan. 7 because neither messiah is the literal Son of God. The Talmud then tried to explain what will happen and what other powers would be involved.

OBJECTION: <u>Moshiakh ben Yosef was to defeat the power of Esau, brother of Patriarch Jacob, who stands in Jewish tradition as a figure for Rome</u>: (5)

RESPONSE: The book of Obadiah states; "Every man from Mount Esau will be cut off by slaughter from the violence done to your brother Jacob, shame shall cover you and you shall be cut off forever." The brother of Jacob, Esau, could never be Rome as described in Jewish tradition. These are the descendents of Esau known as Edom and their territory is identified in Obadiah 1:17-21. This is not Rome. This again shows an error of the Talmud and why Jewish people should feel free to read the Tenakh without Talmudic interference. Obadiah is speaking of a current and future conflict with the Arabs (Muslims) not the Romans (Pagans/Christians). (6)

SEGUE: It does not matter what the rabbi's and sages believe concerning the people who existed as Edom and who are now part of the Arab nation joined with the Ishmaelites. Although they may feel that an allegory suits their purpose they cannot make the case that God's intention was for them to view Esau as Rome. Unfortunately we will see below that the Jewish discourse concerning Yeshua and Christians will become more trying. (7)

OBJECTION: The Talmud states; "May the apostates (Minim) have no hope unless they return to your Torah and may the Nazarenes and the Minim disappear in a moment. May they be erased from the book of Life and not be inscribed with the righteous." In another section Rabbi Tarphon says if he was being chased by an enemy and his life was in danger he would flee into a pagan temple but would give up his life before entering a Jewish Christian Church." Rabbi Ishmael said "they arouse jealousy, enmity and dissention between Israel and our father in heaven." (8)

RESPONSE: These sayings arose after the destruction of the second Temple. Although most Jews did not follow Yeshua the Jews who didn't believe in Yeshua blamed the Jewish Christians for the disaster of 70 C.E. In other words the majority had to suffer for the convictions of a minority. Could the collective Jewish Psyche have even contemplated Luke 19:41-44? "And when he drew near and saw the city he wept over it, saying, Would that even today you knew the things that make for peace! But now they are hid from your eyes. For the days will come upon you, when your enemies will cast up a bank about you and surround you, and hem you in on every side, and dash you to the ground, you and your children within you, and they will not leave one stone upon another in you; because you did not know the time of your visitation." Since The Jewish people of that time were unable to consider this, the culpability of the event was thus transferred to the Jewish Christians. (9)

SEGUE: Obviously from the discourse of Rabbi Tarphon, the thought of even turning to Christians for help was unthinkable. The issue still comes back to Yeshua. The appropriate rebuttal is against what he taught. One should always try to determine if he sinned. As for the Jewish Christian decision not to defend Jerusalem in 70 C.E. It may be prudent to consider Mark 13:14. Although it appears that Yeshua was referring to the end of time, Jewish Christians may have seen "the end" in the events of 70 C.E. and therefore fled to Petra.

OBJECTION: The Talmud tractate Avodah Zarah states when God brought Israel to Sinai they were not his first choice. He offered the covenant to every other people on earth but they all turned it down. Maharal, rabbinic sage who died in 1609 stated, "This means that He (God) examined their character to see if they possessed a predisposition to the Torah and did not find it in them and this constituted their refusal. (10)

RESPONSE: Let's follow this through. Gen.6:18 God said to Noah, "I will establish my covenant with you" Gen.9:8 "God said to Noah and to his son's with him, Behold I establish my covenant with you and your descendents after you..." What we know is that God made a Covenant with Noah and his son's. Gen.9:24 "Cursed be Canaan; a slave of slaves shall he be to his brothers...Blessed be Shem and let Canaan be his slave. God enlarge Japheth and let him dwell in the tents of Shem; and let Canaan be his slave. What we know is that Canaan and his descendents Gen.10:15-18 were eliminated from the Covenant this includes Sidon,

Heth, Jebusites, Amorites, Girgashites, Hivites, Arkites, Sinites, Arvadites, Zemarites, and Hamathites. The other son's of Ham, at this point, remain, Cush, Egypt and Put. The promise to Noah's son Japheth is growth; however, Shem alone is blessed. This extends to his son's Gen.10:22 "Elam, Asshur, Arpachshad, Lud and Aram. From Shem's son Arpachshad was born Shelah Gen.11:12; Shelah was the father of Eber Gen.11:14; Eber was the father of Peleg Gen.11:16; Peleg was the father of Reu Gen.11:18; Reu became the father of Serug Gen.11:20; Serug became the father of Nahor Gen.11: 22; Nahor became the father of Terah Gen11: 24; Terah became the father of Abram, Nahor and Haran Gen.11:26. Gen.14:15 proves that these words were penned between the book of Joshua 1200 B.C.E. and the 8th Century B.C.E. for it speaks of Damascus, but there was no Damascus 4000 years ago. Gen.15:18 "On that day the Lord made a covenant with Abram." Sarai had a maid Hagar who was Egyptian Gen.16:1. Hagar bore Abram a son Ishmael Gen.16:15-16. At this point of the son's of Ham; Cush, Egypt and Put only Egypt is in a position to receive the Covenant from Abram. God tells Abraham "I will establish my Covenant between me and you and your descendents throughout their generations for an everlasting Covenant Gen.17:7. Therefore, Covenant established with Abraham is everlasting. "God said, Sarah your wife shall bear you a son and you shall name him Isaac. I will establish my everlasting Covenant with him and his descendents after him Gen.17:19. Ishmael, although blessed does not receive the Covenant. Egypt the only son of Ham placed in a position to inherit the covenant is eliminated from consideration. Gen.35:9-12 God changes Jacob's, son of Isaac, name to Israel and promises him what was promised to Abraham and his father Isaac. According to the Talmud, Israel was the last people that God considered for the Covenant but only they had the predisposition for the Torah. The Tenakh proves that God made his Covenant with Noah. Canaan son of Ham was eliminated from consideration. Shem not Japheth was given the blessing. Only Arpachshad son of Shem and his descendents are highlighted because through him and his descendent Terah, Abraham was born. His first born son through the Egyptian Hagar is eliminated from consideration. Isaac receives the Covenant. His son Esau had it but sold it carelessly so he was eliminated. Then his brother Jacob/Israel was given the Covenant and the 12 tribes are descendent of him. The point being made that "every other people on earth were offered the Covenant" is simply not true. Deut. 7:6 "The Lord God has chosen you...out of the peoples that are on the face of the earth...you were the fewest of all the people...it is because the Lord loves you and is keeping the oath which he swore to your fathers" The Talmud is incorrect. Israel was not God's last choice. He picked them not because others rejected his offer but because he loves them and observed his oath to Noah, Shem, Abraham, Isaac, and Jacob.

SEGUE: The Jewish people are God's chosen not his leftovers. This is another example of the learned in Judaism developing a duel reality with the Tenakh. It was exactly this dual tract that Yeshua rejected. He objected to it because it kept the Jewish people from discovering the most precious gift that God wanted to give them. The discourse continues.

OBJECTIION: <u>The Talmud states; "40 years before the Temples destruction and onward there were supernatural omens of the disaster to come...following the death of Jesus.</u> (11)

RESPONSE: In the Babylonian Talmud, rabbi Dr. Epstein, ed Erubin 21b states "My son be more careful in the observance of the scribes [Talmud] than in the words of the Torah. " See Isa. 29:13-14. God does not want the teaching of the Talmud to become more important than the Word of the Lord found in the Written Torah. God says in Isaiah that he will make this "wisdom" perish and will cause their discernment to be hidden. This means that the rabbis will get some things wrong. In Sanhedrin 97 a-b The Tanna debe Eliyyahu teaches the world is to exist 6000 years. In the first 2000 there was desolation; 2000 years for Torah flourished; and the next 2000 years is the messianic era, but through our many sins all these years have been lost. This material refers to events after the destruction of the Temple in 70 C.E. Let's review the content of Sanhedrin 97 a-b. It recognizes three periods: Adam to Abraham (2000) years; Abraham to Yeshua (2000) years. Yeshua to the present falls within what Tanna debe Eliyyahu teaches was the messianic era .and concludes with the words "but through our many sins all these years have been lost." This can only have two meanings:

1. The Jewish people sinned terribly during the past 2000 years. This is why they lost their land and were treated horribly because God being holy and just, could not bless them.

2. Since the Jewish people reject Yeshua (Psalm 69:1-14; Psalm118 22-23; Isa. 53:1-12) the Jewish people lost 2000 years of fellowship and worship with their Messiah.

This also applies to the next tractate. Talmud Yoma 9b "But why was the second Sanctuary destroyed seeing that in its time they (the Jews) were occupying themselves with the Torah, the precepts, and the practice of charity...because therein hatred prevailed without a cause." The question is asked; why was the second sanctuary destroyed? Answer: Because hatred prevailed without a cause. Notice Yeshua's words Luke 19:41-44 "When he drew near the city (Jerusalem) he wept over it, saying 'Would that even today you knew the things that make for peace! But now they are hid from your eyes. For the days shall come upon you when your enemies will cast up a bank about you and surround you and hem you in on every side and dash you to the ground you and your children within you, and they will not leave one stone upon another in you because you did not know the time of your visitation." Being hated without a cause was foretold by King David, the prophet Isaiah and explains the events of Zech 12.

Talmud Rosh Hashanah 31b states that originally they used to fasten the thread of scarlet on the door of the Temple court on the outside. If it turned white the people used to rejoice, and if it did not turn white they were sad... For 40 years before the destruction of the Temple the thread of the scarlet never turned white but it remained red." What occurred exactly 40 years before the Temple was destroyed in 70 C.E.? In 30 C.E. Yeshua was rejected by the Pharisees, Sadducees, and Scribes. He was put to death by the Romans then became the first to be resurrected from the grave three days after being slain (Psalm 16:10, Pro.30:3-4, Isa.53:12, Hos.6:1-3, Dan.12:2-3). There was a 1 in 360 chance that Yeshua was slain when the Passover lamb was slain and like the Passover lamb King David foretold Psalm 34:21 "He keeps all his bones; not one of them is broken." Now we see according to the rabbis, the scarlet thread did not turn white from the time of Yeshua's execution to the destruction of the Temple. It appears that God was speaking to his people. Were his people listening? Compare this with Matt.27:51-53 and Mark.15: 38. The Talmud admits that strange happenings began to occur and these things started at the time of Yeshua's death. Notice Dan.9:26-27. Who then is the Messiah to be cut off before the destruction of the Temple? The number 40 is also significant. Moses on Sinai with God Ex. 34:28, Elijah at Sinai 1King 19:8; Yeshua being tested by Satan Matt 4:1-2, and the Israelites wandering in the desert 40 years. In all instances 40 becomes likened to a time of testing. Just as the logic of the events of 721 B.C.E. and 586 B.C.E. can be used to interpret the events of 70 C.E. so can the logic of testing or proving worthy be placed to the number 40 when determining the number of years between the Crucifixion of Yeshua and the destruction of the Second Temple. (12)

SEGUE: If Yeshua was an insignificant dreamer who the Jewish people rejected, why were there omens of the disaster to come, a disaster that Yeshua predicted? Did the Jews at that time plead a mea culpa concerning the events of 70 C.E.? (13)

OBJECTIONS: <u>The Jewish Oral tradition places the blame on Minim who abrogated the covenant</u>. (14)

RESPONSE: The reasoning follows that the majority will suffer for the actions of the minority. Taking the argument from the Talmud, Jerusalem was destroyed because some Jews accepted Yeshua and abrogated the original covenant, although Jews who became apostates and collaborated with Rome were as numerous as the Jews who believed in Yeshua. The events of 70 C.E. had nothing to do with Jewish sinfulness, or Jewish rejection of Yeshua who claimed to be the Messiah. They also make no issue of the fact that the dead remains of Yeshua were never recovered. If that had happened, the Christian movement never would have started. To blame the total destruction of Jerusalem and the Temple on a small minority in their midst is another error portrayed in the oral tradition. In fact Yeshua and those who followed him were a threat to the legitimacy of the Jewish establishment which consisted of those who ran the Temple, mostly Sadducees, and those who controlled the Sanhedrin, mostly Pharisees.

SEGUE: The original Covenant could not have been abrogated as stated in the Objection because God swore upon his name to sustain it. The New Covenant was announced at Passover 30 C.E. Those who believed in the New Covenant saw it as the ultimate fulfillment of the intent of the original Covenant. Where the original promised to preserve a remnant of the children of Israel, the New provided a permanent atonement and thus fulfilled the Old Covenant in its entirety. (15)

OBJECTION: <u>The Jewish sage Abahu concurred; "If a man tells you, 'I am God' he is a liar; if he says 'I am the son of man,' in the end people will laugh at him.. The next objection based on the same theme states; "I am the first and I am the last and aside from me there is no God." The Talmudic explanation states that God has no father, no son, and no brother.</u> (16)

RESPONSE: The initial comment is based on a verse from the Torah. "God is not a man that he should not tell the truth; neither the son of man that he should repent: he has said it and will he not do it? This is part of Balaam's reply to Balak. Within the context of Num. 22 & 23 it means that God can be trusted because he is without sin unlike a man. Abahu concludes from this that God will never be a man or be called the son of man. Let's look at the Psalms chapter 2. The Kings of the earth and other earthly rulers will take counsel against Yahveh and his Anointed (Messiah). Who is this Anointed? He will be the King. David then says "I will tell of the decree of the Lord. He said to me 'You are my son. Today I have begotten you". What we learn from this is that the Messiah, King and Son are the same. Psalm 45 speaks of the Divine throne enduring forever. "Therefore God your God has anointed you. Here God is anointing someone whose "Divine" throne will endure forever. This has not happened yet. Why? Psalm 110 "The Lord says to my Lord 'sit at my right hand until I make your enemies your footstool". The Lord is sitting at the Lord's (Yahveh) right hand. (17)

The next objection stems from Isaiah 44. Abahu omitted the beginning of this verse in his argument. "Thus says the Lord, the King of Israel and his Redeemer, The Lord of hosts." Here the Lord is identified as the King of Israel, but there is another Redeemer who is the Lord of hosts. We received indications of this from Gen.1:26, 3:22 and Isa.48:16. "I have not spoken in secret from the beginning." See the Genesis quotes. "There I am, the Lord God, and His Spirit has sent me. The Talmudic explanation is proven incorrect by the scripture. (18)

SEGUE: At this point the discussion departs concerning the oneness of God as determined by Jewish Oral tradition and the triune nature of God. The discourse continues in the next section concerning the first chapter of Genesis.

OBJECTION: Regarding Gen. 1:26 "in our image" Rabbi Yochanan, a 3rd century Palestinian sage reported a tradition about a conversation between God and Moses. When Moses came to "in our image" he stated "What a pretext for heresy you have given to the Minim. I am amazed! God replied Write and he who wishes to err let him err." (19)

RESPONSE: This is put forth by Rabbi Yochanan as proof concerning how Gen.1:26 should be interpreted. It is however beset with problems. The 3rd century sage, meaning he spoke 200 years after Yeshua, cites a tradition where God and Moses have this discussion. The 3rd Century C.E. Sage cites a tradition about an event that occurred over a millennium before Yeshua. In this conversation Moses speaks of the pretext to heresy this could give the Minim. God and Moses are having a conversation about "Heretical" Christians some 1400 years before any Christians existed! This tradition is not part of the Tenakh, but yet it is portrayed as being true. Are Moses and God speaking about future Christian heretics? This is not likely. What is more likely is that the sage made this up as a way of dealing with this problematic scripture. In Deut.18:15-18 who was the Prophet that Moses was speaking of? These traditions are what separate the Jewish people from their Messiah. The Prophet Isaiah speaks of the Jewish people honoring God with their mouth and lips, but following the traditions of men i.e. the oral Torah known as the Talmud. If the oral traditions were to be considered like the Tenakh where are the references in the Tenakh that point to them? Isaiah points out that these traditions have unfortunately superseded the scripture for his people. (20)

SEGUE: It becomes clear that the oral tradition was developed in order to interpret "problematic" scriptures. What we see is the oral tradition taking on the importance of the word of God. When the Messiah came and told his people that their sages got it wrong, meaning the oral tradition with all its errors, He pointed towards a main reason why the Jewish people could not accept their long awaited promise, the Messiah. (21)

OBJECTION: Jewish tradition cites the following; "Because Abraham obeyed my voice and observed my safeguards, my commandments, my decrees and my Torahs." This indicated not only the written but the oral Torah. (22)

RESPONSE: Once again it seems as though we have a disconnection from the Word of God and commentary. The verse cited does not come from the first five books of the Bible. It comes from an oral tradition that is viewed by Jewish people as being scriptural. The point being that Abraham already had the Torah i.e. law. As observed this quote is not part of the Bible. The argument is also made regarding Torahs i.e. laws. Since the Rabbi's already have 613 laws to observe, the Torah applies to these laws, not one Torah in written form and one Torah in oral form. There was no Mosaic law in 2000 B.C.E. during the time of Abraham. In Genesis it states that Abraham was righteous because he believed God. This same book of Moses goes on to display that God blessed Abraham because he obeyed God's voice. There is no mention of performing or fulfilling 613 laws. The Talmudic tradition was created to give credence to the rabbi's argument. It's not in harmony with the intent of written scripture which points to salvation through the blessed hope. (23)

SEGUE: The Mosaic Law was not known to Abraham. Abraham's faith in God made him righteous. He trusted God. A person can keep numerous laws but still not trust God. A person can keep numerous laws but still not possess the faith of Abraham. Despite this the first book of Moses portrayed Abraham as less than totally honest and displayed a lack of faith. He also appeared willing to save his own skin and risk that an Egyptian may want to have relations with his wife. Abraham clearly sinned. Therefore; Abraham was not considered righteous because he kept the law. Abraham was deemed righteous because of his faith. (24)

OBJECTION: Rabbi Simeon ben Yohai stated the Messiah will come if all Israel observed two Sabbaths. Rabbi Yochanan said the Messiah will come when a generation was either entirely righteous or wicked. The argument goes that repentance will bring the Messiah. To the Jews it would be clear that the Messiah had not come in the first century. (25)

RESPONSE: The rabbis obviously don't know. They do know that they must reject the Christian explanation because to accept that would mean that the rabbis of the past got it wrong. In the Gospel of Matthew Yeshua stated, "O Jerusalem, Jerusalem killing the Prophets and stoning those who are sent to you! How often would I have gathered your children together as a hen gathers her brood under her wings and you would not! Behold your house is forsaken and desolate. For I tell you, you will not see me again until you say, Baruch ha ba B'shem Adonai 'Blessed is he who comes in the name of the Lord.'"(26)

SEGUE: According to Rabbi Yohai, Israel must observe two Sabbaths. This is his opinion not Sacred Writ. Rabbi Yochanan covers all bases by saying that Messiah comes when people will either be righteous or wicked. Wicked people don't repent only people who do bad things and want to get righteous repent. As for the carpenter from Galilee what kind of person was he?

OBJECTION: Jesus had a bad habit of making inappropriate remarks about women. He was cast out of Rabbi Joshua's circle because of a series of misunderstandings he conceived and for instructing others in his heretical ideas. Jesus was so hurt that this suffering motivated him to stray in his beliefs and his teachings. Jesus states the following according to the Talmud; "I have learned this from you: everyone who sins and causes other people to sin will not receive the opportunity to repent." Jesus is referred to as a wayward fellow man. He practiced magic and led astray and deceived Israel. He went astray because of his own character flaw. (27)

RESPONSE: This entire encounter is related to Yeshua's strained relationship with Rabbi Joshua ben Perachya. This Rabbi was mentioned before. He actually lived 100 years before Yeshua was born. There is a serious credibility problem with this set of Jewish beliefs. Yeshua states in the Gospel of Matthew in regard to women "I say to you everyone who looks at a woman lustfully has already committed adultery with her in his heart." In John's Gospel a woman was caught in the act of adultery. She's about to be stoned but Yeshua challenges the one without sin to cast the first stone. After they depart Yeshua said "Has no one condemned you...neither do I condemn you; go and sin no more."

This is the same Yeshua who has a bad habit of making inappropriate remarks about women? Again in Matthew's Gospel Yeshua states, "Every sin and blasphemy will be forgiven men but blasphemy against the Holy Spirit will not be forgiven...Speaking against the Son of Man will be forgiven but speaking against the Holy Spirit will not be forgiven." The Yeshua of the Gospels says nothing about not receiving the opportunity to repent. As far as practicing magic, we find no evidence that Yeshua was involved with conjuring up spirits, omen-taking or fortune telling. In terms of healing people Isaiah spoke of this in Isa.35:5 and 42:7. Then in Matt.11:5-6, Yeshua speaks about how the blind see, the lame walk, lepers are cleansed, the deaf hear, and the dead are raised. Which of these actions deserve Talmudic ridicule if not true? If Yeshua deceived people then explain why the book of Acts was written? They would have been aware of his deceit. Finally another episode that illustrates Yeshua's character flaw can be found in the Gospel according to Luke, "And when they came to the place called the skull there they crucified him and the criminals one to the right and one to the left and Yeshua said "Father forgive them for they know not what they do." (28)

SEGUE: According to the objection as stated above, a Jewish person must believe that Yeshua had bad intentions concerning women. He (Yeshua) was rejected by a Rabbi who was dead before Yeshua was born in Bethlehem. Yeshua's internal torment caused him to teach others heretical ideas. He caused other people to sin and therefore was not afforded the opportunity to repent. He practiced magic, deceived Israel and had a character flaw. If any of this were true, what then happened to Yeshua after he was crucified?

OBJECTION: Onkelos was the Nephew of Titus the Roman General who destroyed Jerusalem in 70 C.E. Onkelos, who was considering conversion to Judaism used magic to raise the spirit of Titus from hell where he was burned. The Spirit of Titus stated that Israel was the most highly esteemed in the afterworld... Onkelos then raised the spirit of Jesus who also agreed that Israel was highly esteemed. Onkelos then asked Jesus about his punishment in hell. Jesus answered 'boiled in excrement'. "Everyone who mocks the words of the wise is punished by boiling excrement". The rabbis viewed boiling in excrement as a symbolically appropriate punishment. (29)

RESPONSE: In this instance the "truth" in the Talmud comes from a goy relative of the man who destroyed Jerusalem in 70 C.E. and an avid practitioner of magic i.e. he conjured up spirits. According to the Torah in the Book of Deuteronomy "Anyone who practices divination, a soothsayer or an astrologer or sorcerer or a charmer or a medium or a wizard or a necromancer for whoever does these things is an abomination to the Lord." In the First Book of Samuel, Saul violates the Lord's command in Deuteronomy. The medium conjures up what is supposed to be the Spirit of Samuel the Prophet. The Medium at Endor then declares "I see a god coming up out of the earth." Saul "knew" it was Samuel so he bowed with his face to the ground. The Book of Leviticus states, "Regard them not that have familiar spirits, neither seek after wizards, to be defiled by them. A man or women that practices divination of spirits shall surely be put to death. In the Book of Chronicles it states concerning Manasseh King of Judah, He observed times and used enchantments and used witchcraft, and dealt with familiar spirit and with wizards: he wrought much evil in the sight of the Lord to provoke him to anger. The Talmud places its trust in the testimony of a goy necromancer, an abomination according to the Lord. Therefore these "gods' came up out of the earth and the Jewish people believe this a genuine account of Yeshua in the hereafter. In actuality the entire actions of Onkelos are an abomination to the Lord. Despite these biblical truths, this story is included in the Jewish tradition as being true. (30)

SEGUE: In order to assure themselves that they did not reject God's Messiah, alternate stories were devised. In this case a story was invented that was in opposition to what God had forbidden in his written word. Since this account comes about via a means that God forbids, it is not and cannot be true let alone be included as part of Judaism.

OBJECTION: God revealed the Torah with its oral explanation to the Jewish people. Jesus was dismissive of the Torah's oral transmission. He cast aside the wisdom of the elders. Believers in false religious ideas see this reality in a distorted form. (31)

RESPONSE: Where does the written Torah state that it cannot be interpreted without the tradition of the elders? Did the Prophets claim that their Prophesy could only be interpreted with the tradition of the elders? Were the Elders also the Prophets of the Tenakh? NO! The Jewish people had the written Torah and the Oral Torah yet still treated the Prophets shamefully. You can agree that the Prophets were treated shamefully yet when Yeshua comes to the Judeans in God's name he is also treated like the Prophets yet some Jewish people account this for good. Does the tradition of the Elders, The oral Torah, prevent Jews from coming to Yeshua?

Yes! If the Elders did well by rejecting Yeshua why was Jerusalem destroyed 40 years later? Why didn't God reward the Jewish forefathers for rejecting Yeshua's false ideas? If Yeshua is the Messiah and your forefathers rejected him the destruction of Jerusalem and a 2000 year Diaspora become understandable although not the only reason why these events occurred. Given the Roman occupation in 63 B.C.E. by Pompey the Great, clearly God was not pleased with the Jewish behavior. The Gospel of Mark written 58 C.E. states according to Yeshua that Jerusalem and the Temple would be destroyed. It occurred as predicted 12 years later. (32)

SEGUE: The question then comes in this section, was Yeshua wiser than those who wrote the oral tradition? Perhaps our individual journey will depend on how people answer this question. The objection declares that Yeshua distorted the Law yet people who practiced what he preached live good lives. Something does not add up.

OBJECTION: <u>According to the Oral Tradition, Esau becomes the persecutor of Jacob therefore Esau stands for Christianity</u>. (33)

RESPONSE: If this analogy is to be taken literally then Rome/Christianity is/are the elder brother of Jacob. This is false on both counts. Judaism came before Christianity and Israel predates Rome. Then who is Esau? The one who planned to murder Jacob Gen.27:41-42. The one who married Ishmael's daughter Gen.28:9. The one who married Canaanite women Gen.36:2. Also see Gen.28:8. Esau is Edom Gen.36:1, 19. Amalek is a son of Esau Gen.36:16. Yahveh promises that Amalek will be wiped out forever Ex.17:14-16. Yahveh is against all of Edom Exek.36:5; Amos1:11-12. Edom is listed together with the Ishmaelites conspiring to destroy Israel as a nation Ps.83:1-12. For all these reasons Esau cannot be Rome or Christianity. The Elders of the oral tradition would once again be incorrect. However, if this representation was meant to be figurative one could understand how pre-modern Christianity seemed like a type of Esau since the pre-modern professing Christians were notorious for persecuting the Jewish people.

SEGUE: The problem is continual. In a literal sense the elders continually disregard their own scriptures for the stories of the oral tradition that are inaccurate. Esau's descendents in reality are followers of the Arab Prophet. The written scripture describes a different reality.

OBJECTION: <u>The Talmud claims to tell Jewish history as genealogy. Esau's children founded the city and later the empire of Rome. Rome would fall and be replaced by the Kingdom of Messiah after people repented. This would vindicate Jewish tradition</u>. (34)

RESPONSE: Genesis lists the offspring and dwelling places of all the Chiefs of Esau (Edom). None of the places mentioned can be confused with Rome. They are all south and east of modern day Israel. Rome is approx.1000 miles northwest of the lands of Edom. The oral tradition became the Talmud, the written oral tradition, from 400-430 C.E. Rome was allegedly founded in 758 B.C.E. by two brothers Romulus and Remus. There is no mention of the son's of Esau. There is a reason for that. These folks were still in the Arabian desert. Edom and the folks mentioned in Psalm 83 are all Arab peoples more specifically the Muslim nations that surround Israel. When the Babylonian Talmud was written, no later than 430 C.E., Muhammad was not yet born. That occurred in 570 C.E. The Edomites described in the Psalms are Arab Muslims not the progenitors of modern day Italians. The Talmud once again misses the mark. (35)

SEGUE: This section proves conclusively that the elders were not Prophets. They did not foresee Islam. They could see no further than the Romanized Christianity of their day. Esau becoming Rome is not an accurate analogy.

OBJECTION: <u>Rabbi Naftali Zvi Yehuda Berlin a.k.a. called Netziv stated Esau has long been understood by the Jews as a type of Rome</u>. (36)

RESPONSE: According to the Rabbi, this has long been understood. The problem is that reality has changed which proves that Esau and Rome are not compatible. The Talmud should be updated to show that this literal interpretation was and is outdated, irrelevant, and incorrect.

SEGUE: Perhaps there have been other rabbis who have studied these issues and realized that the ancient sages and elders missed the mark.

OBJECTION: <u>German Rabbi Jacob Emden praised the Nazarene for bringing about a double kindness in the world. He strengthened the Torah of Moses majestically...not one of our sages spoke out more emphatically concerning the immutability of the Torah</u>

and he did much good for the Gentiles by doing away with the pagan gods. He also bestowed on them ethical ways. He blames errant scholars among the Christians who insisted Jesus intended to displace the Torah and abrogate its commandments among the Jews. (37)

RESPONSE: We have a minority Jewish opinion concerning the good that Yeshua brought to the world. Rabbi Emden contradicts the sages and elders. Yeshua strengthens the Torah, does good for the Gentiles. Yeshua did not set up worship of pagan gods. Yeshua was ethical. The good rabbi has his finger on the pulse. Some early Christian scholars got it wrong concerning the abrogation of the commandments. Not being Jews they couldn't conceive of Judaism with Yeshua. They believed the Church replaced the Synagogue when in reality the Church, believers in Yeshua, is commanded to love and be longsuffering with the people who worshipped in the Synagogue.

SEGUE: Here we begin to have a coming together. Rabbi Emden sees Yeshua as a force for good not bad. The question we may never know is if Yeshua was considered a personage for good among the Jews, where would his place be in the Jewish faith? At this point, he has no status among the people of Israel.

OBJECTION: Unlike Christianity and Islam, Judaism was never intended or suited to be a mass religion. 16th Century scholar Rabbi Ovadiah Sforno summarized "And now if you hearken well and observe my covenant, you shall be to me a kingdom of Priests and a holy nation meaning this was a call to share God with other peoples and to instruct all of mankind to call on the name of the Lord. God's instruction to the Jews at the moment of revelation of the Torah was to bring the knowledge of the Lord to humanity. (38)

RESPONSE: Since Judaism was never intended or suited to be a mass religion, how then could the Jews within Judaism instruct all of mankind to call upon the name of the Lord? Did Judaism do this? More specifically did the people that rejected Yeshua, for Judaism dismisses him as the Messiah, act as priests to the Gentiles? How did the gentiles come to embrace the God of Abraham, Isaac, and Jacob? Didn't this occur through St. Paul the Apostle to the Gentiles whose theology Jewish people cannot and will not accept? It makes no sense to say Yeshua got it wrong and Paul got it wrong yet through them and their teaching western civilization has been a blessing. As far as the Jews and the covenant that Rabbi Sforno quoted notice Jer.31:32. God speaks through the Prophet Jeremiah and tells Israel that they have broken the original Covenant so God is making a New Covenant that is not like the original covenant. Those who accepted this New Covenant, both Jews and Gentiles, brought this knowledge and worship of the God of Abraham, Isaac, and Jacob to the nations. The People of the original covenant did preserve the Old Covenant and became a minority people who excel in law, politics, the arts, science etc...In this capacity the Jewish people have been a blessing to the world.

SEGUE: It cannot be argued that knowledge of the God of Abraham was spread throughout the world by the followers of Yeshua. According to Rabbi Sforno, the Jewish people are supposed to be sharing the Hebrew God with the peoples of the world. Jewish people brought this word to the Gentiles but more specifically it was the Jewish followers of the rejected Jew Yeshua who are specifically responsible for bringing this light to the Gentiles.

OBJECTION: According to rabbinical tradition if the Jews deserved to be redeemed the king would come on the clouds. If the Jews did not deserve a King, God would send the Messiah anyway, but he would come humbly upon a donkey: (39)

RESPONSE: Let's be clear, nowhere from Genesis to Malachi does the Bible say "If the Jews deserve it this will happen if they don't that will happen". Enter the Talmud that gives the above explanation. Why? Because if they didn't come up with the either or scenario what remains? He who they rejected remains. Once again the Talmud keeps God's chosen from their eternal promise.

SEGUE: Talmudic tradition continually had to come up with alternate explanations of the biblical fulfillment of the biblical prophesies. In the 15th century Jewish community leader Don Vidal ben Benvenista was charged to argue the reign of Messiah from Jewish tradition. Don Vidal apparently was not convinced of the position that he was charged to defend and at a later time became a believer in Yeshua. (40)

Chapter 3 Notes

1. Klinghoffer, Why the Jews Rejected Jesus, PP.74-75; M.Sanhedrin 7:5;
2. Klinghoffer, Why the Jews Rejected Jesus, PP.76-77; Goldstein, Jesus in the Jewish Tradition. PP.148-154
3. B. Sukkak 52a; Klinghoffer, P.84
4. Zech. 12:10; B. Sanhedrin 98b; Klinghoffer, P.84
5. B Baba Batra 123b; Obadiah 1:18; Klinghoffer, P.84
6. Obadiah 1: 9-10
7. Gen. 36: 3-4, 9-10, 13, 17, 19
8. B.Berachot 28b; B. Shabbat116a; Klinghoffer, PP. 116-117
9. B. Yoma 39b; Klinghoffer, P.117
10. Katz, Exclusiveness and Tolerance, P.141; Klinghoffer, PP. 215-216
11. B Yoma 39b; Klinghoffer, P.117
12. Schoeman, Salvation is from the Jews, PP. 111-134; Ex. 7: 7; Deut.34: 7
13. Matt.24: 1-2; Luke 19:41-44
14. Lamentations Rabbah1:1; Klinghoffer P.117
15. Matt.26:28; Mark 14:24; Luke 22:19-20
16. Herford, Christianity in Talmud and Midrash, J Taanit 65b; Ex. Rabbah 29:5.
17. Num. 23:19; Ps. 2: 1-9; 45:6-7; 110:1; Klinghoffer P.130
18. Isa. 44:6; Klinghoffer P.130

19. Genesis Rabbah 8:8; Klinghoffer, PP.133-134
20. Isa.29:13
21. Mark 7:1-13
22. Genesis Rabbah 64:4; Klinghoffer, P.135
23. Gen.15:6; 22:15-18
24. Gen. 12:10-20; 20:1-18
25. B Shabbat 118B; B Sanhedrin 98A; Klinghoffer, P.141
26. Matt.23:37-39
27. B. Sanhedrin 107b; B. Sanhedrin 43a; Klinghoffer P.143
28. Klinghoffer, Why the Jews Rejected Jesus, P.142; Matt.5:28; John 8:3-11; Matt.12: 31-32; Luke 23:33-34
29. B Gitten 56B-57A; Klinghoffer, P.144
30. Deut.18:10-14; ISam.28:7-14; Lev.19:31; 20:27; IIChron33:6
31. Klinghoffer, Why the Jews Rejected Jesus, P.145
32. McDonald, Believers Bible Commentary, P.1318; Mark 13:1-2
33. J. Nedarim 3:10; Klinghoffer, P.146
34. Genesis Rabbah 44:15-17; Klinghoffer, P.148
35. Gen. 36:1- 43; Ps.83:1-12
36. Klinghoffer, Why the Jews Rejected Jesus, P.188
37. Falk, Journal of Ecumenical Studies, 19:1; Klinghoffer, P.189
38. Klinghoffer, Why the Jews Rejected Jesus, PP. 198, 217-218
39. Zech. 9:10; Klinghoffer, P.78
40. Maccoby, op. cit., P.174; Klinghoffer, PP.170-171

Chapter 4

Does the Tenakh Equate To The Life Of Yeshua?

OBJECTION: <u>In the Bible one finds no internal clues that God or the Prophets are to be understood as speaking of two Israel's—one good (Christian) and one bad (Jewish). Israel is...sometimes good and sometimes bad.</u> (1)

RESPONSE: The first book of the Torah states, "Your descendents shall possess the gate of their enemies, the nations of the earth will bless themselves because you have obeyed my voice." In the book of Deuteronomy Moses makes clear that those who obey God's voice will be blessed. "I will stir them to jealousy with those who are not a people." This point is driven home again in the Tenakh. It states people who are not biologically from Abraham, Isaac, and Jacob shall embrace the God of the Hebrews. According to the Prophet Isaiah the destruction of the Kingdom of Israel is decreed where only a remnant will return. There will only be a few survivors. In Isa.28:16 who or what is the "tried stone, cornerstone, sure foundation?" Isa.29:10 states that "a spirit of stupor poured out on Israel." The argument is made that the Jewish religious leaders got it right. Isaiah states that blindness shall come upon Israel. Is Isaiah trying to distinguish between observant Jews and non-observant Jews? Let's continue. The Redeemer comes from Zion to redeem those who turn from sin. Here it is not all those who are physically Israel but all those who turn from sin. The prophet continues to say those who did not seek God will find him a people not called to him. So anyone not seeking God shall be excluded from the promise. The prophet Hosea states Israel his own people walk in a way that is not good after their own thoughts. God tells the ancient Kingdom of Israel that they are not his people and this kingdom will be destroyed. The Assyrians accomplished this in 721 B.C.E. Yet in the future Israel, those who strive with God, will be called "Sons of the living God." Israel and Judah in that day shall come together meaning all those who strive with God and the Jews. Again the Lord speaks through the Prophet Hosea "It shall come to pass in that day...I will say to them that were not my people, you are my people, and they will say you are my God." This has happened to those who knew not God but do through belief in Yeshua the Messiah. In Chapter 11 of St. Paul's letter to the Romans it states that God has not rejected his people. God speaks of Gentile involvement in his salvation plan in Deut.32:21. Gentile believers should be humble. If they are not they, Gentile believers, can also be broken off from God. Gentile believers should continue in God's kindness, especially to the Jewish people or be cut off. Gentile believers should not be conceited. Rom.11:30 states Gentiles only receive mercy because of God working His purpose through the Jewish people. Therefore, the Gentiles should show the same mercy to the Jewish people that God has shown to the Gentiles. Don't think that those who believe in Yeshua are more special than the Jews. The misconception is that there are not two Israel's only one. (2)

SEGUE: As we go through this journey, the opinions of Jewish sages do not appear to be the only stumbling block. Discussions about Yeshua between Gentile Christians and Jews in the middle ages were for the most part heated. It appears that much of the Jewish reply in terms of apologetics or polemic stem from these discussions. Certainly from a Rabbinical point of view most of these "discussions" were held under varying degrees of duress, and Jewish arguments from the Talmud were generally rejected or held to have less weight than anything recorded in the New Covenant. The purpose of this work is not to necessarily justify, from the Christian point of view, those discussions but to bring reconciliation between the son's of Abraham, Isaac, and Jacob and the one that modern Jews have been taught to reject. The difference is that the Christians of the middle ages did not appear to have a vision of Jewish people believing in Yeshua within the synagogue or Jewish setting. Today many Gentile believers within established Christian denominations have this vision. As we learn more about the place that the Talmud has to post-Temple era Jews, coupled with past Jewish suffering in "Christian" lands, Jewish resistance to reconciliation becomes known.

OBJECTION: Gen 49:10 "The Scepter shall not depart from Judah nor a scholar from among his descendents until Shiloh comes and unto him shall be the gathering of the nations." Jews claim that Shiloh was the name of a locality in Israel. Christians claim this was also a designation for Messiah. The source for this identification is an ancient translation the Rabbis claimed was revealed at Sinai but lost then rediscovered in 90 C.E. by the famous convert to Judaism Onkelos. (3)

RESPONSE: Another translation from the Hebrew Bible states, "The Scepter shall not depart from Judah or a lawgiver from between his feet until he comes to Shiloh and unto him shall the gathering of the people be." The first part of this verse states that the ruler shall come from Judah. We know in Isa.11:1 and IISam.7:12 the Messiah must also be a Descendent of Jesse, His son David and David's son Solomon. The Genealogies in Matthew and Luke show that Yeshua was a descendent of all. This creates a problem for a Jewish Messiah who just shows up in the next few years. How do we validate that he is from the tribe of Judah, the house of David, and through David's son Solomon? (4)

SEGUE: Both Jews and Christians are correct concerning the term Shiloh. Shiloh (Rabbinical perspective Shiloah) was a town in Ephraim northeast of Bethel and site of the tabernacle. Shiloh also means the "sent one or the one who brings peace". In this instance a town cannot come but a "sent one who brings peace" can. This sent one will bring the tabernacle with him.

OBJECTION: <u>There is forgiveness of sin without the shedding of blood.</u> (5)

RESPONSE: The rabbis base this upon the precedent set by the first Diaspora (Babylonian captivity). For well over 70 years, no Temple sacrifices were feasible (even after the Persian conquest, since it was decades before the Temple in Jerusalem was re-sanctified). Many Jews in the Diaspora never aliyah'd to the Temple in Jerusalem even after it was built, or only did so once in a lifetime, as it was a long, costly, arduous, and sometimes dangerous journey. The precedent was renewed during the Seleucid occupation and desecration of the Temple, and again when the Hasmoneans corrupted themselves and the Temple by seizing the high priesthood for themselves despite not being of the Aaronic line (they were Kohanim, but of a different clan) and combining the priestly authority with the monarchy (one of Saul's most grievous sins). More importantly, even the Levitical sacrifices were only a temporary, incomplete "covering" (kapporot) for sin – animal blood could not make atonement for human sin – only a pure human's blood could cleanse as opposed to merely cover. The priests thus were never finished, but Yeshua's work was finished. It is the incompleteness/insufficiency of animal offerings AND the rabbinical formula of repentance, prayer, fasting, and charity (tzadakah) and other good works (mitzvot) to permanently and completely ATONE for sin that makes it essential that a perfect man (Messiah Yeshua being the only one) die for the sins of mankind. Before 66 C.E., Jews could still make it to Jerusalem. King Solomon stated what the Jews should do in exile IKings 8:47-50. What then is God's standard? His standard is Lev. 17:11. Chapter 17 starts with the Lord speaking to Moses with the caveat which the Lord has commanded. "For it is the blood that makes atonement for the soul" What God states is the standard for the forgiveness of sin. In IKings Chapter 8, King Solomon spoke of a special situation. (6)

SEGUE: What the Jewish people think and what the rabbis opine are their opinions and do not carry the weight of "The Lord Said and What the Lord commands." Accepting Yeshua and his sacrifice would satisfy this command of the Lord, but the Jews must first accept Yeshua's purity AND "remember" that blood atonement is necessary and sufficient for the cleansing of sin.

OBJECTION: <u>The Torah states, "God is not a man that he should be deceitful or a son of man that he should repent." The Talmud states, "If a man tells you I am</u>

God, he is a liar. If he says I am the son of man in the end people will laugh at him." (7)

RESPONSE: If a man tells you he is God, and that is the end of it, he would either be a liar, a fool, or a madman. This passage from the Book of Numbers specifically deals with the discourse between Balaam and Balak. Balaam was not telling Balak what he wanted to hear from Balaam's God. The reply declares if God were solely flesh and blood he would lie and therefore need to repent. The issue becomes not that God cannot become man but rather if that man is dishonest and must repent he cannot be God. The Talmud goes on to say if any man says that he is God he is a liar and if he says I am the son of man people will laugh at him. If a man tells you He is God, and He does wondrous miracles before multitudes of people in the Name of the God of Israel, the God of the Patriarchs; and He promises that He will be crucified and resurrected; and hundreds of people see Him crucified and then resurrected and accept a horrible martyrdom rather than recant their witness (a witness which does them and their families no earthly good) – THAT Man is indeed the Son of Man, and the Son of God, God in the flesh.

Dan.7:13 One like a son of man, he will be in human form but from everlasting. This messianic figure will be in human form but coming with the clouds of heaven cannot be human like us. Mic 5:2 The ruler of Israel will be born in Bethlehem. Yet his origin is from everlasting from the beginning. Here a child is born who has an origin that predates his birth! Zech.12:10, who is the one in human form who has been pierced and why do the Jewish people weep over him? Zech.14:3-16. Here the Lord will fight and he's in physical form because his feet stand on the Mount of Olives. He comes with his holy ones. They are heavenly but in human form. The Lord will become King. This Lord will be worshipped in person in Jerusalem. So God, the Lord, has existed, lived in human form, and will be worshipped. The burden of proof is then placed on those who accuse Yeshua of deceit. They must prove his deceit. This would disqualify him. As far as the Talmudic quote, 2000 years later millions believe in him and those "people" are not laughing at him.

SEGUE: What was expressed concerning God not being man was an attempt to discredit Yeshua. The problem again rests with the authority sanctioned to Jewish oral tradition vice relying on the Tenakh for its interpretation. What do these same folks believe Moses had to say about this topic?

OBJECTION: Moses forewarned the Jews that God would test their love for him by rising up, in their midst, prophets and dreamers who would lure them from the true path of monotheism and observance of the commandments. Could the true Messiah be someone who founded a religion that told the Jews that these very same commandments were not good? (8)

RESPONSE: Obviously, the passage refers to Yeshua. The Jews rejected Yeshua so how were they lured from the true path? The Jews have benefited by rejecting Yeshua right? Did the events of 70 C.E. or 73 C.E. or 135 C.E. show God's favor with his people? The Jews passed the test by rejecting Yeshua the false prophet and dreamer. Yet through him knowledge of the God of Israel came to the Gentiles. Is this a bad thing? The Jewish people had no control of their own land for almost 2000 years. Where was God's favor in this? Matt. 19:17 "Why do you ask me what is good? One there is who is good. If you would enter life keep the commandments." Matt.19:18-18; Yeshua names the commandments. Also Mark10:18-19. Matt. 22: 37-40; Yeshua quotes Deut. 6:5 and Lev.19:18 then stated "On these two commandments depend all the law and the prophets." John14:15; "If you love me you will keep my commandments." John15:10; "If you keep my commandments you will abide in my love, just as I have kept my fathers commandments and abide in his love." Based on these New Covenant texts the argument does not distinguish between what Yeshua said concerning keeping the biblical commandments and Jewish Talmudic or traditional laws. Yeshua certainly held the commandments received by Moses in the highest of esteem. Yeshua largely rejected rabbinical teaching and the Oral Law. He stated that these were great burdens the rabbis heaped on the backs of the people without lifting a hand to help bear the load. He explicitly rejected rabbinical teaching on the causes of misfortunes and physical handicaps, on details of Sabbath observance, on taking oaths, etc. Yeshua summed up the Ten Commandments, and indeed the "heart" of Torah, with His restatement of the 1st Commandment "Love the Lord thy God" which implicitly includes the 2nd "Have no other gods before me" (make no idols); the other 7 are summed up in "love thy neighbor as thyself." The Patriarchs walked with the LORD without benefit of the Torah.

SEGUE: The Jewish premise stated in the "Objection" is faulty. It still seems that this line of dispute is more directed at medieval respondents than the Yeshua of history who clearly held the commandments as only good. Molding an argument that does not fit the object of the dispute displays more of a need to discredit Yeshua than to seek the truth in all openness with a contrite heart.

OBJECTION: There was nothing in Jewish tradition that laid tremendous importance on whether or not one acknowledged any person apart from 'our Father who is in heaven: (9)

RESPONSE: Deut. 18:17-18 "The Lord said to me (Moses)...I (GOD) will raise up for them (The Israelites) a prophet like you (A Prophet like Moses in terms of stature and importance to Israel) from among their brothers. (Moses was a Levite). This prophet would come from one of the other tribes, (Judah) and I will put my words in his mouth (John 5: 19-47) and he (the Prophet to come) shall speak to them (Israel) all that I command him. And whoever will not give heed to my words which he shall speak in my name I myself will require it of him."

SEGUE: No one in Judaism approaches the status of Moses. Only the Jew Yeshua approached this status and to Christians surpassed Moses status. Both spoke for the Lord. Both performed miracles. Both were deliverers. One delivered people from bondage to slavery the other from bondage to sin. Moses led the Israelites to the Promised Land but did not enter because he disobeyed God. Yeshua led people to the paradise of God, the spiritual, but was rejected by his people and has not sat on his throne in Jerusalem. Moses indeed established a religion; Yeshua completed the work of that religion and re-established a personal relationship with God the Father. The religion of Moses codified right and wrong behavior. Yeshua spiritualized right and wrong to the hearts of men and announced a New Covenant. Only Yeshua fulfils the intent of Deut 18. John chapter five explains this Jewish concern very well and places in context Moses words which occurred 1200 years earlier. (10)

OBJECTION: The preeminent condition that would cause Messiah to appear was repentance. (11)

RESPONSE: These words were declared approx. 1200 B.C.E. In 721 B.C.E. the northern 10 tribes were taken into captivity by Assyria as indicated in IIKIngs17:5-18. Why? They broke the commandments and would not listen to God's Prophets. Those 10 tribes were never reestablished. Their identity lost. We know the Samaritans were a mixture of Israelite and Assyrian but were not accepted by the southern tribes of Judah, Benjamin and the Levites. In 586 B.C.E. Babylon conquered the Southern tribes and took them into captivity. 200 or so years before the event in Isa.44:28; 45:1 Isaiah speaks of Cyrus King of Persia by name and refers to him as "my Shepherd" and his anointed "Messiah." Cyrus delivers the southern tribes from Babylon. IIChron36:15-28 states the reason that the "Jews" were punished was because they kept mocking God's messengers and his Prophets. This is what made God angry and led to the captivity. The Jews were then returned to their land. Yeshua predicted the following. Luke 19: 41-44 "Would that even today you knew the things that make for peace! But now they are hid from your eyes. For the days will come upon you when your enemies will surround you and hem you in on every side and dash you to the ground you and your children within you and they will not leave one stone upon another in you because you did not know the time of your visitation." In 70 C.E. this all came about. The example described above displays that rejection of God's prophets and their words brings God's wrath. If the Jewish people did right by rejecting Yeshua why were they so severely punished? If not Yeshua what Prophet was rejected? The Prophets last spoke 400 years before Yeshua's birth. If it was not Yeshua who was it?

SEGUE: Deut. 30 speaks in terms of sin->exile; repentance->restoration. This section does not speak of the Messianic reign. What it does say is that the Jewish people sinned and they were exiled. They repented and were restored. According to Deut.30 they sinned. The result was 70 C.E. The restoration was announced in 1948 although some Jews always maintained contact and presence with the eastern Mediterranean coast.

OBJECTION: Jewish people acknowledge that IISam.7:14; Ps.2:7; 72:11, 86:9 and Dan.7:13-14 refer to the Messiah, but not Jesus. (12)

RESPONSE:_What do we learn from the scriptures listed above? "I shall be his Father and he will be a son to me." It also states "The Lord said to me, You are my son, I have begotten you this day." The nations shall prostrate before God and also the Davidic King; He shall come in the latter days on the clouds with power and great glory. The Jewish point of view states that the Davidic king will be "served" yifl'chun which also means worship. The Jewish people can not accept the worship translation because it violates the Shema. The creator of all things is God "Elohim." He also gave man the ability to create life. When men create life or become a Father the offspring takes on the surname of the Father. Elohim is the surname of the Divine. He is Yahveh. His Messiah is Yeshua, meaning Yahveh's Salvation. They are both Elohim together with the Ruach ha Kodesh. See Gen.1:26; 3:22, and Isa.48:16-17. How can one who is only human, the Jewish version of messiah, have all nations bowing before him, come on the clouds, and establish an unending kingdom? This messiah will never die? How then can he be the Talmudic Messiah? Only the coming Lord in glory will not die and reign forever.

SEGUE: The scriptures as cited above can only be fulfilled with two separate events spanning an undetermined number of years. The one human messiah, ben Joseph, ben David scenario does not fit. The messiah to come is accurately described as God's son and the Lord. Only within this context will he be able to accomplish what no man could accomplish in this extremely troubled world.

OBJECTION: Regarding Ps. 22 the Jews can only have been baffled as to why this Psalm would be relevant at all. (13)

RESPONSE: This would not have baffled the Jews who witnessed the crucifixion. They were witnesses of what occurred. It was only after these things occurred that the purpose of the scripture became known. For in Yeshua's particular death, a death that he could not have staged, the scripture came to a specific fulfillment. For Jews who could not interpret the scripture without the Talmud telling them what to think, it is not surprising that other Jews would be baffled.

SEGUE: The issue now becomes, was King David speaking of a specific event in the future?

OBJECTION: Ps.22:16 Nitzachon Vetus stated that the word given in the Latin translation as "they pierced" were written in the Hebrew original not as "karu" but as ka'ari "like a lion". The proper rendering being "For dogs have surrounded me a pack of evildoers has enclosed me like a lion at my hands and feet." On point after point Christian exegesis was found to be dubious to anyone who could read the Bible for himself in its original language. (14)

RESPONSE: The Hebrew Bible by Alexander Harkavy stated "For dogs have compassed me the assembly of the wicked have enclosed me like a lion they threaten my hands and my feet." Both versions agree that dogs (gentiles) have surrounded the object of this Psalm and that they are bad people. The first version says "like a lion at my hands and feet" the other version states "like a lion they threaten my hands and feet". "The last clause has been the subject of much discussion involving questions as to the genuineness of the Hebrew word translated "pierce". According to Strong's Biblical Dictionary, 'airy' H738 means a (young) lion, based upon the primitive root H717 'arah' to pluck or gather. However, it also notes that "pierced" is an alternative translation. A common Hebrew literary form, similar in function to the "blank verse" of English, has a descriptive or allegorical phrase, and then follows it with another similar allegory. Thus, "For dogs have compassed me an assembly of the wicked have enclosed me..." works well. But "Like a lion they threaten my hands and feet" has a clear grammatical problem. Similarly, a "pack of evildoers" or a "pack of dogs" can enclose, but a lion cannot – lions hunt in solitary fashion, and lions crouch and leap – they don't surround like dogs, wolves, or coyotes. The prefix ka' is a connective that ties the "lion" to the preceding phrase or term (in this case, the "enclosed me"). Though not quoted in the New Covenant, the remarkable aptness of the description to the facts of Yeshua's history together with difficulties attending to any other mode of explaining the clause in the Hebrew justify an adherence to the terms of our version and their obvious meaning. Both versions agree with dogs who are a pack of evil doers or assembly of the wicked. In the Jewish version the dogs i.e. evil doers equal a Lion. The biblical commentary states that the Hebrew word cannot be made intelligible to the English reader. Let's look at Psalm 22 in its entirety. Verse 1a Yeshua quotes the opening phrase of this Psalm from the cross. (See Matt.27:46, Mark15:34). The object of this Psalm is suffering yet his praise for God continues. Psalm 22:6-8 "scorned by men and despised by the people; mocked, ridiculed. If God delights in him let God deliver him". Matt.27:39, 43; Mark 15:29; Luke 23:35. Psalm 22:9-11 King David is either speaking about his father, Jesse, or the object of his Psalm is speaking of the God who took him from the womb and kept him safe. Since my mother bore me you have been my God. What infant would know these details except the one who is from God? The text does not say that the object of the verse KNEW God from birth, but that he was dependent upon God from birth. Taking comfort in these words reality thrusts upon him. He is surrounded by angry people Matt.27:24, 27-31, 39-44. Psalm 22:14-15 He is now bleeding to death, his heart is being pressed, it's hard to get a breath, his bones are out of joint, his strength is leaving him and he has great thirst (see John19: 28-30). We can be confident that King David who died when he was old in his royal palace NEVER experienced this – a graphic description of the agony uniquely caused by crucifixion. Crucifixion was unknown in King David's time (first known practice of this form of torturous death were the Assyrians, centuries later). This indicates the prophetic nature of the passage. Psalm 22:16-18 He is surrounded by evil people who either have pierced his hands and feet or are like a lion at his hands and feet. People are staring at him. His bones ache from being out of joint and these evil people are casting lots for his clothes (see Matt 27:35; Mark15:24; Luke 23:34; John 19: 23-25). Regardless of ones decision concerning "pierced" or "like a lion" the object of David's Psalm is being put to death. He is bleeding, his bones are out of joint, he is surrounded, his mouth is dry and while he is being killed people are casting lots for his clothes. So we know that he has been undressed and his death is a slow death. The New Covenant account establishes that this is the crucifixion of Yahveh's Salvation (Yeshua). (15)

SEGUE: Regardless of which translation you prefer for Psalm 22:16, it describes an event that occurred 1000 years after David's lifetime, that David, filled with God's spirit, foretold it. David also spoke of other issues relating to our topic.

OBJECTION: Although Psalm 45:6-7 seems to speak of a Divine King; "Your throne endures forever. Your royal scepter is a scepter of equity you love righteousness and hate wickedness. Therefore God, your God has anointed you with the oil of gladness above your fellows." This cannot refer to Jesus. According to verse 9 at your right hand stands the queen in gold of Ophir." (16)

RESPONSE: The first part of Psalm 45 is reinforced via Psalm 2:2, 7 "The Kings of the earth set themselves and the rulers take counsel together against Yahveh and against his Messiah"..."I will declare the decree: The Lord has said to me, You are my son: today I have begotten you." This explains how God can speak to God. The king messiah is begotten of God. Now how about that queen? Ezek.16:10-14 speaks of a woman adorned like this who could be Israel because it also describes her past unfaithfulness. In John 3:28-29 John the Baptist alludes to the Bride being Israel and Yeshua the Bridegroom. IICor.11:2 St Paul considers the Bride of Messiah the Church. In Rev.22:17 the bride is telling the Messiah to come to his bride. Who wants Messiah to come? Israel and the Church both want this. If the queen is the bride of the Messiah this proves that the bride is an allegorical bride. It is also possible that the queen is not King messiah's bride. The queen could be his mother. Luke 1:46-55. Mary acknowledges being The Lord's handmaiden and quotes 1Sam.2:1-10 and states that "all generations will call me blessed." This again shows that the queen does not have to be the bride of the King and not a physical mate. Although Psalm 45:8-17 makes it clear that this is a Psalm about David himself, and his thanksgiving and joy in all that God has done for him, closing with the promise God gave to him for his seed, the closing verse would not have been true had not Yeshua come and restored the hidden glory of the House of David to the eyes of the world. (17)

SEGUE: The point of the previous response was that marriage terminology is consistent when speaking of the Messiah. The New Covenant uses it referring to Israel and the Church. The point is also made that the queen referred to could be the king's mother not his wife.

OBJECTION: King David would not have prayed as he did if God's standard operating procedure was indeed to hold humans to strict Judgment. (18)

RESPONSE: In Deut.27:26 God is speaking to the nation of Israel hence the ending "and all the people shall say Amen". In Psalm 103:10 and 143:2 David speaks of the individual not the nation. To the individual the theme is that God is merciful. "For in your sight no man living shall be justified." Now look at Ex.34:6-7. God forgives all sins even the sin of falling short of his standards. Although God forgives all sins this does not keep Israel or individuals from punishment. The blessings and curses laid out in Deut.26-27 are both individual and collective. Individuals will be blessed for obedience and cursed for disobedience. If the society does not encourage obedience and punish disobedience, it will collectively be cursed as well. Each individual is accountable for himself before the Lord. Leaders/elders, priests, and prophets will also be held accountable for their performance as reflected in collective obedience or disobedience. God is merciful – He has made provisions for the temporary covering of sin (the Levitical sacrificial system – which also requires penitence of the heart lest God reject the sacrifice) and the permanent cleansing of sin (the ultimate sacrifice of the Lamb of God, Yeshua).

SEGUE: The point being made here is that forgiveness and punishment are not mutually exclusive. A murderer may be sorry for what he did, but he still must be punished. The other issue being discussed is that the object of a particular scripture helps determine its interpretation. For instance if I as an individual am attacked I am not to carry out justice as I see fit. That would be up to the authorities; however, if a group of people like a nation is attacked it is important for that nation to defend itself or even defeat the enemy lest the enemy think that the nation that was attacked is weak and thus invite more violence. On a spiritual level Moses spoke to the nation. Yeshua spoke to individuals to the human heart.

OBJECTION: Nitzachon Vetus cites Ps 110:1 "The Lord says to my Lord Sit at my right hand until I make your enemies your footstool." If both Father and son are God, presumably they share the same will. The Psalm seems to state otherwise. So does John 5:30 "I seek not my own will but the will him who sent me." Does this mean that they have two wills so that one wants what the other does not? According to them the two are one entity yet Jesus says I seek not my own will." (19)

RESPONSE: In the first instance, there is no division of will – the Father invites the Son to sit in the place of honor in heaven until it is time to establish the millennial kingdom on earth – there is no reason to believe the Son would not want to sit at the Father's right hand. In the second instance, they have distinct wills, but their wills are in perfect alignment because the Son knows the perfection of the Father's will and abides in it. In a Father and Son relationship the Son is subordinate to the Father. The Father loves the Son and will give all that he has as an inheritance to an obedient son. In this case the Son can decide or make decisions based on his free will just like our free will, but this son exists to please his father even to the point of self sacrifice for his father's creation.

SEGUE: It is interesting how the Objection tries to put constraints on God. Try this on. The family is the building block of society. Free will is a gift that God has given his creation because the Father, Son, and Holy Spirit exercise free will. Their exercise in free will results in cooperation, unity, creation, and teamwork. God is our model. This is why we were made in God's image so that through our free will we would act like God. All of these things are summed up in another word—Love.

OBJECTION: <u>Any biblically literate Jew in 30 C.E. would know the prophesy in question (Isa. 6:9-10/Matt.13:14-15) had been fulfilled long ago and could prove nothing about Jesus:</u> (20)

RESPONSE: Let's go with this reasoning. The Prophesy was spoken in 754/740 B.C.E. The Northern Kingdom of Israel is destroyed by Assyria in 721 B.C.E. Then Babylon destroys the Southern Kingdom of Judah in 586.B.C.E. The Northern tribes are lost but some come back to be known as Samaritans. The Samaritans are a mongrel race formed from the remnant of the apostate northern tribes that was not carried off by the Assyrians and the various races the Assyrians brought in to resettle the land. The bulk of the northern tribes' population, already deep in apostasy, assimilated into the rest of the Assyrian Empire – they are not a distinct population anywhere in the world. The Southerners make it back by 517 B.C.E. from Babylon. According to the stated objection, after these events the Judeans would understand the scripture related to events in the

8th century B.C.E. Here is what we know about their understanding. Judeans had contempt for the half blood Samaritans. We must also position Dan.9:24-27 with events to come after Yeshua's death whereby a messiah is cut off then Jerusalem and the second temple are destroyed. What did Moses say? Lev. 26:18-46; Deut. 28:15-69. Basically if you do evil you will be expelled. In 70 A.D these people who have understanding are thrust from a functioning Israel for 2000 years. If they had an understanding and were doing the right thing why did the events of 70 C.E. occur? Matthew was right their understanding was yet to come. Many 2nd Diaspora Orthodox, and later Khasidic & Conservative rabbis since the 2nd century have asserted that the Jews were expelled from the Land and the Temple destroyed as a punishment for the corruption and sinful disobedience of the Jews -- especially of the Kohanim, Levites, and the Sadducees who dominated the Temple organization and the Sanhedrin. They don't deny that the Jews of Yeshua's' day and after were sinful, but deny that accepting Yeshua was the right/good thing to do, or that Diaspora and destruction of the Temple were the result of rejecting Yeshua as Messiah. Rather, they assert that following the Pharisaical teachings of the rabbis was what was necessary to purify the hearts and minds of the people and prepare the way for Messiah to come and restore the Temple - both in the 1st century and today. (21)

SEGUE: Since we just saw that the application of this passage in Matthew's Gospel is a better explanation, what other verses challenge us with a duel or incorrect interpretation?

OBJECTION: Isa. 7:14Young woman (Almah) as the word is used in Hebrew could be married of single, sexually experienced or not. One might also mention that Jesus' name was not Emmanuel: (22)

RESPONSE: What was not stated is that "Almah" is used in seven other instances in the Bible where the woman is also a virgin. There is another reason why Almah is the perfect word here instead of the other rendering. If the word "strictly meaning virgin" was used that woman could not have been married. Mary was married. She was also young with child yet untried. Mary was with child and yet was very much a virgin; she was betrothed, not yet married. Almah means virgin. The Jewish translators who created the Greek Septuagint over a century before Yeshua's' time knew that Almah meant virgin, and used the appropriate Greek term parthenos, meaning a young unmarried woman who preserved her virginity (not the Greek term for young woman, or for a wife). This is a big difference. Betrothal is more than a modern "engaged," but definitely not married - not cohabiting, not bound in a covenant before God and the community. Betrothal was a time of testing to prove the virginity of the young woman prior to the formal marriage. She was treated as if she was married, and was expected to remain loyal to her betrothed.

In terms of the word Emmanuel once again we run head long into Judaic literalism vice "Who was Yeshua (Yahveh's Salvation)? He was Emmanuel (God with us). Yeshua is what the Messiah came to do while Emmanuel is what the Messiah is. (23)

SEGUE: The issue concerning the word "virgin" and Emmanuel does not end the discussion of Isa. 7:14. There are other issues to address.

OBJECTION: Isa. 7:14 According to Joseph Kimchi the word translated virgin actually meant maiden. The prophesy actually applied to King Ahaz of Judah as a sign to him. Therefore it could have no future implication. The Nitzachon Vetus noted that the verse actually says "has conceived and will bear a son" therefore this would exclude Mary who wouldn't be born for centuries later. (24)

RESPONSE: Kimchi is guilty of an anachronism -- a maiden was by definition a virgin. A woman who was no longer a maiden was no longer a virgin – she either was a wife, a widow, or a whore. In Isa.7:10 -13 God asks King Ahaz to ask for a sign. King Ahaz refuses choosing to trust in Syria instead. The Lord then gives a sign anyway. Since Ahaz did not want a sign there is nothing here stating that the sign would apply to the time of King Ahaz. Let's also not lose sight that Ahaz was wicked IIKings 23:12; IIChron.28. He also burned his own son as an offering. IIKing 16:2 Ahaz was 20 when he started to reign. He died when he was 36. His son Hezekiah was good and started to reign when he was 25. If Hezekiah was Ahaz biological son then he had to be 11 when he fathered Hezekiah. We do know that the mother of Hezekiah was Abijah who was the daughter of one Zechariah. The Hebrew Bible by Alexander Harkavy states "the young woman will conceive and bear a son." When this prophesy was given Ahaz was already into his reign. Since we have proved that Hezekiah was born when Ahaz was 11 Ahaz either jumped the gun with Abijah or Hezekiah was adopted. Either way this prophesy could not apply to him. It was impossible. Who was God with us Emmanuel? Matt.1:20-25 The young married virgin Mary has the child. The Angel states that the child must be named Yeshua meaning Yahveh's Salvation. He will also be called Emmanuel; God is with us, because he is the Son of God Luke 1:31-35. If the Jewish argument persists that this could not mean Yeshua then look at the following concerning Hezekiah. IIKings18:5-6 He trusted in the Lord God of Israel so that after him was none like him among all the Kings of Judah not any that were before him." It is clear that the only possible candidate for the fulfillment of Isa. 7:14 was Hezekiah, yet he was already born which disqualified him. Furthermore, he was not Emmanuel "God with us" because he was the son of evil Ahaz and Abijah. There is another fact that brings this into clarity. Isa. 9:5-7 let's see if this can apply to Hezekiah. Once again this relates to the child of Isa.7:14 for this child will be special. Government upon his shoulder, this could be Hezekiah. His name will be called Wonderful, Counselor (of the) Mighty God, (of the) Everlasting Father, Prince of Peace. Of the increase of his government and peace there shall be no end upon the throne of David and upon his Kingdom to order it and establish it with judgment and with justice forever." Was Hezekiah the Prince of Peace? In IIKings 7-8 Hezekiah rebelled and smote the Philistines. The increase of his government and peace there shall be no end upon his Kingdom from the time it is established forever. In IIKings 20:16-20 Isaiah tells Hezekiah that nothing will be left for all will be carried to Babylon. It occurred in 586 B.C.E.; therefore the prophesy excludes Hezekiah. Then to whom does this apply? The context is for the future Messiah King. The Jews no more had earthly peace or an earthly king after Yeshua than before; but, as Yeshua said to

Pilate, "My Kingdom is not of this world." (John 18:36-37) Messiah had to come first as a suffering servant, the perfect Lamb of God, to die for the sin of mankind and establish the kingdom of heaven's claim on earth. Messiah would then return as the conquering king to re-establish the throne of David on earth when the Father made "his enemies to be his footstool." After this King arrives there will be peace and his Kingdom will be established forever. Dan.7:13-14 Daniel the Prophet speaks of the same event. The Son of Man comes with the clouds of Heaven to the latter days and all the earth shall serve him. His Kingdom will be eternal. The Jewish argument is that this did not happen with Yeshua, but the story is not over. Mark 16:19 After he spoken to them, the Lord Yeshua was taken up into heaven. Luke 24:51 While he blessed them he parted from them and was carried up into heaven. Acts 1:6-11 So when they had come together they asked him Lord will you at this time restore the kingdom of Israel? He said "It is not for you to know times or seasons which the Father has fixed by his own authority. But you shall receive power when the Holy Spirit has come upon you and you will be my witnesses in Jerusalem and in all Judea and Samaria and to the end of the earth. And when he had said this as they were looking on he was lifted up and a cloud took him out of their sight. And while they were gazing into heaven as he went behold two men stood by them in white robes and said Men of Galilee why do you stand looking into heaven? This Yeshua who was taken up from you into heaven will come in the same way as you saw him go into heaven."

SEGUE: After establishing the object of Isa.7:14 surely there are other verses that will point to him or establish that we must wait for another. Let's see

OBJECTION: Isa.35:5-7, Isa.42:1-4, 49:1-6, Ps.78:2 have not been totally fulfilled by Jesus. One can argue that some of these verses were partially fulfilled but none of them were totally fulfilled so Jesus could not be the Messiah. (25)

RESPONSE: What we know; Yeshua healed all who wanted to be healed. His gentle Spirit comes through in the Gospels. Those living far from Israel delight in him, He was named while still in his mother's womb, and Yeshua spoke in parables. It is true not all aspects of the prophesies were fulfilled. If this becomes a stumbling block recall Mic.5. He will be born in Bethlehem yet Dan.7:13-14 he will come on the clouds of heaven with great power and glory. Two different events will occur. One has already occurred. We, you and me, are anticipating the next event. That event will be the Main Event.

SEGUE: The presupposition is that all the scriptures relating to the Messiah must be fulfilled during one event. On the surface this certainly makes sense, but when confronted with the dichotomy of Daniel 7 and Micah 5 this opens the probability of two events. If this is so, how do we deal with terms that seem to indicate one or the other?

OBJECTION: In the context of the term "servant" Isaiah 44 speaks of Israel because the context makes sense. The "servant" as elsewhere in Isaiah is none other than the people Israel: (26)

RESPONSE: Let's explore this. The Objection states the servant is always the same even if one can't make sense from the application. Look at Isa.44:6. This verse appears to imply the messiah, "Thus says the Lord, The King of Israel and his Redeemer, the Lord of hosts: I am the first and I am the last and besides me there is no god." In Isa.49:3 it doesn't say "you are my servant Israel" It says you are my servant, O Israel, in whom I will be glorified." According to the reasoning displayed in the Objection, the servant is the people Israel. Isa.49:5 states "the Lord that formed me from the womb to be his servant (Israel or Messiah) to bring Jacob again to him, that Israel be gathered unto him." If the servant is Israel then Israel is to bring Jacob to him (God). Israel and Jacob are the same because Israel was Jacob before becoming Israel (Gen. 32:28). Therefore, Messiah must be this servant. Isa.49:6 states, "It is the right thing that you should be my servant to raise up the tribes of Jacob to restore the remnant of Israel." If the servant is Israel then Israel will raise up the tribes of Jacob? Jacob and Israel are the same. One is despised and equated with the servant. Israel is not the Holy one for it says "to a servant...Princes also shall worship." That's not Israel. It is Messiah. In Isa.50:10 it says "Who is among you that fears the Lord and obeys the voice of his servant (Israel or Messiah)? Obey the voice of his Israel or his Messiah?" Isa. 52:12 "The Lord will go before you; and the God of Israel will be your rear guard." Here the Lord and the God of Israel are distinguished by the one at the front the other at the rear. Once again the term Israel is not them but "him", "you", and "he". It is Messiah not the People of Israel. Isa.53:2 "and when we see him (when we Israel see Israel?) there is no beauty that we should desire him (Israel)." Messiah is a much better fit. Israel makes no sense in these passages. Isa. 53: 3 how can the people of Israel be called man? "He (Israel was despised)", can't be the Patriarch for he was long dead so if it is the people of Israel then "we esteemed him not (Israel will not esteem Israel?)." This again makes no sense. Messiah is the right fit. Isa.53:4 If he, us, we, him are all Israel this makes no sense. The entire chapter only makes sense when we consider this to speak of messiah. Isa. 53:6 states, "The iniquity of Israel shall fall upon Israel or Messiah?" Isa. 53:8 "cut off" See Dan.9:26. If Israel has done no wrong then who are "my people who have transgressed?" In Isa.53:10 it states "He shall see his seed." After the resurrection he will see the seed he planted with his followers grow. The people of Israel like any other people are sinful. How can they "bear their iniquities" Isa.53:12 says, "remove the sin of many and made intersession." This is not the people of Israel. It is Messiah. This speaks of the life, death, and resurrection of Yeshua the Messiah.

SEGUE: If Israel/Jacob must be brought back to God by "My Servant," it is clear that Israel/Jacob (a.k.a. B'nai Yisroel; Children of Israel) has not been obediently following God. We can now see that the servant is Messiah, but does this mean that the context of Isa.53 also relates to the Messiah?

OBJECTION: <u>Isaiah 53 positively indicates that the servant will not lose his life for he will see his offspring.</u> (27)

RESPONSE: Sin can only be atoned through death and the shedding of blood (Lev.17:11). Isa.53: 8 says "he was cut off out of the land of the living." He was killed. The fascinating spin comes from the Objection that refuses to recognize redemption because many Jewish people can't consider that the Talmud may have gotten this wrong. The final passages of Isaiah 53 speak of the one who died for sin being rewarded with many followers with his seed, his spirit that leads to eternal life whereby his resurrection is foretold. The meaning of Isaiah 53 seems clear once one can conceive of the Servant Messiah as dying and being resurrected. Israel cannot be sacrificed to bear the sins of Israel. That would be equivalent to saying that Israel dies to bear its sins, yet is immortal as a people – that somehow the collective Israel is without sin, and does not die, but individuals who are "of Israel" and are sinners somehow die for their own sins and those of others. This is clearly NOT the intent of Lev. 17!

SEGUE: From God's point of view, we who chose to serve him are his children. Not biologically, but like an adopted son. One who cannot claim the same biology, but one who invites the same Spirit, the Spirit of God, to reside within his or her being.

OBJECTIION: Isaiah 53 the Jewish version- The man of sorrow is God's nameless servant. Rabbi Solomon bar Isaac (Rashi) 1040-1105 stated that the servant was the Jewish People. It was Isaiah's way to speak of Israel as if Israel were one man. Proof Isa. 41:8; 44:1-2. The speaker in Isaiah 53 was the Gentile nations that oppressed Israel. Gentiles will see at the end of history that people should be forgiven through the suffering of Israel. Israel bore the illness that should have come upon us. Abraham Ibn Ezra 1093-1168 spoke that the latter would see his seed, prolong his days, and divide the spoil with the strong. Jesus did none of these things. The context of Isa.51-54 proves this. (28)

RESPONSE: The scripture in question actually starts with Isa. 52:13. "My servant shall prosper be exalted, extolled and be very high" The Jewish position is that the servant must be the People Israel. Isa.41: 8-9 It is clear here that the servant is Israel who God has chosen. It is by context the people Israel. In Isa.42:1-4 this servant has God's spirit put upon him and brings forth judgment to the Gentiles. He does not raise his voice or break anything. He will not be discouraged until he judges the earth. The Islands wait for his law. This servant is not the people "Israel". This is messianic by its context. See Luke 4:16-21. In Isa.42:8-19 the servant is blind. This is certainly not the Messiah. Isa.42:17 points to the Israelites in the desert. Isa.44:1-2 agrees as does Isa.44: 21 with Isa.41: 8-9. Isa.49:1-7 refers to Isa.42:1-4. God is glorified in this servant. See Isa.42: 5-6. This servant cannot be Israel because this servant will bring Jacob to him and will gather Israel. This chapter refers to the Messiah by its context. In Isa.50:10 who is speaking? God is speaking through Isaiah telling the people (Israel) to obey his servant. This servant is messianic. So we learn that the servant is either Israel or the messiah depending upon the context. Isa.52:14 see Mark 14:65, John 18:22, Mark 15:15-20. The context of Isa. 52:13-14 fits the New Covenant accounts not Israel the people. In the context of Isa. 53 Isaiah the prophet is speaking. Isaiah is an Israelite and when he states "we esteemed him not" he is describing how Jews view Yeshua. To say the "we" is humanity does not fit for the Jews also constitute "we". Isa.53:4 "we did esteem him stricken smitten of God and afflicted" Israel views Israel as smitten of God? This wording would be very awkward. The verse applies to Yeshua. Isa.53:5 Israel was wounded (pierced) through our transgression? How can this be in light of Lev.26 and Deut.28 where God clearly states that Israel's own sinfulness brought woe to the nation? See Acts 2: 22-36. In Isa.53:6 it states that "The Lord has caused the iniquity of us all to fall on him." Wouldn't the Jewish people be included in the phrase "us all"? The iniquity of all falls on Israel? Isa.53:7 Israel goes to its slaughter but does not open its mouth? In 721 B.C.E. against Assyria, 586 B.C.E. against Babylon, 63 B.C.E. against Rome, the destruction of Jerusalem 70 C.E., and the Bar Kochbah Rebellion 135 C.E. Israel opened its mouth and resisted in every instance. See Matt.26:63; 27:12, 14; Mark14:61, Luke 23:9; John 19:9-11. Isa.53: 8 "For he was cut off out of the land of the living through the transgression of my people he was stricken." When was Israel killed? A remnant always remained See Lev.26 Deut.28. If Israel was cut off through the transgression of Isaiah's people, then it is clear that the people of Israel were transgressors, and thus not without sin and thus not able to serve as the sinless Redeemer from sin. Who are my people? If Isaiah is speaking it is the Jews. If God is speaking it is Israel. "My people" in the 8th century B.C.E. were never the Gentiles. Isa.53:9 "His grave among the wicked and his tomb with the rich; although he had done no violence nor was there deceit in his mouth." The servant who was killed with the wicked and buried with the rich did no violence and spoke no deceit. Argue as you may want but this in no way is Israel. See Matt.27:38; Mark 15:27; Luke 23:32-33; John 19:18-19. "With the rich" Matt.27:57-60; Mark 15:43-46; Luke 23:50-53; John 19:38-42. Isa.53:10 states, "It pleased the Lord to bruise him; to put him to grief and consider it an offering for guilt." It pleased the Lord to bruise Israel? Only to the extent that Israel sinned and deserved punishment not that sinful Israel could redeem Gentiles through Jewish suffering. Israel was punished because of their transgressions not someone else's sins. The guilt offering pleased God. The act was selfless. This does not describe Israel. Luke 24:25-27. "He shall see his seed, he shall prolong his days and the pleasure of the Lord shall prosper in his hand". For this to happen he must be alive see Ps.16:10, Matt. 28:16-18. He who was dead now claims millions of spiritual descendents who worship him. Isa.53:11 "He shall see the travail of his soul and shall be satisfied; by his knowledge shall my servant justify the righteous before many and he shall bear their iniquities." God will be satisfied by watching Israel suffer? Israel will justify the righteous and bear their iniquities? The Jewish people have the capability to do this? Matt 3:17; 17:5; 27:46; Mark 1:11; 9: 6-7; 15:34; Luke 3:22; 9:35; 23:36; 24:39-48. Then in Isa.53:12 it states, "Therefore I will divide him a portion with the great and he shall divide the spoil with the strong because he laid open his soul to death and was numbered with the transgressors and he removed the sin of many and made intercession for the transgressors." God will divide Israel a portion with the great and Israel will divide the spoil with the strong because Israel died and was numbered with transgressors and Israel removed the sin of many and Israel made intercession for transgressors? This cannot be the people Israel. The people Israel cannot divide the spoil with the strong because they never died. How can the people Israel who have sinned remove the sins of others and make intercession for the sinners? They can't. We are in agreement that Yeshua was publicly executed between two thieves. The four Gospel writers give us accounts of conversations with Yeshua after he resurrected. Those who comment about Yeshua in the Jewish oral tradition definitely see Yeshua as a transgressor. Why? Since Yeshua rejected the tradition of the elders he is being rejected. By doing so did he sin? If so, where does the Tenakh say that if one rejects the oral tradition he commits sin? Rejecting the traditions of the elders would be grounds for various punishments, but not death – plenty of Sadducees, etc. rejected the traditions of the elders and weren't threatened with execution. Yeshua is rejected as a transgressor because he claimed to be like/equal to God by claiming to be the Son of God; by claiming "before Abraham was, I AM." This would be a "cardinal sin" - a capital crime punishable by stoning - if it was NOT true. But given the miracles He performed, the timing and nature of his birth, etc., it could be seen that it WAS true. The sin of the Jewish leaders of the day was that they refused to acknowledge the miracles Yeshua performed in the name of the God of Abraham, Isaac, and Jacob. If Yeshua did not resurrect why did his followers risk their lives and eventually all die for this lie some 30 to 60 years after the crucifixion? How can the future prophesy come true since this event has not yet occurred? Matt. 24:27-30; Mark 13: 24-27; Luke 21: 25-28; Rev 19: 11-21.

SEGUE: The Objection states that the meaning of the term "servant" is always Israel. Within the context given the servant is sometimes Israel but not always. The reason is that it is not possible for the people of Israel to fulfill those scriptures. However, one did come who fulfilled specific parts of these scriptures. Yeshua flatly predicted that certain portions of these prophecies would not be fulfilled until he returned. The fact that Yeshua spoke of a future time does not mean that those prophecies will never be fulfilled, just not yet. The fact that he did fulfill most of them illuminates the point.

OBJECTION: <u>Slaughter of the Innocents does not refer to the event described in Matthew. It refers to the exiled Jewish people.</u> (29)

RESPONSE: Jer.31: 9-13/10-14 Speaks of Israel's restoration. This segment begins with "Hear the word of the Lord". A new thought begins with Jer.31:14-15. "Thus says the Lord" Rachel cries for the children of Ramah (the region around Bethlehem) because her Children were no more." Now a new thought or paragraph begins with Jer.31:15-16 "Thus says the Lord." The verses cited before and after Jer.31:14-15 reference Israel and the eventual restoration from Babylon. The cries from Rachel specifically go out to children who are no more, who exist not. They are dead. The latter verses speak of the children taken away in the captivity to Babylon who will return. Why, because they were not killed. The new thought of Jer.31:14-15 speaks about an event in a specific place. That event happened. Matt.2: 16-18. Although not named specifically by outside historians like Josephus, Herod's barbarity and brutality are beyond question.

SEGUE: Jeremiah 31 contains more than a few scriptural verses that have diverse interpretations. The Key to the verses cited above is that this event specifically happens in the environs of Bethlehem. The children of the restoration could never be referred to as "her children were no more". Those babies killed by Herod's henchmen were "no more".

OBJECTION: Jeremiah 31:31-34 "I will seal a new Covenant with the House of Israel and the House of Judah". The author of Nitzachon Vetus replies the Prophet Jeremiah does not write "the new Torah of Jesus". Therefore this was written about the current Torah so that God would write it on their hearts so that they would no longer forget it. If this New Covenant of Jesus is referred to why does the Prophet not mention the other nations who supposedly will also have Jesus law of love inscribed within them? (30)

RESPONSE: Jeremiah 31:31-32 foretells "'Behold, days are coming,' declares the LORD," when I will make a new covenant with the house of Israel and with the house of Judah; not like the covenant which I made with their fathers in the day that I took them by the hand to bring them out of the land of Egypt, My covenant which they broke, although I was a husband to them," declares the LORD." Jeremiah is writing in the 6th Century B.C.E. The old Covenant had been broken by the Jews and a new one, a different one was needed. From the Jewish point of view when did the New Covenant occur? It hasn't. So the Jewish people are operating under a broken covenant with their God. The Old Covenant was established with Abraham, Isaac, Jacob, and Joseph, was codified, formalized and ratified by all Israel at Mt Sinai. The New was sealed on Good Friday, which was during the Feast of the Unleavened Bread. The result will be that God will forgive iniquity and remember sin no more. Jer.50:4-5 states that Israel and Judah will realize in tears as a result of the Babylonian captivity that they need a new and everlasting covenant realizing that the old Covenant was broken. What was foretold here was the destruction of both Babylon and the remnants of Assyria by Persia (the ancient center of the Medes and Persians was northeast of Babylon). This was fulfilled when the Persians allowed the Jews to return to Jerusalem to rebuild the city and the Temple – they went, weeping tears of both anguish and joy. They are seeking "an everlasting covenant" – and indeed, while Israel sins in many ways subsequent to the end of the Babylonian captivity, it does not collectively and officially turn to pagan gods ever again. Rabbinical Jews believe they have kept this covenant because they have never collectively worshipped images/idols again. We can assert, based on faith, that the New Covenant discussed in Jeremiah 50 is the same as that discussed in Jeremiah 31 and that both are the covenant established in Yeshua on the cross. However, the Jews can assert that the New Covenant is simply the rejection of the old tendency to mix pagan worship in with worship of the one true God. See Matt.26:17-19. The Last Supper occurs at Passover. Matt.26:26-29; Mark 14:22-25; Luke 22:14-20. The New Covenant completes the Old, it does not supersede it, as the Lord said Himself – not one dot or stroke of the Law will be changed or erased. Instead of needing constant correction and teaching and punishment, the Law will be engraved on our hearts – we will know it and we will fervently desire to live it. As for the Gentiles, Jesus Himself said that "salvation is from the Jews" and that a man does not put a light under a bushel (basket) but puts it on a stand so that it may illuminate everything. Yes, the Covenant is first to the Jew, then to the Gentile. But if the Jews reject it, the Gentiles will accept it and be blessed by it, to the consternation of the Jews who thought they had an "exclusive" on God's love. May it never be so! He is the God of ALL Creation, not just mankind, and God of ALL mankind, not just the Jews. Therefore the New Covenant is different. The key to the New Covenant is its provision to forgive iniquity and deal with sin. These elements are present. Who was worthy to make this New Covenant? The King of Israel who will be known by his riding on an ass on a colt the foal of an ass. It happened as described in these Gospel accounts Matt.21:1-11; Mark 11:1-11; Luke 19:28-40; John 12:1216. This same person will bring peace and rule the earth Matt.25:31-46; Mark13:26-27; Luke 21:27-28. The Messenger to come before the King of Israel was John the Baptist. See Matt.3:1-6;

Mark1:1-9; Luke 3:2-6 and finally Matt.11:7-15. Malachi then states after the coming of the Messenger, the Lord will enter the Temple. Matt.21:23; 24:1; Mark 11:15, 35:13:1-2; Luke 19:45. The Jewish polemicist makes the point that there is no mention of other nations. The New Covenant was needed because Israel and Judah fractured the Old Covenant so this was directed at the Jewish people. There are other scriptures that address this. Isa.42:1-4 states that the Nations/Gentiles will await Gods chosen his servant. The Spirit will be upon this servant Isa. 61:1-4. See Luke 4:16-19 and then referring to the Gentiles Matt. 8:10-11 states "Truly I say to you not even in Israel have I found such faith. I tell you many will come from east and west and sit at table with Abraham Isaac and Jacob in the Kingdom of Heaven."

SEGUE: The Objection fails to address Israel's sin. Their ancestors sinned to the point of rupturing their covenant with God. The point being that the Jewish people have been called out to be holy. Yeshua is the only one who announced this New Covenant. This is the Covenant that welcomes both Jews and Gentiles.

OBJECTION: Rabbi Ishmael's 13 rules of exegesis from Sifra were believed to be given by God at Sinai. Therefore the key to interpreting the Torah comes from the oral tradition which Jews believe was revealed with the written law. The Talmud states that "242 C.E." was supposed to begin the days of the Messiah, but because of our sins which are numerous, the redeemer has been delayed. (31)

RESPONSE: The Key to interpreting the Tenakh comes from the Tenakh itself. Concerning the Messiah;

Dan.9:24-27 "70 weeks are decreed concerning your people (Israel) and your holy city (Jerusalem) to finish transgression (Israel is guilty of a transgression; this will change) to make an end to sins (not just Israel but globally) to make reconciliation for iniquity (not as Jews do today through the day of atonement, but accepting an act that makes permanent reconciliation) to bring in everlasting righteousness (This can only happen through the Messiah King) to seal up the vision and prophesy (At the end of the 70 weeks visions and prophesy will cease) to anoint the most holy place (Jerusalem when King Messiah reigns from his city). Know therefore and understand from the going forth of the word to restore and build Jerusalem to the coming of an anointed the prince there shall be 7 weeks (This occurs in Neh.2:1-8 when Artaxerxes gave the word or command in 445/444 B.C.E.)." If 7 weeks is to be taken literally the beginning and ending of this time still leaves us in the same year. This would also mean that the anointed Prince had to show up in 445/444 B.C.E.); "and during 62 weeks it shall be built again with street and trench but in a troubled time." Daniel is speaking from the 6th century B.C.E. He sees Babylon coming to an end at the hands of Persia. Cyrus, an anointed, the leader of the Medes and Persians is the conqueror of the Babylonians. See Isa.44:28. In the 8th century B.C.E., Isaiah predicts 200 years before Cyrus is born that Jerusalem will be rebuilt. It specifically states the foundation of a new Temple shall be laid. In IIChron.36:21-26 and Ezra 1:1-5 it states Jerusalem will lay desolate for 70 years, 586-516 B.C.E. Cyrus, King of Persia, in the first year of his reign in Babylon 516 B.C.E. states that God wants him to build God a house at Jerusalem. In Ezra 6:14-15 this was accomplished in the 6th year of the reign of King Darius. Cyrus spoke about the house of God but Artaxerxes granted that

Jerusalem be rebuilt in the 20th year of his reign 445/444 B.C.E. So this is the starting date of Daniels prophesy. Could Jerusalem be rebuilt in 62 weeks? That's 1 year 2 months and two weeks. Was Jerusalem rebuilt during this small amount of time? Did an anointed appear at that time? Was this a troubled time for Israel? The answer to all of these questions is no. "After 62 weeks the Anointed (Messiah) shall be cut off and shall have nothing and the people of the prince that shall come will destroy the city and the sanctuary and the end therefore shall be with a flood and unto the end of the war desolations are determined." Was an anointed "cut off" during this time? How could the city and sanctuary be destroyed during this time when it had not been rebuilt from the time of the Babylonian captivity? Was there a war involving the Jews in the 5th century B.C.E.? The answer to all these questions is no. The weeks therefore described by Daniel are not literal weeks. What we do know is that Jerusalem and the Temple were eventually rebuilt and that they were destroyed again by Titus of Rome in 70 C.E. during the Roman war against the Jewish rebellion that started in the year 66 C.E. Since we know this from history it becomes plain that the weeks that Daniel speaks of are weeks of years. Therefore the 7 weeks are 49 years. This is the span of time from the word to rebuild Jerusalem to the coming of the anointed prince. 63 weeks now remain. The actual construction will take place over 62 weeks of years or 434 years until completion. This spans the rise of Alexander and the defeat of Persia in the 4th century B.C.E.; the Reign of Antiochus Epiphanes IV in 168 B.C.E. and the subsequent Maccabean revolt. Greece was defeated by Rome in 68 B.C.E. and Rome conquered Palestine in 63 B.C.E. These were truly troubled times. We have now accounted for 69 weeks of years or 483 years. The first week deals with the going forth of the word to rebuild and the coming anointed at the end of this construction process, but the actual construction process lasts 62 weeks of years or 434 years. Rev 11:2-3 defines 42 months as 1260 days. When one divides 42 months into 1260 days we arrive at 30 days per month. Therefore 7 weeks or 49 years equals 17640 days (49 X 360). In order to calculate this into our solar calendar we must divide 17640 days by 365.25. The quotient equals 48.3 years. We then subtract 48.3 from the 20th year of the reign of Artaxerxes. The starting point is 445/444 B.C.E. less 48.3years. This brings us to 397/396 B.C.E. We have now accounted for 7 weeks of Daniel's prophesy. The next 62 weeks or 434 years must be calculated from 397/396 B.C.E. 434 years equals 156,240 days (434 X 360). 156,240 divided by 365.25 equals 427.8 years. Since there was no year zero when moving from B.C.E. to C.E. we must add one year. Moving 427.8 years ahead from the year 397/396 we arrive at 32/33 C.E. See Dan.9:26. After the 62 weeks of years, "the anointed shall be cut off." After this in 70 C.E. Titus, son of Vespasian the Roman emperor, came and destroyed Jerusalem including the Temple. This happened during a war with Rome and Jerusalem was left desolate. Eventually The Emperor Hadrian forbade Jews to enter Jerusalem. This occurred after the Bar Kochbah rebellion of 135 C.E. "And he shall confirm the covenant with many for one week and for ½ of the week (3 ½ days) he shall cause sacrifice and offering to stop and for the overspreading of abominations shall be one who makes it desolate until the consummation which is determined, is poured out on the desolate." One from the ancient Roman empire (Europe, Middle East, North Africa) will make a 1 week or 7 year agreement but after 3 ½ years he will force Jewish rituals to cease. This means that yet again in the future the Jewish Temple will be rebuilt. Otherwise how could this person from the area of the ancient Roman Empire stop Jewish rituals? He will cause an abomination and make the holy place desolate however this person will eventually be made desolate. The Bible and known history help us interpret the scripture and unlock the true meaning.

SEGUE: The point being made by the Objection is that according to Jewish tradition the coming of the Messiah was forecast after 242 C.E. The coming of the Messiah is determined by God through his prophets. The Tenakh describes Messiah's coming, its timing, and its reason. The Tenakh, like Messiah, is from God, and foretells the coming of God's Messiah. The Talmud is from men, and it cannot teach or explain more than what men know. The Rabbis are NOT prophets and are not anointed as such. The Talmud can teach much about men, but cannot teach about God, since it is not written by God nor inspired directly by God the way the word of Moses or Daniel or Jeremiah was divinely inspired.

OBJECTION: In Dan. 9:22-27 the sequence of years begins with the return of Daniels compatriots to the Holy land to rebuild Jerusalem. The figure 483 years equals 69 weeks of years minus 1 week or 490-7 = 483. So the end point of the period of 69 weeks is 7 years before 70 C.E. That is 63 C.E. Daniel states that in the very end of the 70th week a foreign power will destroy the city and sanctuary. The anointed one dies after the 63 years as verse 25-26 make clear. Since Jesus died around 30 C.E. he cannot be the Messiah. (32)

RESPONSE: Dan.9:25 "Know therefore and understand from the going forth of the commandment to restore and rebuild Jerusalem unto the anointed the prince shall be seven weeks". This occurs at Neh.2:1-8. See previous response. The time table begins with the command to restore and rebuild. This occurs in 445/444 B.C.E. The time does not begin with the return of Daniels compatriots but rather the granting of permission to do so. We also know that the Jewish people claim no coming of a Messiah 49 years after the "going forth of the command to restore and rebuild Jerusalem." This would bring us to 397/396 B.C.E. The Jewish people do not claim a messiah at that time. The only other candidate that we can consider, other that Yeshua, is Eleazar who made the stand against the Romans at Masada. In 73 C.E. he and 952 other Jews killed themselves. No one followed him after his death so he is eliminated. Next there is Bar Kochbah. He was killed by Rome in 135 C.E. After his death the Jewish people were dispersed and the Jewish people don't follow him so he's eliminated. Dan.9:26 "and during 62 weeks it shall be built again with street and trench even in troubled times." The scripture does not say "after the seven weeks" it immediately jumps to 62 weeks. The 7 weeks (49 years) of commanding Jerusalem to be rebuilt to the coming of the Messiah are added to the 62 weeks (434) years it takes to rebuild Jerusalem during trouble times. "Then shall the Messiah be cut off and there shall be none to succeed him; And the people of the prince that will come will destroy the city and the sanctuary; and the end will be with a flood and unto the end of the war desolations are determined". What the scripture says is after the rebuilding period of Jerusalem the Messiah will be killed. After Herod the Great completed building the Temple complex at Jerusalem Yeshua was put to death. The Roman General Titus comes in 70 C.E. and destroys Jerusalem and the Temple. The point of view espoused above states that we must count backwards from 70 C.E. One week (7 years) before 70

C.E. is 63 C.E. According to the Objection we must now subtract 483 years from 63 C.E. This brings us to 420 B.C.E. The time table starts with the "going forth of the commandment to restore and rebuild Jerusalem." The restoration and rebuilding of Jerusalem was well underway by 420 B.C.E. Therefore, starting with 70 C.E. and working backward does not work and is not accurate. Now back to our story. Dan.9:27 "And he shall confirm the covenant with many for one week: and for half of the week he shall cause the sacrifice and oblation to cease and for the overspreading of abominations he shall make it desolate even until the consummation and that determined shall be poured upon the desolate." The Jewish version states that the "the prince that will come" is the same person as the 'he' in Dan.9: 27. Let's see. This person would have to be consistent with the historical Titus general of the Roman Legions that destroyed Jerusalem in 70 C.E. Did Titus, son of Emperor Vespasian, make an agreement with the People of Jerusalem for 7 years? NO. Did he cause sacrifice and offering to cease for 3 ½ years? The Jewish revolt started in 66 C.E. We can make a case for four years not seven. Did Titus cause sacrifice and offering to stop? Before this the Jewish people had fallen into depravity according to Flavius Josephus, who was the Roman appointed Jewish historian of the era. They were not in a righteous state when Titus and his legions arrived during Passover. Titus did not make an abomination to God. The Jewish People rebelled. Just as some in Jerusalem were glad to see Yeshua meet his end on the cross so did Titus visit destruction upon Jerusalem and its inhabitants. It can be argued that he destroyed Jerusalem and the Temple and thus left it desolate, but did the verse "poured upon him the desolator" refer to Titus? No. He became Emperor of Rome in 79 C.E. and the Arch of Titus finished in 81

C.E. still stands in Rome outside of the Coliseum. The personage to conclude the 70 weeks of Daniel is still on the horizon. In Dan.9:26 Jerusalem and the Temple are destroyed. In Dan.9:27 this person will make an agreement with Jerusalem. In order to make sacrifice and offering stop, the Temple must be rebuilt. He will do abominations against God and "upon consummation, the ending of all things, this desolater shall be made desolate." This is yet to come. (33)

SEGUE: By going into detail concerning "the Prophesy of weeks" included by Daniel the Prophet we learn that no one could fulfill the scripture except Yeshua of Nazareth. When one comes to this realization they accept Yeshua as the Anointed.

OBJECTION: The Flight to Egypt as explained by the Prophet Hosea did not refer to Jesus leaving Egypt as a small child. (34)

RESPONSE: "When Israel was a child I loved him, and called my son out of Egypt." Hos.11: 1 Israel/Jacob, God indeed did love him. If we are to take this verse to apply to the Egyptian captivity there are some problems. This is not talking about the descendents of Israel. Why, God loved Israel referred to as him not them. Furthermore; Israel/him was old when he went to Egypt Gen.46. What we see is that Israel was referred to as him not them so the descendents of Israel are not referred to nor is Israel/Jacob because he died in Egypt Gen. 50 and therefore could not be called out. If this did refer to the Israelites in Egypt being called out it still would not apply since they were in captivity after Jacob/Israel's death. Israel in this sense refers to Messiah as Emmanuel referred to Messiah. Israel, one who strives with God, was loved by the Father who sought the child's protection Matt.2:13-15. After Herod's death God's son was called out of Egypt to return safely to the Galilee.

SEGUE: There are two views with this passage. One looks backward and the other forward from Hosea's time. If Hosea is looking backward this passage is not a Prophesy. If he is looking forward then this is a Prophesy. In the context of Hosea 11:1-5, it is equally clear that God is ALSO referring to His calling His son Israel out of Egypt. Yeshua can only be equated with the term 'Israel' to the extent that the Prophet Isaiah refers to Israel/Jacob and Messiah as "The Servant of God". During his lifetime Yeshua was referred to as the Son of David, or Son of Man, or Son of the Living God. Conversely, the Children of Israel are frequently referred to by God in the Tenakh as Israel, just as the Jews are the descendants of Judah and were often referred to as Judah, and Israel was referred to as Ephraim (Joseph's younger son who was favored by Jacob over the elder and whose tribe dominated the northern kingdom). Hos.11:5 makes it clear that they will not RETURN to the land of Egypt, but rather Assyria will rule and consume them because they refused to turn back to God despite the prophets' calling to them on God's behalf. By all accounts Hosea is a prophet. Who therefore is the "son" Hosea speaks about? See Proverbs 30:4.

OBJECTION: "Tell the daughter of Zion" "Rejoice greatly Oh daughter of Zion" then Zechariah speaks of one animal not two. It seems that Matthews's account of this event is a bit confused. (35)

RESPONSE: The key here is that "daughter of Zion" is being addressed. This also occurs in Isa.62:11. The details of Zech.9:9 point to a greater fulfillment in Isaiah where it states "Behold your salvation comes". The argument goes on to say "The colt thrown in there by the Gospel is extraneous." I looked up the verse in the Hebrew Scriptures revised by Alexander Harkavy through the Hebrew Publishing Company of New York. In this publication the verse states, "Riding upon an ass and upon a colt the foal of an ass" This is exactly what Matthew quoted. "Mounted on a donkey, even on a colt, the foal of a donkey." This is not a reference to two separate animals, but in a traditional Hebrew poetic usage, a general reference followed by a specific one - mounted on a donkey - specifically, a colt of a donkey. BUT... the "and" <u>is</u> there in the original Hebrew of Zechariah. In Hebrew usage, the "and" is a connective, not meant to imply two animals, since no one rides two animals simultaneously, especially a mismatched pair of an adult donkey and a donkey colt. This is an example of an argument whereby if nothing can be found to disprove the claim of Yeshua then find fault with the gospel writer. In essence, run away from the one that promises life eternal with Abraham, Isaac, and Jacob.

SEGUE: The Objections that are encountered at this point will be dual in nature. The criticism is levied against Yeshua or one of his followers. The criticism is valid if it is true. Let's continue to discern where we can find the truth.

OBJECTION: <u>Regarding Zech.12:10 it is a fine example of how cryptic the prophets can be, providing many</u>

a foothold either for Jewish tradition or Christian interpretation: (36)

RESPONSE: This is a literalist argument concerning "whom they have pierced" implying the Romans did the literal piercing. This is addressed in Act 2:22-28. "Men of Israel...you crucified and killed by the hands of lawless men." This according to Matt.27:22-23; Mark 15:13-14; Luke 23:21-23; John 19:15-16 states that the Judeans thought, desired, and confessed that they wanted Yeshua crucified. They were complicit in his piercing and therefore responsible, as were the Romans, for the events of that day.

SEGUE: One who plans murder is as guilty as the people who carry it out. From an ethical or legal basis capitol punishment was inflicted on Yeshua. Who did he harm? He was killed because his point of view was at variance with those in power. Therefore those who planned his passion were also guilty. The Judean leadership was approved and appointed by the authority Rome. If they approved of Yeshua their position would have been at risk. In fact, they had been marginalized by Rome and therefore approved of Yeshua's demise.

OBJECTION: Zech.12:10 has nothing to do with Jesus. It wasn't the Jews who pierced Jesus with nails and a spear at the crucifixion it was the Romans John19: 34-37. (37)

RESPONSE: Matt.26:59 "Now the Chief priests and the whole counsel sought false testimony against Yeshua that they might put him to death." Matt. 26:65-66 "Then the high Priest tore his robes and said, He has uttered blasphemy...what is your judgment? They answered,

He deserves death." Matt.27:1 "When morning came all the chief priests and the elders of the people took counsel against Yeshua to put him to death." Matt.27:12 "But when he was accused by the chief priests and elders he made no answer. Then Pilate said to him, do you not hear how many things they testify against you?" Matt 27:20 "Now the chief priests and elders persuaded the people to ask for Barabbas and destroy Yeshua." Matt.27:22-23 "Pilate said to them, what shall I do with Yeshua who is called Messiah? They all said, let him be crucified! And he said why? What evil has he done? But they shouted all the more, Let him be crucified!" Matt.27:24-26 "Seeing that he was gaining nothing but that a riot was beginning Pilate said, I am innocent of this man's blood. See to it yourselves. And all the people answered, Let his blood be on us and our children! Then he released Barabbas and having scourged Yeshua delivered him to be crucified." Acts 2:22-23 "Peter said, Men of Israel hear these words; Yeshua of Nazareth a man attested to you by God with mighty works and wonders and signs which God did through him in your midst as you yourselves know-this Yeshua delivered up according to the definite plan and foreknowledge of God you crucified and killed by the hands of lawless men." Some facts: Yeshua was arrested by the Judeans not the Romans. The Judeans conspired to kill Yeshua not the Romans. The Judeans brought Yeshua to Pilate. Pilate did not request him. Pilate sentenced Yeshua to death only after he saw that a riot was breaking out. The intent of the Judeans was to have Yeshua crucified. Although the Roman authority carried out the wishes of the Judeans, for Pilate washed his hands, the Judeans were complicit in the crucifixion of Yeshua for they wanted him dead therefore Zech 12:10 applies. There is no other explanation for this. No one fulfills this except Yeshua and it will be through this, the scars of his passion, that the Jewish people will recognize him.

SEGUE: This question cries out, who was pierced? If Yeshua had died in another fashion, like stoning or drowning, or natural causes Zech.12:10 would make no sense. The truth is he died through scourging and being nailed to a tree, therefore the passage has significance. Yeshua was wrongly accused by the priests and scribes – the Temple leadership – and it was they who cornered Pilate and coerced him into crucifying Yeshua lest he be reported to Rome as tolerating a would-be rebel against the Emperor who claimed to be King of the Jews. It was on this basis that Pilate had the Lord crucified. He emphasized this – when the priests complained about the placard over the cross, Pilate insisted that it said what it said correctly. Whatever Pilate may have thought about Yeshua, he rationalized the crucifixion on the basis that Yeshua asserted that he was the king of the Jews, and thus a threat to Roman authority. One did not call oneself a king in Augustinian Rome and live (on earth) to tell about it. The Jews, through their priests, and the Romans, through Pilate and their troops, were BOTH guilty of the blood of Yeshua. Indeed, this was as it should be. Yeshua died for the sins of ALL mankind, Jew and Gentile, priest and commoner, rulers and ruled. No living man on earth dare blame another for the death of Yeshua – each of us bears equal blame! God asked His Son to die for us out of love for each of us, and the Son out of obedience to the Father and out of love for each of us willingly did so.

OBJECTION: <u>Micah 5:1-2 Messiah will come from Bethlehem, from David's lineage, to be born, soon</u>

<u>thereafter the exiles return to Israel, Messiah will reign over the earth and establish peace.</u> (38)

RESPONSE: Yeshua was born in Bethlehem and is David's descendent. His genealogy from Matthew and Luke confirm it. Messiah's origin is from days of old. If the Messiah is only human his origin is from 9 months before he was born. How does this translate into days of old? Yeshua claimed to be the Son of God therefore his origin was from days of old. In Yeshua's day the Jews were not exiled. Although Israel was reestablished in the 20th century the Jews are still scattered today. If Yeshua were not the Messiah born in Bethlehem from David's family, the Messiah must be born in a mostly Muslim/ Christian Bethlehem and prove his Davidic lineage. This is not at all probable in our day. Some of the exiles have returned but Messiah will complete the task. How could he, meaning Yeshua, complete the task if he was born 2000 years ago in Bethlehem? See Dan.7:13-14. No human being could reign over this world and bring peace unless he is also the Lord. Yeshua stated, "Before Abraham was, I AM." The Jews present knew EXACTLY what He meant, which was why they sought to stone Him for it on the spot. Because He WAS who He said He was, they could not do so. Also, there was still a sizeable Jewish Diaspora in Jesus' day. There were Jews in Rome, across the Greek lands (Achaean peninsula and Asia Minor), and in Mesopotamia and Persia, and up into the Caucasus and down into Arabia Felix (the Hejaz). Judah was quasi-autonomous in Yeshua's day – though its autonomy was steadily diminishing due to the Jews' rebelliousness. The Jews lived under their own law and traditions, subject only to paying taxes to Rome and accepting the presence of Roman troops and Roman civil law. Today, the Jews of Israel live under SECULAR law, and the Orthodox are not much freer in many ways than they were under Pilate. The Temple has not been rebuilt – the State will not allow it for fear of the anger of allies and enemies alike, and most Jews in Israel don't care – they think the Temple and the Levitical sacrifices are primitive revolting rituals. As for if anyone born today could prove they are of the line of David; only GOD knows who are the heirs of David, and could raise one up if He chose to do so. The Christians of Bethlehem are a mix of Arabs, Arameans, Syriacs, and Greeks. The Talmud posits two Messiahs, but the Tenakh does not.

SEGUE: 2000 years ago Bethlehem was a Jewish town. Today it is not. This does not mean that a savior could not be born there but Bethlehem's significance as the city of David is now replaced with manger square, a steady decrease of Christians and an increasing Muslim population. How a person born in this age could prove that he is an offspring of Jesse, David and Solomon will be anyone's guess. The Talmud in other passages spoke about two Messiah's Ben David and Ben Josef. It wouldn't make sense for ben Josef to be born In Bethlehem. Ben Josef gets killed so ben David must be born in Bethlehem. This creates the problem of who is the character of Dan. 7: 13-14? Yeshua was born in Bethlehem the city of David and will return as King of kings and Lord of lords.

The Messiah of Israel HAD TO APPEAR before the destruction of the second Temple. Here's why. IIChron.7:19-22 states that if the people forsake the statutes and commandments of God and worship other gods the people will be removed from the land and God's house will also be cast out i.e. destroyed. Since the Temple was destroyed in 70 C.E. we can conclude that God was displeased with his people. Dan.9:24-27 states that prior to the destruction of Jerusalem and the sanctuary (Temple) an anointed (messiah) shall come, be cut off and have nothing. Verse 24 also states that the atonement for sin and bringing of everlasting righteousness shall also occur before this destruction. Hag.2:3-9 states that the former (Temple) was glorious, before its destruction. However, in the next House (Temple) "I will fill this house with splendor...the latter splendor of this house shall be greater than the former." The difference between the first and second Temple is that the Lord of Hosts fills the second Temple with His splendor. The Lord of Hosts visits the second Temple. In Mal.3:1-5 The Lord of Hosts states that 'The Lord whom you seek will suddenly come to his Temple...who can stand when he appears? According to the scriptures the Messiah will be cut off and fulfill the atonement for sin before the destruction of the Temple. Just prior to these events the Lord will come to his Temple and fill it with splendor for the scripture states he appears i.e. will be seen in his Temple. Since the Temple was destroyed in 70 C.E. Yeshua is the only anointed who was cut off and appeared in the Temple before its destruction. As a point of emphasis Yoma 39b in the Babylonian Talmud states that the sacrifices offered by the High Priest on Yom Kippur from 30-70 C.E. were not accepted by God because the thread of scarlet never turned white but remained red. God no longer accepted the Temple sacrifices as a covering for sin because Messiah became our atonement as predicted by the prophets prior to the destruction of the second Temple. (39)

Chapter 4 Notes

1. Klinghoffer, Why The Jews Rejected Jesus, P.126
2. Gen.22:17-18; Deut.32:21; Isa.1:9, 10:22-23; 59:20; 65:1-2; Hos.1:4, 6, 9-11; 2:23-24; Rom.11: 1, 11, 15; 11:12-13, 20, 30
3. Klinghoffer, Why the Jews Reject Jesus, P.163
4. B.Gitten 56b-57a; Matt.1: 1-7; Luke 3: 23-32
5. Klinghoffer, Why the Jews Rejected Jesus, PP.111-112
6. MacDonald, Believers Bible Commentary, PP.354-365
7. Num.23:19; J.Taanit 65B
8. Klinghoffer, Why the Jews Rejected Jesus, P.127
9. Klinghoffer, P.48
10. Lindsay, The Messiah, PP.39-45
11. Deut 30: 1-10; Klinghoffer, P.140
12. Klinghoffer, Why the Jews Rejected Jesus, PP.69-70
13. Klinghoffer, P.83
14. Klinghoffer, PP.168/9
15. Jamieson, Fausset and Brown, Biblical Commentary P.415
16. Klinghoffer, P.205
17. MacDonald, Believers Bible Commentary, P.620
18. Ps.143:2; Klinghoffer, Why the Jews Rejected Jesus, P.111
19. Klinghoffer, PP.174/5

20. Klinghoffer, P.80
21. Jamieson, Fausset and Brown, Biblical Commentary P.503; MacDonald, Believers Bible Commentary P.938
22. Klinghoffer, Why the Jews Rejected Jesus, P.65
23. Lindsay, The Messiah, PP.56-57; Lockyer, All the Messianic Prophecies of the Bible, P.62
24. Kimchi, op. cit., P.55; Klinghoffer, Why the Jews Rejected Jesus, P.167
25. Klinghoffer, P.209
26. Klinghoffer, P.81
27. Klinghoffer, P.82
28. Shereshevsky, Rashi's and Christian Interpretations" Jewish Quarterly Review 61 (1970), P.77; Rashi on Isa.53:1-2, 4; Klinghoffer, PP.165-166
29. Klinghoffer, PP.65-66
30. Berger, op. cit., P.90; Klinghoffer, P.168
31. Exodus Rabbah 47:1, B Sanhedrin 97B; Klinghoffer P.139
32. Dan.12:9; Klinghoffer PP.207-208
33. Josephus, The Wars of the Jews, Volume 1 Book V
34. Matt.2:15; Klinghoffer, Why the Jews Rejected Jesus, P.66

35. Vermes, Jesus the Jew, P.22; Jaynes, The Origin of Consciousness in the Breakdown of the Bicameral Mind, PP.232-233; Matt:4:24; Klinghoffer, P.78
36. Klinghoffer, P.78
37. Klinghoffer, P.208
38. Klinghoffer, P.34
39. Strobel, Finding the Real Jesus, PP.48-61

SECTION II:

JEWISH DISCOURSE REGARDING THE NEW COVENANT, ST. PAUL, AND YESHUA

Chapter 5

The New Covenant: Misrepresentation of Man or Inspired Writ of God

OBJECTION: We have no record in the New Covenant ever publicly volunteering that Jesus was the long awaited Messiah: (1)

RESPONSE: Matt.16:16-17; 22:42-45; Luke 24:25-27; John 4:25 argue the point otherwise. On some occasions Yeshua is queried with the terms Messiah (Christ) Son of God, Lord, Son of David and Son of Man all included. Messiah had a political connotation, which would have led a larger audience to believe that he came to drive out the Romans and thus was threatening to Rome. He clearly did not come for this purpose. How could he have won over the Gentiles if he made war on them? He came to save not slay. Yeshua acknowledged to the High Priest and to the Pharisees, as well as to John the Baptizer's followers, that He was the Messiah. He was acknowledged as such by many, including John the Baptizer, the apostles, etc.

SEGUE: The verses cited above are displayed here. Simon Peter replied, "You are the Messiah the Son of the Living God." Yeshua answered, blessed are you Simon for flesh and blood has not revealed this to you, but my Father who is in heaven. Yeshua asked them "What do you think of the Messiah? The Pharisees said the Son of David. Yeshua said David inspired by the Spirit said,

"The LORD said to my Lord, sit at my right hand until I put your enemies under your feet? (Ps.110:1) If David calls him Lord how can he be his son? O foolish men and slow of heart to believe all that the prophets have spoken. Was it not necessary that the Messiah should suffer these things and enter into his glory? The woman said I know that Messiah is coming; when he comes he will show us all things. Yeshua said to her, I who speak to you am he."

OBJECTION: The New Covenant makes little sense where it is clear that the cumulative confrontations between Jesus and the Jewish religious leadership led to their hostility against him. (2)

RESPONSE: The hostility that the Jewish religious leaders felt toward Yeshua started almost immediately. The question is why? In Luke 4:16-19 Yeshua quotes from Isaiah and claims its fulfillment. Later after he forgives a crippled man's sins the man is healed. Yeshua did and said things early on that associated himself with God. The learned Jews could not accept this. So to them Yeshua became a blasphemer. Eventually they were publicly embarrassed in discussions with him. This combined with the repercussions that would occur had the masses crowned Yeshua as King Messiah led them to want Yeshua destroyed. Yeshua was twice on the verge of being stoned -- very explicitly for the alleged blasphemy of claiming to be the Son of God, or for being God incarnate. He also asserted that His authority was greater than the scribes, Pharisees, and priests, and that He had authority to teach the Law greater than Moses. It was quite clear whom He was saying He was -- and quite clear that the majority of the Jews refused to believe whom He said He was despite the miracles and signs and the fulfillment of prophecies with which the learned were very familiar -- they were expecting Messiah to come, but not as a suffering servant, and not as both God and Man.

SEGUE: Another problem was a class problem. Judeans considered themselves more sophisticated than their northern neighbors the Galileans.

OBJECTION: The Galileans were country bumpkins, but the Judeans in the south with its rabbis and priests would know better. (3)

RESPONSE: There was a degree of legitimacy to this attitude. The Galileans generally didn't know the Torah or the Tenakh as well as the Jews in and around Jerusalem. Prior to the broadcast media era -- rural folk usually were less educated and had few opportunities to keep up with things than urban folk. The Objection also presupposes that educated Jews always get it right. The problem not addressed by this Objection is one that Yeshua addressed with the Judeans, their pride. Are we supposed to believe that all the religiously learned are the most spiritual vis a vis the poor and simple? Those in the south were involved with Religion, their status in religion among the people and the politics that was Jerusalem. Yeshua's message was for the individual and the poor to enhance their status vis a vis the well to do, more knowledgeable in the south, who thought too well of themselves. Yeshua did not shy away from confrontation with the "southerners." The New Covenant has many accounts of discourse which leave the better educated "southerners" on the short end of the dialogue. Yet are we to assume these same people for sure could spot the true Messiah? In fact many Judeans followed Yeshua, including at least two Sanhedrin members, Nicodemus and Joseph of Arimathea. But what was required of great and small alike was child-like faith.

SEGUE: The better educated and more sophisticated don't always get it right. Those who are better educated do not necessarily love more than the less educated. The more educated do not necessarily make better husbands and wives. Why then is there this assumption that the Judeans would recognize messiah before Galileans? The Judeans SHOULD have recognized the Messiah before the Galileans, because more of them were familiar with the indicative prophecies in Daniel 9, Isaiah 51-53, Psalms 2 and 22 -- and they were expecting Messiah's advent. The problem was selective reading -- they didn't want to accept that Messiah would necessarily come first as a suffering servant -- they wanted liberation from the pagan Romans.

OBJECTION: <u>He was adulated by a following from Galilee, famous for their ignorance, knowing no better, they thought Jesus uniquely had Judaism all figured out. To the extent Jesus' better informed listeners understood this; it was unsurprising that they should regard his approach to Torah with suspicion</u>. (4)

RESPONSE: Here the point is made that the Galileans were ignorant and the Judeans more learned. This applies to matters of intellect but not to matters that are spiritually discernable. How was it then that these same Galileans, together with St. Paul brought the words of Yeshua to the world? Further, it was clear that something profound had happened to these Galilean apostles -- note the difference between Simon

Peter's impulsive behavior and simple, single-phrase sentences in the Gospels and his careful, well-thought-out plans and lengthy, insightful, Scripture-based preaching in Acts. Similarly, John the Apostle began following Yeshua as a teenager -- he had no higher learning -- but clearly from his writings was brilliantly insightful about the Tenakh and human nature. The same would apply to Yeshua's half-brother James. The same people who were belittled by their co-religionists brought Yeshua's words to a world that embraced them through persecution. Who brought the knowledge of the God of Abraham and his Messiah to the world in the first century C.E. those ignorant Galileans or those better informed Judeans? This section appears to bear witness to the Gospel accounts that detail the conflict between Yeshua and the rabbis. The rabbis debate with Yeshua but continually come up on the short end. So the learned Rabbi's cannot outwit Yeshua of Nazareth. Wasn't Yeshua also a product of the Galilee?

SEGUE: God often uses the unassuming and meek, not the most intelligent and wealthiest. When one possesses knowledge of the past one learns that the learned and powerful often get it wrong. The events of 70 C.E. should prove as an exclamation point.

OBJECTION: We need not accept the historical truth of all this (the Gospel accounts are probably not true) ...I cannot find any reason to deny the basic tenor of the Gospel depiction of the reception Jesus got from many of his fellow Jews. (5)

RESPONSE: This assertion casts doubt on the Gospel account yet it does not disagree with the Gospel premise concerning Yeshua and his people the Jews.

This tension is understandable. Yeshua son of Joseph claims God is his Father, Yeshua forgives sins and people are healed, Yeshua gives a more spiritual than physical interpretation of Scripture. This means if he's got it right other learned Jews may have gotten some issues wrong. Who wants to be religiously wrong? No one! Therefore Yeshua's interpretation and his claims must be disregarded miracles and healings explained away.

SEGUE: Miracles of healing had an impact on individuals and families in a personal way. Yeshua didn't perform any miracles that made people rich or hurt someone else. How could these events not have an impact on the community at large? The miracles persuaded many, but the rabbis' answer -- that these were essentially satanically inspired magic tricks, not the work of God (they alleged that God would not violate the Sabbath by healing on the Sabbath -- implying that their misinterpretation of the Law was binding on the Lawgiver!) -- was sufficient to fool many Galileans and Judeans alike. Ultimately, the Father determined who was to be given grace sufficient to salvation, then as now, and those whom the Father gave unto the Son were saved.

OBJECTION: A Jew at the time, upon hearing (or witnessing) such things might seek out or see what this was about but no more than that. Admittedly I don't know of a sage of this century to whom the rabbinic sources attribute the power of resurrection. Unlike the Gospel writers, the Talmud doesn't make a fuss about this. The Jews were based on being grounded in the Talmud would have seen miracles, even if witnessed with their own eyes as proof of spiritual potency, but nothing more than that. (6)

RESPONSE: The Egyptian magicians in Moses day performed a miracle. Did they claim to perform this miracle in the name of the God of Abraham? No. This tells us that another force can also perform miracles. Are we to expect that the God of Abraham was causing miracles for Pharaoh and Moses? No. By the way Moses and the God of Abraham won the contest. Yeshua performs miracles in the name of the God of Abraham. Why does God permit miracles from one who was a fraud and equated himself with divinity, including resurrection from the dead? Another miracle (healing) occurs after Yeshua forgave the man his sins Matt.9: 1-8. How does one who is a false prophet, a fraud, do these deeds in the name of the God of Israel, forgive sins, while God permitted him to heal and work wonders? Did his power come from the source that performed miracles for Pharaohs magicians or did this power come from the God of Abraham? If it comes from the God of Abraham why then is this man considered a fraud? The prophet Elijah performed at least one resurrection. He and others among the prophets, most notably but not exclusively Moses, performed miracles, all in God's name. (7)

SEGUE: The Book of Exodus states that the sorcerers and magicians performed enchantments. According to the Torah these practices are not of God, in fact are harmful, therefore they are considered an abomination before the Lord. This was indicative of the moral downfall of Judah, Jacob's son and progenitor of the Jews, and also of King Saul. The key difference is that sorcerers and magicians claim secret/special/hidden knowledge and access to spirits or pagan pseudo-gods, while God's prophets and Yeshua stated that they only knew/spoke/did what the God of Abraham, Isaac, and Jacob put into their minds and mouths to do. (8)

OBJECTIONS: Perhaps the Gospel writers are true to Jesus own teaching which had the tendency to walk on both sides of the street, heads I win tales you lose: (9)

RESPONSE: I cannot think of any of Yeshua's teachings which were ambivalent or mutually contradictory. They did often contradict the Pharisaical rabbis, the priests, and the secularized Sadducees' views of the meaning of the Law and the prophets -- but they vehemently disagreed with each other, too, as Yeshua demonstrated. Yeshua stated that IF John the Apostle did not taste death before His Return and the establishment of the Kingdom on earth, what was it to Peter? The Lord did not say that would happen, only that it was not Peter's concern -- no man was to know when Yeshua would return in Glory -- not even He Himself knew, only the Father. For instance St. John saw the Son of Man's coming -- in a vision, which is preserved for us as the Revelation of John. There also appears to be a problem with Yeshua stating that the Kingdom of God is among you, followed by the Son of man will come with power and great glory. In terms of the former, Yeshua was the awaited King however; he could not establish a Kingdom against the will of the Jewish people. Therefore, the scripture was fulfilled by their rejection of him. The Son of Man/Messiah had to come, preach, be rejected by most, and then humiliated, killed, resurrected, and assumed into heaven before He could come in glory to establish the Kingdom. If He had not done so, no man or woman on earth could have lived in the millennial Kingdom! Only the saved could enter that Kingdom -- the unsaved would all be in hell, awaiting final judgment and the Lake of Fire.

St. Peter also saw Yeshua in the Kingdom to come. If other Apostles saw this it wasn't recorded; however, they did witness the ascension Acts 1: 9-11. The Lord also spoke of a future event whereby Israel will welcome his return. (10)

SEGUE: The Objection above indicates that the gospel writers cannot be right no matter their testimony. The reason they cannot be right is that it would make the Jewish position less than correct. Thus we are left with the dilemma. If Yeshua is the Messiah but the Jewish people by and large reject Him, the Jews are left "in the outer darkness, where there is weeping and gnashing of teeth." The Jewish people, totally confused by secularism and assimilation, today have little religious identity remaining and not much more cultural identity in a post-Yiddish world. The only thing left with which to define their identity is their rejection of Yeshua -- those who wish to follow Messiah must be willing to die to their own people as much today as has been true since the 4th century C.E. Unfortunately Jews and Christians are not united in the hope of Messiah -- they are divided by it, as they have been for centuries. This will remain true until "the fullness of the Gentiles" are brought into the Kingdom.

OBJECTION: <u>The claim to descent from Judah was through his mother's husband Joseph. If Jesus was not Joseph's son he cannot be the Messiah If he was Joseph's son he cannot be the son of God. Understand</u>

then they are refuted by their own words, by the book of their error, namely the New Covenant. (11)

RESPONSE: What is omitted is that there are two genealogies. Matt.1:15 & Luke 3:24. Matthat and Matthan is the same person. These names are actually much closer then Sinai and Horeb. Jacob and Heli were brothers. Jacob the father of Joseph died. Then Heli who was Mary's father became legal guardian of Joseph. In both Genealogies he is a son of Judah, and son of David. Luke's Gospel States, "The Angel said the Holy Spirit will come upon you and the power of the most high will over shadow you therefore the child to be born will be called holy, the Son of God." (12)

SEGUE: The New Covenant never states that Yeshua was Joseph's biological son. Joseph was Yeshua's legal guardian. Mary was the biological mother who was also a descendent of David. The Holy Spirit satisfied the God part and Mary satisfied the biological part. Joseph was also of the same lineage. Therefore, the New Covenant is not the book of our error rather it is the book whereby we meet our Lord and find salvation.

OBJECTION: The genealogy in Matthew only proves that Joseph was a son of David. Joseph could never pass on by adoption that which he doesn't have. Because Joseph descended from Jeconiah (Matt 1:11) he fell under the curse of that king that none of his descendents could ever sit as a king upon the throne of David (Jer.22:30; 36:30). Luke 3 traces Joseph's genealogy not Mary. Even if Luke 3 traces Mary to King David, tribal affiliation can only go through the father (Num1:18; Ezra: 2:59). Furthermore; this lineage goes through David's son Nathan not Solomon (Luke3:31) the scripture says it must go through Solomon (IISam.7:14; IChron.17: 11-14; 22:9-10; 28:4-6). Luke 3:27 lists Shealtiel and Zerubbabel in the genealogy. These two also appear in (Matt 1:12) as descendents of the cursed Jeconiah. If Mary descends from them, it would also disqualify her from being a messianic progenitor. (13)

RESPONSE:_Joseph was the legal guardian of Yeshua being Mary's husband. Biologically, through Joseph Yeshua was not from his lineage of David, yet as the legal guardian of Yeshua he becomes David's descendent legally. There is also another genealogy in Luke which differs from the Matthew genealogy. This is widely held as the lineage of Mary, the mother of Yeshua, daughter of David. Luke 2:4-5 states that Joseph was in Bethlehem to be enrolled with Mary his betrothed. Mary is also being enrolled in Bethlehem. Why? Because she was a daughter of David thus making Yeshua a Legal and Physical Son of David. (14)

Had Solomon's descendent Jeconiah been a biological ancestor of Yeshua, the Messianic claim by Christians could not hold water. The issue then returns to Solomon. Concerning Luke's genealogy being a contradictory genealogy of Joseph, notice the following; Matt.1: 15-16 Matthan the Father of Jacob, and Jacob the father of Joseph the husband of Mary. Some versions say that Matthan begat Jacob and Jacob begat Joseph. It is clear this is the biological lineage of Joseph. In Luke 3: 23-24 the terminology changes. Yeshua is the supposed son of Joseph the son of Heli who was the son of Matthan. First, one can be a son of a man without being of biological descent. In this case Joseph being the son (in-law) of Heli. Heli and Jacob share the same father

Matthan so it appears that they were brothers and Joseph and Mary are cousins. (15)

Num.1:18 states that they registered themselves by father's houses and Ezra 2:59 states "they could not prove their father's houses or their descent whether they belonged to Israel." In Matthew we have the legal genealogy of Yeshua's legal father not his biological Father. The Gospels of Matthew and Luke prove that Yeshua belongs to Israel. So who is Yeshua's Father? Matthew's Gospel goes back to Abraham; however, Luke stated Enos the son of Seth, the son of Adam, the son of God. Adam was created by God and considered his son; furthermore, the lineage in Luke contains no prohibitions concerning this lineage. (16)

Concerning the lineage through Solomon the scriptures clearly identify Solomon as the one whereby Solomon's house will be established forever. Here is the qualifier. IChron. 28:7 I will establish his Kingdom forever IF he continues resolute in keeping my commandments and my ordinances as he is today." God's promise is conditional on the behavior of Solomon and those who would follow. We know this is true because God puts a halt to this lineage. (17)

We must also compare and contrast Luke 3:27 with Matt. 1:12. In Matthew Jechoniah is the father of Shealtiel and Shealtiel is the father of Zerubbabel who is the father of Abiud. In Luke, Joanan was the son of Rhesa who was the son of Zerubbabel who was the son of Shealtiel who was the son of Neri. If Neri is the biological father of Shealtiel then how can Jechoniah also be the biological father of Shealtiel? He cannot. The descendents of Jechoniah are under the curse.

Since the Shealtiel of Luke's Gospel is the son of Neri he and Luke's Zerubbabel cannot be the same people so the genealogy in Luke's Gospel allows for Yeshua's biological descent.

SEGUE: If Joseph and Mary were not descendents of David I would not be writing this book and we would not have a difference of perspective. Furthermore, Joseph and Mary would not have traveled to Bethlehem to fulfill the census requirements of the Roman Emperor. Why then was Yeshua called a Nazarene?

OBJECTION: <u>He shall be called a Nazarene</u>. (18)

RESPONSE: According to Matthew, "He went and dwelt in a city called Nazareth that what was spoken by the prophets might be fulfilled." Although he lived in Nazareth of Galilee, the Nazarene described by the Prophets derives from the root "Natsri" where the term Nazarene is derived. This term describes one acquainted with pain. Just as Nazareth would be held in low esteem among the Jews (John 1:46) so also Messiah would be held in low esteem and be familiar with Natsri, pain. Who are these prophets? David Ps.22:7-8, 14, 16, 34:20, 35:11, 38:11, 41:9. 55:12-14, 109:2, 25; Zech. 11:12, 12: 10, 13:6-7; Isa. 50:6, 52:14, 53: 1-12; Mic. 5:1, Ex. 12:46. These therefore are the Prophets who spoke of the Nazarene, the one acquainted with pain and therefore a Nazarene. There is a confusion that commonly develops between Nazarene and Nazirite. The former applies to one from that rather unpleasant and unimportant Roman garrison town in Galilee. The other applies to a formula for holy vows of purification taken by Jewish men to prepare them for a special task. Nazirites were to ingest no grape products, were not to cut their hair, and were generally to live according to the rules for priests in the Torah. The most famous Nazirites in the Bible were Samson (a failed Nazirite who didn't keep his vows) and the prophet Samuel, who was raised by his mother as a Nazirite in answer to her vow. The whole thread of "familiar with pain" certainly would apply to Messiah -- who was prophesied to come as the "suffering servant." (19)

SEGUE: The fact that Yeshua was familiar with pain and Nazareth of the Galilee was a town ridiculed by the Judeans was commonly known at that time. The Objection above is posted because it is an apparent success in displaying that the New Covenant Authors are fools. This again points to the educated Jews even though the source of scriptural inspiration is a spiritual force. Therefore, one must be open to that Spirit vice permitting Jewish tradition to dictate how one is to discern and think.

OBJECTION: <u>The equation of Jesus with God is an artifact of decades long after Yeshua died.</u> (20)

RESPONSE: The Book of Acts gives an account of this realization being with the Apostles, after the resurrection, the ascension and certainly after Pentecost. Given the events as described they realized that Yeshua is God and their Messiah. The Objection cannot entertain these ideas so one must fish for an alternate explanation. In the sense of being "educated Jews" this term places the objection above Matthew and John, who were eyewitnesses, Mark, a Jewish contemporary, and the Greek Physician Luke. For the record Matthew records that an Angel appeared to Joseph in a dream, God spoke to the disciples from a cloud, An Angel spoke to women at the tomb after the crucifixion. Luke records that the Angel Gabriel spoke to the Father of John the Baptist, Mary mother of Yeshua, angels speak with the shepherds, and the risen Yeshua speaks to the men on the road to Emmaus. In John the risen Yeshua appears to doubting Thomas. These signs and the risen Lord and being imbued with the Holy Spirit would have provided enough convincing. If the OBJECTION were true, then why did the Jews twice try to stone Him, and why did the Jewish leaders and the mob they riled up ultimately condemn Him and turn Him over to be crucified? Either He said who He was, and was wrongly attacked for it as a blasphemer, or He didn't say who He was, and this OBJECTION MIGHT be valid, but then the Jews framed and arranged the execution of a man who was completely innocent even by their own rules because he never equated himself with God. (21)

SEGUE: The Objection that Yeshua was the Son of God did not develop till many years later does not reconcile with the facts. One must ask the question, why did the Apostles believe that Yeshua was the Son of God? Yeshua was publicly executed. Three days later his guarded tomb was empty and shortly after that he appeared to his disciples. It was this event and the ascension that convinced them that Yeshua was more than a man. The time frame for them to realize this was less than one month vice 10 or more years after the event. The Jewish leaders, as was reported even in the Gospels, claimed that Yeshua's followers bribed the guards to open the tomb and steal the body so they could claim that Jesus had risen. Of course, this would not explain why all those men and women accepted brutal torture and death just to perpetuate a claim about a dead man rising that did nothing to bring them any wealth, power, influence, social status, or security.

Were they all insane? Were they so committed to a lie that they clung to it under torture, and shared it with others including their own families?

OBJECTION: <u>It is generally thought...the Trinitarian doctrine...was not part of the original Gospel text... From these expressions it's a long leap to the Nicene Creed</u>: (22)

RESPONSE: It is generally thought by whom? I'm not finding that in my Christian texts, so therefore these folks must be non-Christians. Yeshua frequently spoke of the Father, Himself and the Counselor. These Trinitarian views were introduced during his pre-resurrection lifetime. It can also be argued that a foreshadowing of the Trinity was introduced by the Prophet Isaiah. "From the time it came to be I have been there" the speaker has been there from the beginning. Who is the speaker? This speaker is sent by the Lord God and his Spirit. He who was there in the beginning (John 1) was sent by God and his Spirit. What else do we see? The Lord is the Redeemer. In the Jewish Talmudic context Messiah cannot be Lord nor redeem Israel. This same Lord is the Holy One of Israel. Since only God is Holy in this sense the Talmudic messiah cannot be the Holy one of Israel. In the Christian context the Messiah is sent by God with his Spirit. He is the Holy one of Israel since he is also a descendent of Israel. The term Elohim, as used frequently from the very beginning of B'reshis/ Genesis, is a plural. There is also usage of pronoun-like forms such as "we," and a clear distinction between the Ruakh HaKodesh -- the Holy Spirit, and some other aspect of the Godhead, right in the opening chapter of the Torah. While the term Trinity came later and the three aspects of the Godhead only appear in the same sentence in one of the Epistles, it is clear that there is a distinction in all of Yeshua's speeches, especially in the Gospel of John. (23)

SEGUE: The Objection indicates that the Trinitarian doctrine was developed much later. Basically it is something that most rational minded folks would not consider. What cannot be denied is that the concept of Father, Son and Holy Spirit was present in all of the Gospels which were first century documents. The book of Acts has various references to the Father Son and Holy Spirit. The entire New Covenant is compiled from first century documents.

OBJECTION: Clearly the idea of the divine Jesus is the product of an intellectual evolution. It is hard to see how such a notion could ever have taken hold so quickly after his death, as it did. (24)

RESPONSE: In one sense the idea of a divine Yeshua is an intellectual evolution yet the argument displays amazement that the idea took hold so quickly. Are we to believe in a quick evolution? Paul in approx. 50 C.E. wrote that Yeshua is Lord and that God is his Father. This Objection also refuses to consider other evidence such as Yeshua resurrected and Yeshua Ascending. These events can be located in Matt.28; Mark16; Luke 24; John 21, 22; and Acts chapter 1. Yeshua declared His divinity before His crucifixion, and people understood His claims -- hence seeking to stone Him and ultimately arranging His crucifixion. Simon Peter clearly stated Yeshua's divinity at Pentecost -- within a year of the Lord's crucifixion and resurrection, and others among the apostles and disciples were expressing similar things as recorded in the Book of Acts (and even in

Josephus' History) from very soon after Yeshua left this earth. (25)

SEGUE: The reason why there was no "evolution" of Yeshua's divinity was because His divinity was established by hundreds witnessing His resurrection. Without the resurrection there would have been no Christianity. All doubt was removed by this event. The result was that the Apostles and later St Paul could establish the logical foundation of their faith in Yeshua crucified and resurrected and endure the persecution and suffering that they experienced.

OBJECTION: How could Matthew, Mark, and Luke forget to mention such a momentous fact that God Himself had walked the earth in human form? (26)

RESPONSE: The Synoptic Gospel writers tell the story to their audiences. Matthew was a Roman collaborator, a tax collector from what today we'd call a secular background, but back then he would have been considered a Cynic. Mark wrote the most generic Gospel accessible to almost anyone (not just Judeans) who regardless of beliefs had already heard something about Yeshua, seeking to clarify and provide a clear, accurate, almost journalistic account. Luke wrote to Gentiles in general, though in the Holy Land, the vast majority of Gentiles were culturally Greek. John was writing what became the last of the four Gospels and was writing to the early church, which was primarily Jewish. Scriptural proof was important to the Hellenistic Jews. The Jewishness of Yeshua was important to the Judeans, the philosophy of the parables was important to the Greeks and stressing the divine nature of the messiah helped describe the resurrection and His promised return. All of the Synoptic Gospels provide at least one statement by Messiah Himself that was clearly understood at the time to be a direct claim to divinity -- a claim that usually led to either an attempt to stone Him and/or hysterical denunciations of His alleged blasphemy. The Gospel writers reflected their own backgrounds and beliefs; they wrote to people from backgrounds similar to their own.

SEGUE: All four Gospel accounts plus the book of Acts describe Yeshua in his post resurrection form. No human being could have endured 100 lashes from the Romans, crucified to a Roman cross for six hours, a spear thrust in the side and then be seen three days later with his wounds still visible but otherwise absolutely fine. During these appearances he could also appear at will, regardless of locked doors and walls. These accounts made his divinity clear-- one either had to brush off the testimony of these martyrs because it conflicted with one's own preferences, or one had to accept the testimony as stated.

OBJECTION: <u>The earliest Christians searched the Hebrew prophets and found some sayings of Isaiah that could be put to use, retrospectively salvaging Jesus' aborted career as Messiah</u>. (27)

RESPONSE: There are several difficulties here. In regard to the other false messiahs there are no accounts of their followers being steadfast unto a martyr's death as to what they saw, including attesting to the fulfillment of various prophesies (David, Daniel, Ezekiel, and Malachi as well as Isaiah). Why would these Christians go through all this trouble if they knew he didn't resurrect? Why would they die terribly holding to this faith? Here's another plausible explanation from Luke 24:13-53. In verses 27 and 45 the risen Yeshua gives the explanation. This explanation also explains why the apostles and disciples behaved as they did after the resurrection. The stated argument above gives no such explanation.

SEGUE: Why on earth would these Galilean bumpkins worry about salvaging Yeshua's aborted Messianic career if they knew he was dead? What was their motive? They gained no wealth, no influence, no fame, no authority by doing so -- only isolation, misery, poverty, and death. If they were so intellectually inferior how and why did they pull this off? Once again the question is answered through the resurrected Messiah.

OBJECTION: <u>John's Gospel cites the first verse of Isaiah 53. Mark and Luke also deploy Isaiah 53. Isaiah is hardly made use of at all in the New Covenants own narratives of his life:</u> (28)

RESPONSE:Isa.53:7/Matt.27:12;Isa.50:6/Matt.26:67-68;27:30; Isa.52:14;53:5/Luke22:64;Isa.53:9,12/Mark15:27-28,Luke22:37;23:34,39-43; Isa.52:13-14/Luke 23:35; Isa.53:6,11/Matt.20:28

When this particular argument is used with a Jewish audience, an audience that is not educated concerning the New Covenant, they are not able, in the realm of fairness, to point out the omissions inherent in this argument. Most Jews who have not had rabbinical education are also unfamiliar with the full text of Isaiah, since large portions are excluded from the cycle of liturgical "Haftorah" readings in the synagogue and have been since the 4th century C.E.

SEGUE: To be fair, Jewish people of good faith and Gentiles who are on the fence need to investigate the scriptures and make up their own mind. However, arguments that can easily be disproved like the above often do not bolster their Objection to reconciliation.

OBJECTION: <u>In the imaginative interpretations of prophesy that the Gospels in fact offer...we can only guess what the historical Jesus actually taught... if you have already accepted his authority to render interpretations of scripture contrary to the obvious meaning of the words. Hos. 6:1-2...citing the resurrection as a proof to a non-Christian, even if it happened is circular reasoning: </u>(29)

RESPONSE: While accusing the Gospel writers of being imaginative, the Objection states that the rabbi's rendered mind bending readings. Why do we have to guess what Yeshua actually taught? We have four gospels that state what he taught plus Jewish records that agree with Christian records concerning why Yeshua was rejected. "Interpretations of scripture contrary to the obvious meaning" This makes an issue of two verses in Hosea where Yeshua never referred to either until resurrected according to Luke. In Matt.12:39; and Luke 11:29-30 Yeshua refers to the "sign of Jonah" before his death. He only makes reference to Hos.6:1-2 after his resurrection. Why? After his resurrection the meaning became clear to his followers. The plural form of Hosea seems to preclude the Messiah. One must consider Gen.1:26; 3:22; Isa. 48:16-17 where God is described in uni-plural terms. The two days/third day refer to a specific event. The Holy Spirit was with Yeshua at his conception according to St. Matthew. In John 14 Yeshua speaks of God's Spirit that will be sent after Yeshua departs. That same Spirit was in Yeshua and with him. In this same fashion the Spirit would be with the Apostles at Pentecost. The "us" spoken of were Yeshua and the Holy Spirit. The Holy Spirit was in Yeshua during his trial. That same Spirit revived the dead Yeshua through Yahveh's command on the third day. The Holy Spirit was with Yeshua during his suffering and experienced His travail. The God "us" Elohim also experienced the joy of resurrection. Finally, the author speaks of the resurrection in terms of circular reasoning. This isn't true. Why? The argument isn't about the resurrection but the change in behavior by his followers, their motivation to make converts, write scripture, and by doing good returning harm to no one. The followers of Bar Kochbah and Sabbatai Zvi never did any of this. Yeshua's followers witnessed his death, his resurrection, and his ascension, and were anointed with the Holy Spirit. This is the only explanation for their behavior. Hundreds of people would not willingly accept ostracism, persecution, arrest, torture, and a hideous execution among the unclean (not kosher) unless they had very powerful reasons to insist upon the veracity and significance of what they witnessed and of that which they gave testimony. (30)

SEGUE: The fundamental argument is that while both the Orthodox Jew and the Biblical Christian accept the Tenakh as inspired, they differ radically on what the Tenakh means. Jews view the Mosaic Law (Torah) as superior to the prophets and wisdom books; Christians tend to put the most emphasis on the prophets and Psalms. Jews accept the rabbinical response to the disasters of the 1st century C.E. (increasingly harsh Roman occupation culminating in the destruction of the Temple, sack of Jerusalem, and the Second Diaspora); Christians accept the response of Yeshua and the Apostles to the disasters of the 1st century C.E. (seeing the destruction of the Temple and the sack of Jerusalem as unavoidable, and while unfortunate, spiritually irrelevant because the body of Messiah was the Temple of the new age). Jews simply have different beliefs about reconciliation (to the extent they even see reconciliation as being needed), and the nature of God. From the rabbinical perspective, if God's nature is love, then why would God have required the blood sacrifice of the one Christians call his son? The reality is that God's nature is not love. God's nature is HOLINESS. God's love and his mercy, like his justice and righteousness and integrity, are all aspects of His holiness. The angels in heaven proclaim "K'dosh, K'dosh, K'dosh Adonai Ts'voros" Holy, Holy, Holy is the Lord Almighty" THAT is the ultimate expression of His nature -- nothing there about love. God chooses to love, but He IS Holy and Just, and that is fundamental to who He is.

OBJECTION: <u>If no verse in the prophets unambiguously presented resurrection as a criterion for recognizing the Messiah-and none does- then such a hypothetical wonder would prove nothing</u>: (31)

RESPONSE: King David, His son Solomon, and Isaiah the Prophet provided Prophesy concerning the resurrection. **Hosea 6:2 also has a valid claim to be Messianic and foretelling a third day resurrection** -- what confuses the Jewish people is that the reference is to "us," not "me." This plays into the Jewish claim that b'nai Yisroel is the suffering servant, and Messiah is solely the conquering king of the Davidic line. We know from elsewhere (incl. Isaiah and Ezekiel) that this interpretation is not correct, since the suffering servant cannot be a worthy sacrifice unless He is pure and without sin or blemish, and the entirety of the Tenakh testifies that at no time has Israel been sinless and without blemish.(32)

SEGUE: The Objection wanted the resurrection scriptures to be interpreted to "their" satisfaction. If this is true then most of the Tenakh is not written to Jewish satisfaction. Although not all Jews have believed that an "oral Torah" was necessary -- the Sadducees and Essenes rejected this, as do modern Reform Jews. The Pharisees believed it, and their successors, the modern Orthodox and Khasidim believe it. Therefore this argument could also be used for all of the other verses in the scripture that need interpretation. The proof can be found in post-resurrection events that changed the behavior of Yeshua's Apostles and Disciples.

OBJECTION: The fact that the resurrected Jesus had appeared, if he did so at all, to so few people was curious: (33)

RESPONSE: In ICorinthians St. Paul speaks knowledgeably stating that Yeshua appeared to more than 500 after he resurrected. Evidence like this explains why folks like St. Paul and the Apostles helped the Yeshua movement spread. Regarding the spread of the Yeshua movement after the crucifixion; the previous argument fails to explain human nature concerning why the early believers risked their lives to witness about this faith. Stating that Yeshua and his followers, who claimed to be witnesses, were frauds and untruthful in their gospel accounts does not begin to explain the spread of the faith in Yeshua. 500+ people is not insignificant by the standards of the time. He did not call up a media event, nor did He go to the Temple or some other highly visible gathering place, during His time on earth after His resurrection. His intent was to reassure and encourage the believers, not to generate a riot. (34)

SEGUE: This argument seems to insinuate that the resurrection may have happened, but if it did, why appear to a select few. Yeshua appeared to those who he knew to reward their faith. It was never the way of the Lord to reward the unbelief of others.

OBJECTION: Even if the historical truth of the resurrection is taken as a given, as something that we can all agree happened, it's still unclear what the event would prove. (35)

RESPONSE: The Objections given in this section are describing why the Judeans rejected Yeshua. It presents doubts, various arguments and reasoning based on the Talmud; however, the statement above is not an objection that can be considered a shining moment. The event of the resurrection changed lives not for evil but for good. The resurrection is the difference between Yeshua, Bar Kochbah and Sabbatzai Zvi. The influence of the resurrection changed art, society, and healthcare. It changed the world.

SEGUE: I must confess that I was a bit perplexed by the objection that was stated above. Had Yeshua displayed himself to all of Israel after his public execution this may not have been enough proof, but had Yeshua slaughtered Roman Legions and booted them out of Israel well that would have been OK. This would not take into account the human spiritual cancer known as Sin. Yeshua came weak, meek, and unassuming, but had he appeared to those who disbelieved this still would not have been what they wanted. Yeshua was prepared for this sort of argument. He gave an analogy in his parable of the beggar Lazarus (Luke 16:20-25); when the rich man died, and was burning in hell, he begged Yeshua to go and warn his brothers that they wouldn't share his fate. Yeshua replied that they had Moses and the Prophets that should be enough. The rich man begged again, saying that if Yeshua went to them, they would believe. Yeshua replied that even if a man came back from the dead to warn them, they would scoff and reject the warning.

OBJECTION: There was nothing ironclad in Jewish tradition at this time either to require or preclude a messiah who will die and be resurrected: (36)

RESPONSE: This objection admits that a dead then resuscitated messiah is possible. What we have here is the Jewish argument basing its opinion on the Talmud. If the early Jews accepted Yeshua the Jewish objection would not exist because contemporary Jews also would have accepted him. Since they didn't contemporary Jews won't either. Although Judaism permits the possibility stated above, Jews conclude that it cannot be Yeshua because the Judeans rejected him; however more than a few Jews accepted him and spread this message to the Gentiles thus fulfilling the words of the Prophet Isaiah. What contemporary Jewry should not lose sight of is that their 2000 year old ancestors who were in positions of authority were appointed by their Roman conquerors. Once it became clear that Yeshua was not going to raise an army to expel the Romans they could not take the chance that an adoring crowd leaning towards Yeshua could bring the fist of Rome against Judea. (37)

SEGUE: Since there was nothing at that time in Jewish tradition that dealt with a "Yeshua like" situation one must remain open to the possibility that God sent his Son the Jewish Messiah into history specifically at that time.

OBJECTION: <u>They approach and interpret scripture in chronological order as seems reasonable, because after all they find that the New Covenant does not arise naturally or logically from the foundation document, the Old Covenant</u>. (38)

RESPONSE: Let's be clear, Orthodox Jewish people interpret scripture as the Talmud tells them to interpret scripture. If the Tenakh pointed to the advent of Messiah then clues were included throughout the journey. The Torah testifies to this. Elohim is "us" uni-plural. Being a descendent from Judah must be proven. The Passover would be central. How did Yeshua arrange his execution to coincide with Passover? Is this happenstance or God's plan? There is no atonement without the shedding of blood. Since there is no Jewish Temple, how is atonement, being achieved? The rabbinical answer has been that it is done the same way it was done during the Babylonian Captivity and until the time the Temple was re-built in the days of Ezra and Nehemiah -- by prayer and fasting and charity. The real issue is that BOTH the Temple AND the rabbinical formula for repentance only provide temporary "covering" of sin -- they do not cleanse it away. Unless sin is cleansed away, it remains, and the sinner cannot appear in the presence of a holy God lest he literally burn up with guilt and shame. CS Lewis' The Great Divorce is a wonderful analogy of the reality of heaven and hell, and why the unsaved can't get into heaven. The benediction contains the essence of God's triune nature. Who was the Prophet to arise from the people who must be obeyed? As stated before the Talmud has hindered Jewish people from recognizing their Messiah. The central focus of the scripture is the Messiah not the law. The law displays our faults but only the Messiah can bring reconciliation with God and ultimately inner peace and world peace. The Talmud was largely created and/ or edited to deny the Messiahship of Yeshua -- we do not have many authoritative Talmudic texts from before the 4th century C.E.; the Targums and other earlier rabbinical writings (which BTW are straight-forward glosses/study notes on the text of the Tenakh) give a very different perspective on Messiah, resurrection, sin and salvation, etc. from what the "modern" post-Akiva/RASHI Talmud conveys. (39)

SEGUE: What is meant by "does not arise naturally"? Every step of the way there are scriptures associated with the birth, life, ministry, passion, death and resurrection of Yeshua. When one assumes that this story does not develop naturally or logically then can we assume that Christians are illogical? Let's test this illogic. Let's say Christians drop Yeshua. This means we'd also drop what he taught. What then would we replace that with? Kindly give Christians that answer. If that answer is the 7 Noachide laws then know that those laws are included within the body of Christian teaching. These laws contain prohibitions against, murder, lying, stealing, worshiping false gods, sexual immorality, and eating the limb of a live animal. It also admonishes us to set up a court system. The Jewish rabbis aren't complaining about Gentiles believing in

Yeshua (though they think it is blasphemous to believe that a man can be God), nor questioning that if they truly followed Yeshua's teachings they would be better, more godly people. The rabbis' complaint is against the idea that Jews are spiritually incomplete, or, worse, sinners doomed to hell, because they don't believe that Yeshua is the Son of God and belief in Him as such is essential to salvation from sin. Also, Paul himself noted that the Gospel is foolishness to the Greek (the logicians of his day) and a stumbling block to the Jew. Believing in Yeshua is illogical -- in that you can't use a logical proof to demonstrate that Yeshua was the Messiah and belief in Him is essential to salvation, because all of these things are built on faith, not logical inductive or deductive argument. However, believing in Yeshua is NOT irrational. If one accepts IN FAITH what the Scriptures teach about God and the Law, sin and salvation in the Tenakh, then what Jesus taught is rational. God is not bound by logic. By logic, who would sacrifice their only son to save hostile strangers? No one! By logic how can either sin or salvation be imputed to someone based on the actions of another? It cannot. The Jews don't mind Christians quoting the Tenakh in the N.T. -- but they insist that the N.T. not use the Tenakh to "prove" what they insist is blasphemous falsehood. Judaism cannot give non-Jews another Messiah. The Jew Yeshua has been a light to the Gentiles for 2000 years as predicted by the Prophet Isaiah.

OBJECTION: <u>It follows that such a savior must have been needed ...all other possible ways of salvation are wrong...Gal 2:21 if righteousness could come through the law, Christ died in vain</u>. (40)

RESPONSE: What is inferred here is that the Jewish way to salvation is the wrong way. We find in Paul's Letter to the Romans that the new Gentile believers in Yeshua have been grafted in. They do not supersede the Jewish people. The point being made that through Yeshua's death grace abounds lest folks become so concerned with the practice of the law that they believe salvation comes through strict observance of the law. This becomes clear where the Prophet Isaiah states that righteous deeds are nullified through an abundance of iniquity. No one keeps the law perfectly. Therefore trust in the Holy one of God who was faithful in all things fulfills the Spirit of the law. The Jews would always have the law as a solid foundation for right behavior. Paul's letter to the Galatians is written to the Churches. The Gentiles did not have the law so Paul points out to them the importance of Yeshua's death to their salvation lest the Gentile believers in Yeshua believe that they could earn their salvation. Ultimately, the Law, like its Author, is perfect. Imperfect men, marred by sin, cannot perfectly keep it, because they cannot perfectly control their imperfect flesh. Only by faith in Yeshua being the Son of God, perfect, wholly God and wholly man; His perfect sacrifice; and in the righteousness the Father imputes to us on account of that sacrifice can we be saved (41)

SEGUE: Think about it, isn't it comforting to know that God loves us so much that he becomes one of us to experience all that we experience. The difference being that he does it right, but despite this he suffers unjustly, as many do, but bestows forgiveness on his persecutors. He rises above death to give us hope. What is troublesome with this? This portrays a God that we can relate to and love. His wish is that we love him also and this comes through being obedient to his teachings thus fulfilling the Tenakh.

OBJECTION: Eusebius wrote that the Jewish Christians in Jerusalem abandoned the defense of the Holy City before it fell. They fled across the Jordan River to a place called Pella or Petra. This is a desertion that their fellow Jews never forgot. (42)

RESPONSE: The history is valid. But it has nothing to do with the validity or lack thereof of the Gospels. The Jewish Christians had warned the Jewish leaders that Jerusalem would fall, and that no Jewish effort could prevent that fall, and that they should flee. But, just as happened to Jeremiah, instead of believing them, they condemned them and fought on in their own meager strength to destruction. The same thing happened 65 years later with the bar Kochbah/Akiva uprising. Nevertheless, this "desertion" DID happen, and the successors of the Pharisees never forgave the Jewish Christians for deserting them. In the Gospels of Matthew, Mark, and Luke Yeshua predicted the events of 70 C.E. In Luke 19:44 He told his followers when they saw certain signs to depart Jerusalem. They were following the Lords command. Why? Whether the Jewish Christians stayed or did not stay Dan.9:26-27 had to be fulfilled. Jerusalem was doomed. No earthly force was going to repel Titus and his legions. (43)

SEGUE: The Christians were not trained warriors like the Romans. Knowing this and the Lords command to depart Jerusalem they departed. They did not aid the Romans. They were not exactly welcomed by the Jews in Jerusalem. Their mission was not to kill Romans but to share the Gospel with them. This was a war that the Jewish inhabitants of Jerusalem helped bring on themselves. (44)

OBJECTION: <u>Some part of the Christian soul would always be troubled by this, disturbed by the apprehension however suppressed that the Jews were right</u>. (45)

RESPONSE: The Prophet Isaiah stated, "He was despised and rejected by men a man of sorrows acquainted with grief and as one from whom men hid their faces and we (Israel) esteemed him not." The Jewish take is that Israel is the one rejected yet how can Israel reject itself? Christians were aware of the scripture. They did not believe that the Jewish interpretation was correct. They were responding to the great commission as stated by Yeshua in the Gospel of Matthew, "All authority in heaven and on earth has been given to me. Go therefore and make disciples of all nations baptizing them in the name of the Father and of the Son and of the Holy Spirit, teaching them to observe all that I have commanded you; and lo I am with you always to the close of the age.".(46)

SEGUE: This has never been my personal experience or the experience of other biblical Christians with whom I am familiar. There have been a few nominal Christians who have converted to Judaism for spiritual reasons (i.e., other than marriage or personal animosity towards the church), but they are even fewer than the number of Jews, including rabbis, who have become Christians.

OBJECTION: <u>Sensitive readers of scripture must have noted the radical disjunction between the Hebrew Bible and the Christian Gospels and Epistles.</u> (47)

RESPONSE: The "radical disjunction" is that the Tenakh creates an unbearable spiritual dilemma, especially for those under the Law, because they cannot live up to it, and the Levitical sacrificial system is dead. There is no prophecy in the Tenakh foretelling a Third Temple until Messiah comes (returns). The Rabbinical formula can only temporarily satisfy the requirements of the Law, even if one takes the practices of the Babylonian Captivity -- which God foretold AND which God foretold would end in a finite period, followed by the restoration of the Temple and of the Jews in the Land -- as a valid precedent. In the Gospel of Matthew Yeshua embraced the Hebrew Scriptures. In the Book of Exodus the God of the Hebrew Scriptures identifies Himself as Yahveh. In the Gospel of Luke Gabriel tells Mary to name her son Yeshua (Yahveh's Salvation). The disjunction appears to "sensitive readers" because the New Covenant is the story of the Suffering Servant. This notion of Messiah is rejected by the Jewish people who see themselves as this servant. When reading the words of the Prophet Isaiah how can the Jewish people make themselves an offering for sin? According to the Book of Exodus that which is an offering for sin must be without blemish. (48)

SEGUE: Yeshua told his followers to Love God with all their being and to love their neighbor as they love themselves. In this he summed up the entire Tenakh. The operative word is love. This love comes to life in the books of the New Covenant. Quotes from the Hebrew Scriptures are found throughout the New Covenant. In this there is no disjunction especially when Christians quoted from the Hebrew Bible to make their point and Jews often quoted from their oral tradition to make their point. Both Christians and Jews regard the Tenakh as the word of God. The oral tradition cannot be viewed the same way especially when one considers the errors that have already been exposed.

OBJECTION: Reversion from monotheism to multiple deities; the problem of Christianity's abrogation of the law...the Holy Spirit had not yet joined the pantheon. (49)

RESPONSE: In the Letter to the Romans, St. Paul makes the point that through the Law sin was made known, but by accepting God's Messiah we enter a dispensation of grace whereby the Spirit of God enters us so that we long to do good. Although this is true we still fail to reach the mark -- we still sin -- because we are still fleshly; which is why we need continuous grace, forgiveness of sins through faith, AND THE IMPUTATION OF MESSIAH'S RIGHTEOUSNESS ON OUR ACCOUNT, as was said of Abraham, his faith was accounted as righteousness. Remember, Abraham didn't have the Law, only the Noahidic Covenant. Following the Law makes no one righteous since all have fallen short and following the Law does not mean that one possesses the proper heart. King David explains in the Book of Psalms that trying to obey the Law after breaking the Law does not bring salvation. God can only have mercy on us and cleanse us if our heart is right. We know sin through breaking the Law and we are born of people who have broken the Law. Where does the heart stand? The dispensation of God's grace cleanses us where we have broken the Law. David acknowledges that he wanted God's Holy Spirit to reside within him. Trying to obey the Law would not take away iniquity already committed. Finally David explains what God wants, a broken spirit, a broken and contrite heart. God does not want a burnt offering if the heart is not set towards righteousness. The Rabbis cannot out-argue the Law. The Law is perfect, and perfectly condemns every imperfect human being who's walked the earth. If the Jews are right, they are as doomed as we are -- they know they have no written assurance from God, no Covenant, that declares them clean without blood properly shed from an acceptable sacrifice, and no blood has been shed from an acceptable sacrifice since 70 C.E. They can argue, assert, pray, hope, wish -- that God will forgive sin based upon prayer, fasting, and charity, but there is no assurance of it -- the Mosaic Law esp. in Leviticus argues against the rabbis. (50)

SEGUE: Pantheon? Christians worship one God. I never met a Christian who believed that he or she was a polytheist. The monotheistic concept is ingrained in the Tenakh and New Covenant. There is ONE God with THREE Aspects: Father/Judge, Son/Redeemer, and Holy Spirit/Creator-- as Yeshua said, "I and the Father are One." The monotheist concept is central to the Tenakh -- indeed, the main reason for the chastisements of Israel was due to polytheism. The Jews are slow, stubborn, and rebellious, but even they finally understood that they absolutely, positively, uncompromisingly had to reject anything even resembling polytheism. The keys are "I and the Father are one" and God speaking to Himself in Genesis 1.

OBJECTION: Jews objected with particular vigor to the Trinity and the Incarnation. Of the two problematic Christian dogmas, the Trinity was the lesser of evils. The Bible seemed clear enough in stressing God's Oneness "Shema" Hear O Israel the Lord our God, the Lord is one. Deut. 6:4. (51)

RESPONSE: The term "Trinity" does not appear in the New Covenant: The first glimpse of the true nature of God is seen in Gen.1:26 where the word "Elohim" is used and therefore "let US make man in OUR image after OUR likeness." This theme is repeated in Gen. 3:22. There is no doubt that the uni-plural word Elohim is used for the one God. In Gen.16:7-13 the Angel (Messenger) of the Lord found Hagar. After the Angel of the Lord made his pronouncements it states in verse 13 "She called the name of the Lord that spoke unto her. You God See me." The Angel of the Lord is referred to as God. In Gen.18 1-2 The Lord God appears to Abraham. "He (Abraham) lifted up his eyes and looked and lo three men stood by him and when he saw them he ran to meet them from the tent door and bowed himself toward the ground." There is no mention of angels just "The Lord appeared unto him." In Gen.22:15-18 the Angel of the Lord is again speaking to Abraham. Verse 16 states, "By myself I have sworn says the Lord". Verses 17 and 18 declare "I will greatly bless thee because you have obeyed my voice". A creation of God, in this case an Angel cannot bless because a person has obeyed the Angels voice. It is clear that the Angel (Messenger) of the Lord is God. In Gen.31:11-13 the Angel of God is speaking to Jacob. Verse 13 states, "I am the God of Beth-el". A creation of God, an angel, cannot be the God of anything. The Angel of God is the God of Beth-el. From Gen.32:24-30 a man wrestles with Jacob. Verse 28 states, "You have striven with God and with men and have prevailed." In verse 30 Jacob called the place Peniel "For I have seen God face to face yet my life is preserved." Notice here God is in human form so God becoming man is possible and within God's perfect will. In Gen.48:15-16 Israel speaks of the God of his fathers Abraham and Isaac and of the God who led him. He then declared, "The Angel (messenger) who has redeemed me from all evil". A creation of God cannot redeem anyone from evil. Only a Redeemer can do this, therefore this Angel is the Lord. From Ex.3:1-6 verse 2 we see the Angel of the Lord appearing to Moses. Verse 4 states "The Lord saw that he turned aside to see God." It continues in Verse 6 "I am the God of your father, the God of Abraham, the God of Isaac and the God of Jacob." Here we have the Angel of the Lord referred to as the Lord and God where the Angel of the Lord is identified as the God of the Patriarchs. In Ex.14:19-21 the Angel of God went before the host of Israel. Verse 21 states, "The Lord drove the sea back by a strong east wind." The Angel of God is the Lord. The theme continues in Ex.32:34 "The Lord Says to Moses... behold my Angel (messenger) shall go before you. Ex.33:11 declares "The Lord used to speak to Moses face to face as a man speaks to his friend." Ex.33: 14 states, "My presence will go with you and I will give you rest." Here we see that "my Angel" is equated with "my presence". Num.6:24 initiates The Benediction: The Lord bless you and keep you. From Deut.28:2 we learn "All these blessings shall come upon you and overtake you if you obey the voice of the Lord your God. Verse 25 then continues. The Lord makes his face to shine upon you and be gracious to you. Notice Luke 7:1-18 "The Lord seeing her (the boy's mother) said, Do not weep and he went up and touched the stretcher...and he said young man I say to you arise. And he who was dead sat up and began to speak and he gave him to his mother. In Verse 26 in the Book of Numbers declares The Lord lift up his countenance upon you and give you peace. Acts13:2-3 corresponds to Verse 26. "While they were worshipping the Lord and fasting, the Holy Spirit said, "set apart for me Barnabbas and Saul for the work to which I have called them." Then after fasting and praying they laid their hands on them and set them off. In Num.22:35 the Angel of the Lord commands Balaam to speak "only the word which I bid you." The story continues in Num.23:16 "The Lord met Balaam and put a word in his mouth." The Angel of the Lord is also the Lord. From Josh. 5:13-15 we learn the man standing before Joshua is the Commander of the Army of the Lord. In Verse 14 Joshua worshipped Him. In Verse 15 "The commander of the Lord's army said put off your shoes from your feet for the place where you stand is holy." The commander of the Lord's army accepts worship. This man was God. In Judg.2:1-5 the Angel of the Lord brought Israel out of Egypt. The Angel of the Lord made the covenant with the Patriarchs. The Israelites are expected to obey the Angel of the Lord's Commands. The Angel (messenger) is the Lord. Only the Lord gives Commands. In Judg.6:20-23 the Angel of God speaks to Gideon. In verse 22 Gideon calls him "O Lord God" For now I have seen the Angel of the Lord face to face. Then the Lord speaks to Gideon. The Angel of the Lord, Angel of God and the Lord are God. From Judg.13:6-22 we learn "A man of God came and he was like the Angel (messenger) of God." Manoah prays to the Lord, God listened; The Angel of God came as a man, then the Angel of the Lord spoke, Notice verse 16. The Messenger of Yahveh distinguishes himself from Yahveh. In verse 20 The Angel of the Lord ascended. Verse 22 declares "We have seen God." Isa.48:16 states, "Draw near to me and hear this; from the beginning I have not spoken in secret. From the time it came to be I have been there. And now the Lord God has sent me and his spirit. Psalm chapter 2 describes rebellion against Yahveh and his Messiah. In response the Lord speaks of His Eternal Kingdom to be established at Zion. Verse 7 declares He who will be King is begotten of the Lord (Yahveh) and is his Son. The Son of Yahveh is to receive the nations and uttermost parts of the earth for his inheritance. Yahveh's Son will dash the rebellious nations. Then there is a warning to the leaders of nations to serve the Lord. If you are impure you will perish. You will be blessed if you put your trust in the Lord. IISam.7:13-14 speaks of Solomon who will build the house of the Lord; however, that Kingdom did not go on forever as promised "I will be his father and he shall be my son". What we learn here is that God is not against having offspring. If he commits iniquity I shall chastise him with a rod and stripes (scourging). In Isa.53:5 the scourging that others deserved was put on Him. The Kingdom promised was ended in 586 B.C.E. by the Babylonians therefore; its application is for another who was to be the Son of the Father. Pro.30:3-4 states, "Who has gone up and come down from heaven. The waters are his and the ends of the Earth are his." He (God) has a name and a Son. Hos.11:1 Here again we see that God is Father and he is amicable to having a son. In this case we know that he called Israel (he who strives with God) out of Egypt, but we also know that Yahveh's Salvation (Yeshua) also came out of Egypt according to Matt. 2:15. We know that Yeshua was part of Israel. Since he did God's will he also strived with God.

SEGUE: The oneness of God is portrayed in the books of Moses, Joshua, Judges. II Samuel, Proverbs, Isaiah the Prophet and the New Covenant scriptures.

Chapter 5 Notes

1. Klinghoffer, Why the Jews Rejected Jesus, P.7
2. Klinghoffer, P.12
3. Klinghoffer, P.43-44
4. Klinghoffer, P.59
5. Klinghoffer, PP.46-47
6. Klinghoffer, PP.53-54
7. Ex.7: 8-13
8. Deut.18:9-14
9. Klinghoffer, P.64
10. Matt. 16:28; Luke 9:27; Rev.19:11-16; IIPet.3:3-10; Zech.14
11. Klinghoffer, P.164
12. Jamieson, Fausset, and Brown, Commentary on the Whole Bible, P.996; Luke1: 35
13. Klinghoffer,P.65; http://www.aish.com/jewishissues/jewishsociety/why_Jews_Dont_believe_in_Jesus.asp
14. Luke 2: 4-5; Stein, PP. 46-50
15. Macdonald, Believers Bible Commentary, P.1379; Lockyer, All the Messianic Prophecy's of the Bible, PP. 56-57
16. Luke 3:38
17. Jer. 22:30
18. Matt. 2:23; Klinghoffer, P.66
19. Macdonald, Believers Bible Commentary, P 1208

20. Klinghoffer, P.67
21. Matt.1:20-21; 17:5-7; 28:5-6; Luke 1:11-23, 26-38; 2:8-14; 24: 13-32, 50-53, John 20: 24-31; Acts 1: 6-11; 2:1-3
22. Klinghoffer, P.68
23. Isa.48:16-17
24. Klinghoffer, P.68
25. Macdonald, Believers Bible Commentary, P.1874
26. Klinghoffer, P.69
27. Ibid, P.79
28. Ibid, P.80
29. Ibid, PP. 86-87
30. Luke 24: 46; Matt.1:18
31. Klinghoffer, P.88
32. Ps.16:10; 17:15; 30:3; Isa. 53:8, 12; Pro.30:4
33. Klinghoffer, P.88
34. ICor.15:6
35. Klinghoffer, PP.88-89
36. Klinghoffer, P.92
37. Isa. 42: 1-4.
38. Klinghoffer, P.110
39. Gen.1:26; 3:22; 49:10; Ex.12:5-7, 21-22; Lev.17:11; Num.6:24-26; Deut.18:15-19.
40. Klinghoffer, P.112
41. Rom.11: 1-36; Isa.64: 6-7; Gal.3:1-29; 4:1-7
42. B. Yoma 39b; Eusebius, History of the Church; Lamentations Rabbah 1:1; Klinghoffer, PP.117-118

43. Matt. 24:16; Mark 13:14; Luke 21:20-22
44. Josephus, The Wars of the Jews, Volume 1 Book V
45. Klinghoffer, P.120
46. Isa. 53:3; Matt.28:18-19
47. Klinghoffer, P.123
48. Matt. 5:17-20; Ex.3:14; Luke 1:31-33; Isa. 53-7, 10; Ex.12:5-7, 21
49. Klinghoffer, P.132
50. Deut.6:4; Rom.7:1-25; Ps.51:1-5, 7, 9-14, 16-17
51. Klinghoffer, P.153

Chapter 6

Christians: Followers of falsehood or adopted Sons of the Father?

OBJECTION: Peter upbraided them harshly and thereby killed Ananias and Saphirra on the spot: (1)

RESPONSE: Peter never laid a hand on them nor did anyone else. He foretold a graphic cause and effect event. No one held a gun to the heads of Ananias or Saphirra. Outwardly they were behaving like the others but decided to keep back a little extra for themselves. Peter after admonishing them accurately predicted their demise. If Peter's brief, simple chastisement so wounded Ananias and Sapphira that they died on the spot (stroke? heart attack?), then how can anyone question Peter's power from the Holy Spirit to convict of sin? If they cannot question that, then how can they question anything else about Peter's ministry? (2)

SEGUE: Perhaps what the Objection really means is that Peter supernaturally killed both of them. If the intent of the Objection was to imply that St. Peter murdered them then that would be slanderous. Peter did not strike them or poison them. He did not plan their demise. The same Spirit of God that allowed him to heal others also dealt harshly with Ananias and Saphirra. The Tenakh is filled with prophets scolding Israel and Judah for failing to properly tithe to support the Temple, Kohanim, and Levites IAW the Torah.

Divine punishment in the form of droughts, plagues, and invasions was promised -- and delivered -- for this failing. So, the concept of divine punishment for failure to keep one's promises about offerings to God has ample precedent. This was a violation of an oath before God, a violation of a commitment to the church, as well as deceit and hypocrisy.

OBJECTION: <u>Do not entertain someone who wishes to lead you astray, like Christian missionaries. Their voice of temptation leads to sin.</u> (3)

RESPONSE: The question remains. The Jewish people reject Yeshua. He was executed yet some two billion believe in him. Bar Kochbah was killed. After he died how many people continued to follow him? Sabbatai Zvi converted to Islam. Does anyone follow him? Who then is the Messiah? How is he described in the Tenakh so that he is recognizable? Therefore the argument follows that those who came before are not for the Jewish people. Who then is the Messiah? Surely one who is so important has been disclosed. In the Book of Proverbs Agur son of Jakeh the oracle asked an important question. "Who has come down from heaven? Who gathers the wind, the waters and the earth? "What is his name and what is his son's name? Surely you know!" The real issue is whether or not a Jewish person has redemption from sin, a living relationship with God, and assurance of eternal life with Him. This can only be obtained through Messiah Yeshua. No other Name under heaven will suffice. No amount of prayer, fasting, and good works can erase sin – only temporarily cover it – and even that was only accepted during the Babylonian captivity; there is no revealed Scriptural Word of God saying that the rabbis have inherited the prophetic mantle and speak for God in asserting that the Levitical sacrificial system can be replaced. (4)

SEGUE: This book makes the point that Jewish people can reconcile with Yeshua and maintain their Jewishness. Jewish people are only led astray if Yeshua is not the promised hope. It is true enough that Yeshua did not set up his kingdom when he came. However he never misrepresented himself. He said from the beginning that he would be persecuted and killed. He also stated that he would rise, ascend, and one day return to earth. He never wrote anything but has predicted the state of affairs in the world. For one to reject reconciliation one must conclude that ones faith without Yeshua is better than faith with him. We read in Jer.31: 31-32 the following: "Behold the days are coming says the Lord, when I will make a New Covenant with the house of Israel and the House of Judah, not like the covenant which I made with their fathers when I took them by the hand to bring them out of the land of Egypt, my covenant which they broke..."

By God's own words through the Prophet the Jewish people broke the covenant. Therefore the Prophet declared that a New Covenant was needed. Jewish people can come into this fellowship i.e. accept Yeshua and worship in a Jewish way thru the Messianic Jewish movement. (5)

OBJECTION: Julian, The nephew of Constantine, became an emperor and renounced Christianity. In 362 he gathered the Jews to go to Jerusalem and rebuild the Temple. Shortly after construction began and earthquake causes gases to escape that burst in flames and destroyed the site. The next year Julian was killed in a battle against Persia. (6)

RESPONSE: It appears as though Julian never made any Christian commitment. He tried to help the Jews build the Temple 292 years after it was destroyed. Shortly after the work begins an earthquake destroys the site. Could it be possible that God was not pleased with his people? An earthquake causes the site to erupt in flames and one year later in battle the apostate Emperor is killed. Jewish dreams went with him.

SEGUE: We either believe in the sovereignty of God or happenstance. When it comes to the Temple Mount I don't believe anything is happenstance. It was not God's plan that Julian who heard the Christian gospel and rejected it would be instrumental in rebuilding the Temple. Was it God's providence or happenstance that the site blew up and was destroyed? Julian received no blessings for renouncing Christianity. Rather he was destroyed. Julian believed that Christianity was destroying the legitimacy and unity of the Augustinian empire, and attempted to yank the empire back to its glorious pagan roots. He also was facing growing threats from Persia in the east, and having been a bookish and highly literate youth, he knew that it would be necessary to secure the support of various partially assimilated peoples in the east in the battle against Persia. His efforts in support of a Jewish effort to *aliyah* back to the Holy Land (called Palestine since the failed bar Kochbah rebellion of 135 C.E.) and to rebuild the Temple accomplished two things: It struck a blow at the legitimacy of Christianity as a "successor" to Judaism, and built up a loyal client regime in the Near East.

OBJECTION: The hateful teaching of the Christians during the middle Ages was that the prophets from their (Jewish) midst railed against their (Jewish) rebellious spirit. The rejection of Jesus was just another in a long succession of Jewish acts of spite against God. (7)

RESPONSE: The Christian assertion, concerning the rebellious Jews of antiquity, was hateful if it was not true. The assertion by the Christians was to include the Jews not exclude them. Basically, Israel has the truth but not the whole truth. In the Book of Exodus God calls the Israelites stiff necked. The Book of Leviticus laid out the punishment for disobedience. According to the Book of Numbers at times the people of Israel despised God and He declared that He would visit their iniquity on the 3rd and 4th generation. The Israelites who came out of Egypt were described as wicked and faithless. In the Book of Deuteronomy it described the woes they would suffer for not hearing God's voice and this included expulsion from the land. Bad choices by the descendents of Israel brought calamity. The Kingdom of Israel rejected the warning of the Prophets and because they remained in sin they were taken to Assyria never to return as a United Kingdom. Jerusalem and the Temple were destroyed by Babylon because the people of Judah ignored the warnings of the Prophet Jeremiah. There is nothing hateful in reminding the Jewish people how their forefathers behaved. Neither is it hateful to place before the Jewish people the words of King David, "The Lord said to my master Sit at my right hand until I make your enemies your footstool." The Lord sends forth David's master to rule. When this occurs the master's followers will be with him when his host come upon the Holy Mountains. Who is David's Master? Of whom does Yahveh speak? Who will reign? "The stone which the builders rejected has become the head of the corner. This is Yahveh's doing it is marvelous in our eyes." The Prophet Isaiah continues this theme, "The rejected stone will become the master for he sits at Yahveh's right hand. This is marvelous in the eyes of Yahveh and David's master. According to the Gospel of Matthew the Master is identified, "Neither are you called master for you have one master, the Messiah." (8)

SEGUE: I certainly would not have worded the argument as it is stated. The New Covenant Authors do not use that terminology. However; it is right to point out that God's Covenant with his people stipulated that they must be Holy. We've seen many examples where they did not live up to their part of the Covenant. To be fair, medieval Christianity sadly had little to do with the Scriptures, least of all the Tenakh, Medieval Christianity was still reacting to the long-irrelevant Jewish ostracism of the church for its refusal to join the doomed bar Kochbah rebellion back in the 2nd century. (It should be noted that Simon bar Kochbah was hailed as messiah by the then greatly respected Rabbi Akiva. Both died in the revolt. Despite having blasphemously endorsed another in a long string of false messiahs, Akiva is still respected as a Talmudic -- aka "oral Torah" -- scholar and rabbi by modern Rabbinical Jews.) Medieval Christendom for the most part viewed the Jews as accursed for their rejection of Yeshua and as a curse on their own societies because of their stubborn resistance to the Gospel. Being non-Christian put them beyond a major aspect of medieval law and custom, and thus extremely alien (like Norsemen, Irish tribesman, or Central Asian barbarians). Incomplete and erroneous abstractions from the Scriptures, made it seem legitimate to ostracize, expel, or otherwise brutalize Jews – they were seen as beyond the scope of Christianity. Few attempts were made to evangelize the Jews, and very few attempted to do so in a compassionate or loving way. To be blunt, the record of "organized" (Catholic and Orthodox) Christianity towards the Jews from the fourth century C.E. forward until at least the Reformation (and in many cases up into the 20th century) is something that warrants a sincere renunciation and apology, not an explanation or justification. The Church in word and deed did nothing over the course of over a millennium to win the Jews to acknowledgement of their Messiah; indeed, much of what the Church said and did (or condoned) on this score scarred and hardened the Jewish survivors into unthinking rejection and hatred of the Name of Yeshua and of His church. How bad was it? Jews found life easier in the Islamic world from the late 8th century through the late 18th, despite the jiyzah (poll tax) and other aspects of Dhimmitude.

OBJECTION: <u>In 1095 on their way to liberate Jerusalem from Islamic occupiers, Crusaders devastated the ancient Jewish communities of the Rhineland. It broke out in Spain in 1391 and again in 1492 when the Sephardic Jews were expelled from Spain</u>. (9)

RESPONSE: There is no excuse for what the Crusaders did to the Ashkenazim in Germany or the events that led to the Sephardic expulsion in 1492. This can be said; Unlike Islam and its founder, Yeshua and his followers did no violence to any Jews nor taught others to do violence to Jews. The early Christian community was persecuted by Rome until the Conversion of Constantine in the 4th century. Although not treated well by Byzantium, professing Christian bloodletting doesn't occur against the Jews until over 1000 years after Yeshua's time. Those who did this to the Jews had no knowledge of the words of Yeshua in St. John's Gospel, "We worship what we know for salvation is of the Jews". Yeshua states the following in St. Luke's Gospel, "Father forgive them; for they know not what they do." In his Letter to the Romans St. Paul stated, "Lest you be wise in your own conceit, I want you to understand this mystery brothers, a hardening has come upon a part of Israel until the full number of the Gentiles come in." (10)

SEGUE: Permit me to give some comfort to the Jewish nation, those who have suffered at the hands of misguided professing Christians. Yeshua states in St. Matthew's Gospel, "Not everyone who says to me Lord, Lord shall enter the Kingdom of Heaven, but he who does the will of my Father who is in heaven. On that day many will say to me Lord, Lord did we not prophesy in your name, and cast our demons in your name, and do many might works in your name? And then will I declare to them. I never knew you; depart from me you evildoers." The Western/Roman Catholic Church was not exclusively at fault. The Orthodox Church became increasingly anti-Jewish after the rise of Islam (and remains all but openly anti-Jewish today). Martin Luther, who initially sought to reach the Jews with the Gospel based upon his revolutionary return to Christianity's 1st century and Scriptural roots setting aside much of the foundation for Jewish fear/hatred of the Gospel and Christianity, was infuriated by the rejections from central European rabbis, and in his latter years was bitterly and aggressively anti-Jewish. His followers remained in that misguided mindset to varying degrees until after it reached its extreme conclusion in the Holocaust. The revelations of the Holocaust finally shocked and sickened the Catholic and Lutheran churches into recanting centuries of anti-

Jewish teaching and practice. The Baptists and Calvinists (Reformed Church, Presbyterian Church) were, by comparison, more tolerant of the Jews as people, and at the forefront of outreach to the Jews prior to the rise of Evangelical and Pentecostal-Charismatic Christianity in the late 19th and 20th centuries. (11)

OBJECTION: Arch-bishop Andreas of Bari converted to Judaism and fled to Egypt in 1078 because Jews often fled to Muslim-held areas. This is according to another convert to Judaism John of Oppido, Italy. (12)

RESPONSE: According to historian Bat Ye'or, Muslims were persecuting Jews in the 11th Century in Spain, Egypt, Morocco, Yemen, and Jerusalem. Either the Priest convert was unaware of this or the story is not true. Would a Christian or Jew wish to live as a Dhimmi? (13)

SEGUE: Stating that Jews in the Middle Ages fled from Christian to Muslim areas without explaining how Jews suffered in Muslim areas does not accurately display the history of Jews living without a state. The Islamic world then as now, went through periods of disorder and division. Jews prospered in Spain and Morocco during the first 2 centuries of the Muslim conquest, but suffered as badly as Christians and "moderate" Muslims during and after the second, predominantly Berber Ahmadiya revolution in Morocco and subsequent invasion of Iberia in the 12-13th century. The Ahmadiya were essentially reactionary, puritanical fundamentalists not too different from today's salafi'ists, and they invaded to replace the pervious Arab ruling elites who were viewed as having become heretical if not apostates in their tolerance of Jews and Christians. This tolerance was seen as weakness which was enabling Christians to march south from their remaining strongholds in Galicia and the Pyrenees. In Egypt and the Levant, persecution of the Jews coincided with xenophobic reaction to the Crusades and later with the Turkish conquest. In these latter cases, the persecution was ethnically-based and political, not explicitly religious. Even in modern times, Arab and Persian persecution/expulsion of Jews was not religious, but ethno-political reaction to the rise of Zionism and a perception that Jews were inherently Zionist and therefore no longer trustworthy as Dhimmis. There was at least some logic to this. Anti-Jewish hatred in increasingly secularized Europe was totally illogical – there was no longer any religious belief, however erroneous, to justify persecution of the Jews. They were just discriminated against or persecuted because they were different. This was not just NAZI Germany, but allegedly tolerant late 19th century France, etc...

OBJECTION: In the 8th century a Jewish work called "The Polemic of Nestor the Priest" was published by a Priest who became Jew in the Muslim east. Then a Deacon named Bobo, who was in the court of Emperor Louis the Pius in the 9th century, crossed the Pyrenees to practice Judaism in Muslim Spain. (14)

RESPONSE: During the 9th century Christians underwent persecution in Spain. Perhaps the conversion of this priest wasn't a eureka of faith. There may have been other motivations in the face of Muslim persecution. In terms of Nestor the priest in the Muslim Middle East one must look at the reality's in that part of the world.

683-684: Muawiya II persecutes Assyrian Christians & destroys churches

704-705: Caliph Walid I crucifies, decapitates and burns the nobles of Armenia to death in the churches of St. Gregory & Church of Xram.

712: 60 Christian pilgrims from Amorium crucified.

717-724: Copts were branded; 24,000 Copts forcibly converted.

744-750: Caliph Marwan destroyed all churches in Tana, Egypt. Parents in Jerusalem were not allowed to share the Christian faith with their children.

761, 784-786, 797, 811-819: Multiple massacres of Christians at Toledo, Spain highlighted by public crucifixions as prescribed by Surah 5:33.

775-786: Abbasid Caliph Al-Mahdi destroyed Assyrian Churches that were previously rebuilt. 5000 Syrians given choice between conversion & death.

781-881: Massacres common at Saragossa against Spanish insurgents.

789: Monastery of St. Theodosius in Bethlehem plundered; monks executed.

Once again the climate in the Muslim world was hostile towards Christians. One must wonder if this was a conversion of conviction or convenience.

805-813, 828: Massacre of Christians at Cordova and Merida Spain.

9th Century: Systematic massacre of Christians at Seville, Spain. (15)

SEGUE: The Christians and Jews were often exposed to harsh Dhimmi oppression in Muslim lands. At times the oppression against Christians was harsher towards them than the Jews. During these periods of more intense persecution some Christians may have found it expedient to become Jews and thus escape the persecution, at least for a time. Under this persecution many Christians - some only Christian in name converted to Islam. Others remained "secret Christians" but converted to avoid material loss, expulsion, or death. For a Christian to convert to Judaism would have been far more difficult, demanding far more training and discipline, and would have still left them as a discriminated-against minority. Persecution of Christians tended to be far more widespread and severe because Christians were the established ruling elite who had actively waged war against and/or had attempted to rebel against Muslim authorities. Christians also tended to have most if not all of the land and visible wealth that was attractive to the Muslim invaders. Jews had been forced to become good at relying upon portable wealth that could be easily moved and concealed. Catholic and Orthodox Christians were not used to living and worshipping in the shadows - their public religious displays and processions led to conflict with the ruling Muslims. The Jews had given up public religious displays with the destruction of the Temple. Jews did not proselytize except to "backslidden" Jews while Christians were obliged to evangelize, but to do so was to risk torture and death at the hands of Muslim rulers.

OBJECTION: Christianity with its Trinity and Incarnation falls short, compared to Islam with its rigorous monotheism. (16)

RESPONSE: Christianity sprang from Judaism. Islam sprang from Polytheism. The founder of Christianity was a Jew. The founder of Islam was raised in polytheism. The founder of Christianity worshipped the God of the Hebrews Yahveh and stated that he was Yahveh's son named Yahveh's Salvation (Yeshua). The founder of Islam discovered his Deity Allah in Polytheism for Allah was a black stone among idols and had three daughters Allat, Uzza and Manat. Yahveh, Yahveh's messenger, and the Ruach ha Kodesh (Holy Spirit) can all be located in the Tenakh. The Islamic deity Allah is never mentioned in the Tenakh. The Holy book of the founder of Christianity was the Tenakh. The founder of Islam developed his own holy book and stated that the Tenakh was corrupted by the Jews. Some Judeo-Christians and Muslims assume that the deity of Jews and Muslims is the same deity. People can believe in one God, but that one God has a name and the name of that deity is absent from each others sacred text. (17)

Let's also take a look at the Seder. There are three Matzos stacked on the table signifying the Cohen, Levites, and Israelites. Later during the Yachats the middle Matzo is broken in half. One half is hidden to become afikomen or dessert. At the Motzee Matzo the matzo on top and half of the middle Matzo that was not hidden is distributed to all participants. At the Koraych the bottom matzoh is distributed to be eaten with bitter herbs. Finally the afikomen is taken from its place of being hidden and consumed. The third cup of wine, the cup of celebration, follows with references to Elijah's empty chair and the door is opened. The leader then instructs all to drink the last cup of wine. These three matzo are stacked as one as the Father, Son, and Holy Spirit. The middle matzoh signifies the Son. He is torn whereby half is hidden or buried. When the top Matzoh and uncovered half of matzoh are distributed this signifies that Yahveh the Father must be accepted with Yahveh's Salvation (Yeshua) the Son. The bottom Matzoh, Ruach ha Kodesh, can then be consumed. When the Father and Son are accepted the Holy Spirit is sent. The bitter herbs to remind us of the bitterness that Yeshua experienced and the bitterness of life, thus the need for God's saving grace. Making a place for Elijah and opening the door reminds us to look to the future for the forerunner must come, but we must also open the door of our hearts. The drinking of the third cup reminds us of His shed blood for the remission of sins and the New Covenant that was established through His sacrifice.

SEGUE: There is nothing within the Tenakh that tells believers to look towards Mecca. Yeshua, who Muslims believe is one of their prophets, says nothing about Mecca. Yeshua left no doubt that his Father was Yahveh. In 619 C.E. Muhammad was willing to worship Allah with the goddesses Allat, Uzza, and Manat i.e. the satanic verses. After abrogating verses were given, Muhammad recanted and once again returned to a stringent monotheism. (18)

<u>OBJECTION: Maybe the Jews, from whom Jesus came and who wrote the scriptural books to which Christians appealed in making their case for his messiahship, really</u>

were right about him all along. No believing Christian could admit this even to himself, but it's obvious. (19)

RESPONSE: The Gospels were all written by 95 C.E. All of the books of the New Covenant speak of Yeshua resurrected. Three of the Gospels and most if not all of the canonical Epistles were written by Jewish followers of Yeshua. These Jews and others over the subsequent centuries who were not blinded by Yeshua-rejecting rabbis eager to preserve Judaism at all costs, found the truth about the promised Messiah in the Tenakh, and recognized Him in the accounts of the Gospels. As a result, Peter held the faith and was crucified up side down. Paul was beheaded for his faith, John died in exile on the island of Patmos, Andrew crucified on an X shaped cross for his faith, Bartholomew murdered in India for his faith, James son of Zebedee murdered by a Judean mob in Jerusalem, James, Yeshua's half-brother, was decapitated in a Judean Christian purge, Matthew martyred for his faith, Phillip martyred in Phrygia, and Thomas martyred in India. All of these people either knew Yeshua or encountered him. They died for the faith because they knew it was true. The only reality that was obvious to them was that Yeshua resurrected from the dead, ascended into heaven before their eyes, and is the Messiah the Son of the Living God. (20)

SEGUE: Since Jews do not think like Christians how can Jewish people presume to know what Christians believe? This I can say with certainty; Biblically literate Christians who embrace Yeshua do not just believe in him. They trust him and love him. The Yeshua of history, the Yeshua of the Gospels is worthy of our admiration and love.

OBJECTION: <u>God has allowed Christianity to flourish – a religion that grew from the root of Judaism. What did he intend to accomplish by this?</u> (21)

RESPONSE: The Israelites were brought into the Holy Land to become a sacred people, holy to God, who would have been distinctive in all aspects of word and deed, and serve as a beacon to lead the world to saving knowledge of God. They failed in this ministry. First the kingdom was divided, then the northern kingdom destroyed and exiled, and then the southern kingdom, unchanged by what happened to the northern kingdom, shared its fate. They preserved the Word, but often did not live by the Word. "But God so loved the world that He sent His only son..." Yeshua and His followers began the next aspect of the holy task of bringing God's Word – and His redemption – into the world; "... first to the Jew, then to the Gentile." In the Book of Acts of the Apostles we find the following; "Gamaliel a teacher of the Torah and held in esteem by all the people said to them Men of Israel take care what you do with these men...So in the present case I tell you keep away from these men and leave them alone for if this plan or undertaking is of men it will fail, but if it is of God you will not be able to overthrow them. You might even be found opposing God!" Unlike the Islamic expansion, Christianity's spread for the first 300 years was by way of reason. This is the only way that Yeshua wanted people to come to him. For Christians God can become known to humanity. He experiences our woes even to death but death cannot hold him. (22)

SEGUE: Christianity became God's revelation to the Gentiles. Although the first Christians were Jews, the Christian faith became more Gentile in nature when the Jews who believed in Yeshua were forbidden from worshipping in the synagogue. These same Jews did not feel comfortable in Christian Churches and Christianity gradually lost its Jewish flavor.

OBJECTION: <u>Drawing Jews to Christ has been the shared fantasy of Christianity since the beginning of the Church</u> (23)

RESPONSE: One man's "fantasy" is another man's faith. To much of the world, the Jews' peculiar belief in God is a fantasy. To the Christian, the rejection of their Messiah by Jews who cling to rabbinical Judaism is a fantasy, based on the idea that the rabbis could know God's will better than those who died to proclaim that Yeshua was the Messiah, and well enough to effectively tear out whole chapters of Torah and Tenakh that did not support their Revisionism. The "fantasy" is that one can be "right with God" without blood sacrifice, despite God's Word in Torah; that good deeds are enough for modern Jews even though they were not enough for ancient Jews. The emphasis of this book is to examine the issues from both sides. The hope is to bring reconciliation between the Jewish People and Yeshua but to also make the non-Jews cognizant of Jewish concerns and their point of view.

SEGUE: The fear of Jewish people through the centuries has been assimilation. The Yeshua of the Gentiles asked them to leave their heritage and embrace Catholicism or Protestantism. The thought of this has been unacceptable to Jewish people. I propose the following: One cannot have Judaism, as defined by the rabbis with Yeshua. One can and does remain Jewish with Yeshua. One retains an intimate and special connection with

God and one's Jewish ancestors, traditions, and feasts with Yeshua, but one cannot have both Yeshua and Judaism. Judaism as it has survived for the past 1900 years is based on the Oral Law which absolutely and unequivocally rejects Yeshua's Messiahship, and based secondarily upon the Torah and adherence to Torah observance, which is superseded by the New Covenant in the Blood of the Savior. Judaism as we have known it for centuries rejects the need or belief in a substitute for blood sacrifice, and instead asserts salvation may be achieved through prayer, fasting, and charitable works. Forsaking ones Jewishness has never been the intention of Yeshua or his disciples. The disciples never left the Synagogue they were thrown out. By removing this obstacle both Christians and Jews can frankly discuss the historic Yeshua.

OBJECTION: <u>Medieval Jews pointed out the low moral atmosphere of Christian communities which reflected the basic untruth of Christian doctrine. Paul taught that the moral law of Christ is written on men's hearts Rom.2:15. Medieval Jews asked given what they knew about how Christians behaved, how could this be true</u>? (24)

RESPONSE: Jews were born neutral, moral free agents, who had to constantly choose the good and reject the wrong, and needed to atone for sin through blood sacrifice (Biblical Judaism) or the Jewish trinity of prayer, fasting, and charitable works (Rabbinical Judaism). It was understood that Jews could and would sin. Christians, who have the Word of God engraved on their heart (viz, Jeremiah 31), who are sealed with the Holy Spirit, are saved -- they are God's Redeemed. So then it is assumed by many non-Christians that they should then be free from sin, or at least free from bondage to sin, and therefore if they do sin, they do so willfully. That indeed would be disgraceful. Therefore what is needed here is a much clearer discussion of the doctrine of sin, highlighting that sin is an inherent condition in the flesh, that salvation saves the soul, but does not save the flesh. The flesh, including the mortal mind, remained tied to sin. Therefore, what is sin? It is selfishness, greed, self-centeredness, rebellion against external authority/restraint, desire for instant and continuous pleasure. This is what the flesh is. The soul of a saved believer should be repelled by/ repulsed by such things, but only through application of spiritual disciplines (prayer and fasting, study of the Word, fellowship, charitable works, etc) does the Christian's soul, with the help of the Holy Spirit, gain control over the flesh and the ability to bend the flesh to the ends of the Spirit. From a Jewish perspective kindly recall why God forbade the Israelites who left Egypt from entering the Promised Land? Throughout the book of Judges, why were the Israelites continually punished? Why was the Northern Kingdom of Israel conquered by Assyria and lost as a people after the captivity? Why was the Kingdom of Judah conquered by Babylon? Why did Rome conquer Judea then destroy the Jerusalem and the Temple? Why were the Jews without a nation and homeland for 1878 years? The answer is they continued to sin so God allowed them to be punished. This does not mean that Judaism is false. It means that the Jews sinned and paid the price for disobeying God and breaking his covenant. Rom.2:15 describes what is called a conscience. Not all people had the law, Gentiles did not, yet many wanted to do good for they had a good heart and wanted to do well. A person can be raised Christian and still desire to do evil like Mafia members, KKK etc... God has put a measure of right and wrong within us. Romans chapter 2 is about Judgment and answers the question of how people will be judged who never received the Torah from Moses.

SEGUE: The false assumption from some Jewish people is that all people calling themselves Christians are cognizant of what God taught in both Covenants. Yeshua said his disciples would be known for how they loved one another. When Jewish people become more familiar with the New Covenant they are able to discern between the phonies and those who live to walk the talk. (25)

OBJECTION: Christians misconstrued Jer.31:31. If God really intended to regard them dead to the Sinai covenant surely he ought to have made that crystal clear and emphasized it over and over. No authentic Messiah would inspire a religion that ended up calling upon the Jews to reject the manifest meaning of Sinai. (26)

RESPONSE: Verse 31 Speaks of a New Covenant and makes a distinction between Israel and Judah. In this instance Israel was taken into Assyria in 721 B.C.E. and never was re-established as a people, although there were remnants from the other tribes who broke with the Israelite rebellion and adhered to Jerusalem. The other Israelites were absorbed into the nations. Judah, Benjamin, and the Levites became known as the Jews. Verse 32 this covenant is NOT like the covenant that God made with those he brought out of Egypt. This is a covenant which they BROKE. God, however; sustains the covenant because He is holy and will not break His word to Abraham, Moses, and David, for their sakes.

Verse 33 This is the covenant that I will make with the house of Israel (no mention of Judah) after those days. I will put my law within them. I will right it upon their hearts. I will be their God and they shall be my people. Verse 34 relates to those who have accepted the Lord's New Covenant. In doing this he forgives their iniquity and remembers sin no more. Those who strive with God (Israel) those who went among the nations accept this. The New Covenant is not like the Sinai covenant that was broken. In the Gospel of Matthew we find; "And Yeshua cried again with a loud voice and yielded up his spirit. And behold the curtain of the temple was torn in two from top to bottom and the earth shook and the rocks were split." After the events of 70 C.E., 40 years later with destruction of the Temple, the sins of the Judeans led to the removal of the old way i.e. Temple worship. What was pivotal was that after the Crucifixion and Resurrection, the Temple was both superfluous and too limiting -- salvation and grace were already forever established and sin was defeated; there was no longer any need for, or value in, the Levitical covering (kipporos) for sin. The Temple system would not spread grace around the world, and was no longer sufficient to witness to God's glory and redemption. That would now be the direct work of the church and the Holy Spirit. God has been speaking to his people since that time. Yeshua does the following in the Gospel of Luke, "And he took bread and when he had given thanks he broke it and gave it to them saying, this is my body which is given for you. Do this in remembrance of me. And likewise the cup after supper saying, this cup which is poured out for you is the New Covenant in my blood." According to the Book of Acts, "After those days" (The Passover/Passion) when the day of Pentecost had come they were all together and suddenly a sound came from heaven like the rush of a mighty wind and it filled the entire house where they were sitting and there appeared to them tongues as of fire resting on each one of them. And they were all filled with the Holy Spirit and began to speak in other tongues as the Spirit gave them utterance." To the rabbis, the covenant spoken of by Jeremiah the Prophet is not fulfilled until the Messiah establishes the Messianic kingdom on earth, which they believe has yet to happen, since Messiah has not yet come. Rabbis and Christians both recognize this covenant to be radically different, but they see it being fulfilled in different ways, just as they see the Messianic promise of "peace" being fulfilled in different ways. Unless the rabbis are brought to acknowledge that no one else in a future time could fulfill all of the Messianic prophesies (Jesus' particular time, as foretold in Daniel 9, and the peculiar aspects of His death, as foretold in Isaiah 53, etc.), they will adhere to their divergent interpretations of "Jeremiah's" covenant and the visibly manifest results of the Messiah's coming. For most of the Jews in the world in this age, this will only happen when Messiah Returns. However, The Prophet Jeremiah specifically described the forgiveness of sin. In the Gospel of Mathew Yeshua said, "For this my blood of the Covenant which is poured out for many for the forgiveness of sins". What does it mean when Jeremiah states "When I make a New Covenant...not like the Covenant which I made with their fathers...? (27)

SEGUE: Did Yeshua call for the Jews to reject the manifest meaning of Sinai? Let's see. Matthew records in his Gospel, "If you would enter life keep the commandments...You shall not commit adultery, you shall not steal, you shall not bear false witness, Honor your father and mother, and you shall love your neighbor as yourself." The Gospel of Matthew continues, "Think not that I have come to abolish the law and the prophets. I have not come to abolish them but to fulfill them. Truly I say to you, till heaven and earth pass away not an iota not a dot will pass away until all is accomplished. Whoever then relaxes one of the least of these commandments and teaches men so, shall be called least in the Kingdom of Heaven. Finally St. John emphasizes the point, "For the law was given through Moses; grace and truth came through Yeshua the Messiah." The Objection as stated is incorrect. (28)

Chapter 6 Notes

1. Ibid, P. 91
2. Acts 5:1-11
3. Klinghoffer, P.131
4. Pro. 30:3-4
5. Luke 18: 31-34; John 16: 5-22; Luke 21: 8-9, 23-28
6. Klinghoffer, P.146
7. Ibid, P.152
8. Ex. 32:9; Lev.26:14-39; Num.14:11-12, 18, 26-35; Deut.28:15-68; 30:17-19; Judg.2:11-23; 3:7-14; 4:1-3; 6: 1-6; 8:33-35; 10:6-9; 13:1; 21:25; IIKings 17:5-24, 18:11-12; IIKings 25: 8-12; IIChron. 36: 11-21; Ps. 81:11-12; Ps. 110:1-4; Ps. 118:22-23; Isa.28:16; Matt.23:10
9. Klinghoffer, P.153
10. John 4:22; Luke 23:34; Rom.11:25-27

11. Matt. 7: 21-23
12. Klinghoffer, P.158
13. Warraq, Why I am not a Muslim PP.225-240
14. Klinghoffer, P.159
15. Warraq, Why I am not a Muslim P.233
16. Klinghoffer, PP.180-181
17. Spencer, The Truth about Muhammad, PP.33-35, 53, 56
18. Spencer, The Truth about Muhammad, PP.78-83
19. Klinghoffer, P.183
20. Kee/Young/Froehlich. Understanding the New Covenant. PP.239-242
21. Klinghoffer, P.188
22. Acts 5:35-39
23. Klinghoffer, P.191
24. Ibid, P.197
25. John 15:17
26. Klinghoffer, P.214
27. Matt.27: 50-51; Luke.22:19-20; Acts 2:1-4; Jer.31:34; Matt.26:28
28. Matt. 19:17-18; Matt. 5:17-19; John 1: 17

Chapter 7

Paul: Hater of Judaism or Apostle of the Most High

OBJECTION: <u>Paul had a radical view of Jesus teaching</u>. (1)

RESPONSE: This refers to Gentile believers in Yeshua meaning there was not a requirement for them to become Jews first. They could come to the Messiah within their own culture. The intention that Gentiles were to sit at the same table with Abraham, Isaac, and Jacob was displayed in the Gospel of Matthew. What is radical about Paul's view when it brought Gentiles to the knowledge of the one true God and to knowledge of his word in the Tenakh? This is clearly taught in Dr. Luke's Acts of the Apostles concerning Peter's vision and his ministry to the family, servants, and soldiers of the centurion Cornelius. There is also the record of the meeting at the Council of Jerusalem, where Paul convinced the rest of the Apostles of the God-given Truth of his teaching, and the message sent out to the churches came from the apostles assembled, saying that Gentiles did not have to convert to Judaism nor were they under the Law of Moses, but only were to refrain from eating that which had been offered to idols, from profanity and sexual immorality, and from unrighteous conduct. (2)

SEGUE: The Judeans of the first century did nothing to bring Gentiles to the religion of Moses because the Jewish religious establishment was not living up to the spirit of the Mosaic Law, but were lapsing again into the same sins of pride, selfishness, abusing the weak and poor, and dishonesty that the prophets so often decried in centuries past. Paul countered this trend by explaining the story of Yeshua, according to the scriptures, and salvation for those who believe through the grace of God.

OBJECTION: Paul depicts Jesus as the likeness of God... not directly equating him with the Divine: (3)

RESPONSE: In St. Paul's letter to the Romans he states, "The Gospel concerning His Son who was descended from David according to the flesh and designated Son of God in power according to the Spirit of Holiness by His resurrection from the dead, Yeshua the Messiah our Lord. He did not spare his own Son, but gave him up for us all; will he not also give us all things with him?" This contradicts the stated Objection. In St. Paul's second letter to the Corinthians he writes, "The Messiah who is the likeness of God" meaning as Yeshua was observed on earth these are the actions and words of God the Father in Heaven as observed in his Son. In St. Paul's letter to the Colossians it says "He is the image of the invisible God." The Objection also fails to mention another verse from Colossians, "We always thank God, the Father of our Lord Yeshua the Messiah." (4)

SEGUE: The Objections when presented to an audience that are unfamiliar with the Scriptures sound convincing; however, this onion must be peeled so that the children of the Original Covenant can research the material and discover the blessed hope promised by the Prophets.

OBJECTION: The Apostle Paul created a new non-Jewish Jesus. (5)

RESPONSE: In St. Paul's letter to the Romans and in many other scriptures Yeshua is referred to as Christ meaning Messiah. St. Paul was constantly quoting from the scriptures in his letters and in his words recorded in the Acts of the Apostles. Most of Paul's letters are written to Gentile believers. Paul meets them within their culture to relate why Yeshua is important to them. The Objection believes Paul is creating a non-Jewish Yeshua. Whether Jewish or the non-Jewish Yeshua, the Apostles, Gospel writers, and anyone opposing the rabbinical interpretation of the Tenakh will be criticized. Undoubtedly Jews would point to several things that aren't in keeping with modern rabbinical interpretation of Judaism, and would note that Paul, like Yeshua, was rejected by many if not most Jews The issue being raised in the objection is that somehow Paul created a Yeshua who had renounced or was denying Judaism. But not only did Paul emphasize Yeshua's Jewishness (when speaking to Jews), he also emphasized his own, and emphasized that Yeshua, and thus Paul himself, came "first to the Jew, then to the Gentile." Paul repeatedly stated that Yeshua was the fulfillment of the promises of the Law and the Prophets, and rejected any argument from Pharisee or Sadducee that either he or Yeshua had renounced the Law. They DID renounce the Pharisaical traditions that went beyond or outside the Law, just as they renounced the Sadducees' rejection of the Prophets, the Judgment, and the Resurrection. (6)

SEGUE: The Jewish argument was that Yeshua was a false Messiah and a blasphemer for stating "I and the Father are One." They question Yeshua's Jewish religious beliefs, not Yeshua's Jewish ethnicity.

OBJECTION: "<u>Paul's teaching spelled the end of any Jesus based religion that could still claim to be Jewish</u>." (7)

RESPONSE: The stated Objection seems to lose sight that Paul had a largely non-Jewish audience. Why should non-Jews become Jews? The Mosaic covenant was not made with them. They were under no compulsion to observe 613 laws. The message was simple. The Tenakh made constant reference to Messiah. Therefore salvation is not only for the Jew but also the Gentile. This was not to be found in Jewish culture, Judaism or the Talmud. Salvation was to be found in the Messiah. Therefore he wanted these new believers to be focused and centered on the one through whom salvation comes. Therefore; the Objection is valid, but with the following caveat. Paul's teachings, and indeed Yeshua's own teachings, make it clear that the Jewish religion had become confused and corrupted, and that true faith from the Tenakh required people to set aside both Pharisaical (modern Orthodox and Khasidic) Judaism and the beliefs of the Sadducees (modern Conservative, Reform, and Re-constructionist) and live by faith in Yeshua's final and complete blood sacrifice for sin (rebellion against God). Christianity is not Jewish. It is universal. Judaism by Yeshua's time had become a man-made set of rules and interpretations by which imperfect mankind sought to reach a perfect God. Christianity was God's perfect outreach to mankind in His power. Also, non-Jews effectively become spiritual Jews by accepting Yeshua as Messiah, Savior, and Lord – they are grafted into the True Vine of the Root of

Jesse. Both Jew and non-Jew are free in Yeshua from the impossible burdens of the Law, freed to live by faith alone, in Messiah alone.

SEGUE: Paul's epistles didn't end the Jewish basis of Christianity. The Jewish Christians were eventually expelled from the synagogue. After the Jewish believers in Yeshua were forbidden the synagogue, Christianity eventually started to lose its Jewishness. As more non-Jews accepted the faith they brought with them their own culture which was not Jewish. By the early 2nd century C.E., the majority of Christians were Gentiles (mostly Greeks), and the church increasingly became Gentile and Greek. Ethnic Jews who believed in Yeshua, and especially their children, were not accepted as Jews by the Jews, but by the 3rd century C.E., to be accepted as Christians, they had to entirely renounce all aspects of Judaism, including circumcision, the festivals, the Sabbath, etc. This first great schism was very much a mutual thing – Rabbinical (post-Temple) Judaism absolutely rejected those who would follow Yeshua, and the churches absolutely rejected those who sought to commemorate their Jewish customs/culture. This remained almost universal until the Reformation, and continued to be the predominant attitude until the 20th century and the evangelical churches movement to rediscover the Jewish roots of the faith.

OBJECTION: "Certain Jewish believers in Jesus...seize him in the Temple. They almost murder him." (8)

RESPONSE: This Objection stated above initially refers to Acts Chapter 21. The Jews mentioned here are Jews in Jerusalem who were stirred up by other Jews from Asia who recognized Paul. There is another incident that occurred in Acts Chapter 23. This chapter mentions Pharisees, Sadducees and a Jewish mob. No mention at all of Jewish believers in Yeshua trying to harm Paul. This is either an oversight that was misstated or the Jewish source is deliberately misleading a Jewish readership who wouldn't bother to check his statements.

SEGUE: Nowhere in the New Covenant do Jewish or non-Jewish believers in Yeshua threaten to do violence to other believers in Yeshua. The early persecution came from those who rejected Yeshua.

OBJECTION: "With Paul, the hints that he was not what he claimed to be were right on the surface." (9)

RESPONSE: Who was Paul? The Acts of the Apostles states the following concerning Paul, "I am a Jew, born at Tarsus in Cilicia, but brought up to this city at the feet of Gamaliel, educated according to the strict manner of the law of our fathers, being zealous for God as you are all this day." When one cannot account for the spread of the Yeshua movement, the suffering his followers were willing to endure, the fact that they harmed no one, the Objection resorts to a subtle character assassination by trying to place doubt where there is none. St. Paul established his credentials because time had passed between his study with Gamaliel circa 32 C.E. and these events that took place approx 56-60 C.E. The Judeans could have proved St. Paul a liar and thus destroyed his credibility. They did not. (10)

SEGUE: Paul claimed to be a Jew by birth, by education, and by lifestyle – and he also equally fully claimed to be a follower of Yeshua whose sole hope for eternal life was in Yeshua, and not in the rituals of the Temple or of the Pharisees. The book of Romans chapters 1-5 is far more explicit on these points.

OBJECTION: "That a family from the Jewish hinterlands of Tarsus in the first century could trace its lineage to Benjamin seems dubious." "The notion that he was ever a student of the great Gamaliel is called into question." (11)

RESPONSE: Where did Paul attain his insight and knowledge of the scripture? This is a learned man who has the capacity to suffer much for what for him was beyond question. Take a few moments to read Acts Chapter 9. As far as Paul's lineage to the tribe of Benjamin examine the First Book of Kings. We know that the 10 northern tribes of Israel never returned after the Assyrian captivity of 721 B.C.E. However, the Kingdom of Judah was identified as the tribe of Judah and Benjamin. The Levites were also in the Kingdom of Judah since they were responsible for the Temple in Jerusalem. In 586 B.C.E. the southern kingdom of Judah was defeated by Babylon and taken into captivity. After 70 years approx. 517 B.C.E. the tribes of Judah, Benjamin and the Levites were allowed to return to Jerusalem by The Persian King Cyrus. If Paul claimed to be a descendent of one of the northern tribes this would be considered dubious. Since the folks that returned were from two tribes plus the priestly class it is entirely possible that Paul knew that he was a descendent of Benjamin. Prior to the destruction of the Second Temple (which happened late in Paul's life), it was quite normal for Jewish families to be able to trace their lineage back to one of the (remaining) tribes: Judah, Benjamin, or Levi. Circumcision records were maintained very carefully, as were birth records, because lineage was extremely important to retaining rights to one's ancestral lands or, for Levites, one's ancestral claim to a posting in the Temple. It was also quite common for gifted students with means (or a benefactor) to come to Jerusalem to study with one or another of the great rabbis of the day; this was the normal way the next generation of rabbis was developed. The Jews of the early 1st century, though living across the Roman world and beyond, still were very much focused upon and tied to Jerusalem. (12)

SEGUE: Paul was obviously educated and knew the scriptures. If he were lying this could have easily been proven. If a falsehood could have been proven against him this would have discredited him as an evangelist. This never happened during his life. May I mention that he gave his life for this belief, a belief that included and encounter with the resurrected messiah.

OBJECTION: "It's interesting to note then the admission in the book of Acts itself that the Jews regarded Paul as "uneducated." "To the more discerning he must have appeared a charlatan." (13)

RESPONSE: Just like the event stated previously, this assertion is in error. The comment linking Paul and the word "uneducated" comes from Acts 4:13. The term is misapplied to St. Paul. The text makes no mention of St. Paul. Peter and John are mentioned as perceived uneducated. Paul/Saul is not mentioned until Acts Chapter 8 and does not convert until Acts Chapter 9. This Objection resulted from an honest mistake, shoddy research or deliberate deceit perpetrated against the Jewish people to keep them from believing in the Gospel of Yeshua Ha Moshiakh.

SEGUE: Paul preached to Jews and Gentiles, the educated and uneducated, and led thousands to faith in Yeshua as Messiah, Savior, and Lord. His teaching was based solidly in the Tenakh, comprehensive, consistent, and logically argued. What the "discerning" would be able to recognize right away was that following Paul in following Yeshua would be to willingly "take up the cross" and face ostracism, poverty, humiliation, and possibly violence and an untimely death. Paul made no effort to hide this – indeed he presented his suffering for the gospel as a worthy investment in heaven.

OBJECTION: "Probably like Jesus before him, Paul thought that he was living in the final stage of history, foreseen by the Prophets." (14)

RESPONSE: Yeshua taught that we were to live as if He would return that very day. Many Pharisees and many around the Temple believed they were living in the Last Days (viz Simeon and Anna the prophetess). The "final stage of history" it might be, but how long that "final stage" might last is something that Yeshua Himself taught that "only the Father knows." (15)

SEGUE: Although the Objection is valid it does not see the church age as the last period before the 7 year tribulation and eventual coming of Messiah Yeshua.

OBJECTION: Jewish tradition understood the slipperiness in Paul. His letters are not logical or even coherent much of the time. It is doubtful that one could get a clear and straight answer from him. Educated and committed Jews in the audience certainly determined this. (16)

RESPONSE: In Col.1:15 the Apostle Paul relates Yeshua to Gen.1:26; 3:22. The Bible interprets the Bible when one considers Isa.48:16-17. This is consistent with the Genesis account and reconciles it to Deut.6:4. Furthermore, it is hard to imagine anyone being blunter and more clear-spoken than Paul in explaining the Gospel to Jew or Gentile. Paul's letters to the church at Rome and to the church at Ephesus were brilliantly clear, specific, and comprehensive. People didn't seek to stone him or drive him out of their synagogues because he was "slippery" or vague or ambiguous. They violently rejected him because he was very clear in teaching the basic reality of human sin, humanity's inability to redeem itself, the need for a perfect sacrifice as redemption, and God the Father's provision of His Son as being the only possible and fully sufficient sacrifice for the sins of mankind.

SEGUE: The slipperiness of St. Paul means that he died in vain. The Objection makes clear that St. Paul couldn't possibly have gotten this right so he is verbally attacked by those who do not agree with him. He is also demeaned as not logical or coherent. This Objection is focused towards a Jewish audience that may buy the explanation without examining the sources.

OBJECTION: *The Gentile Problem "Paul* did not require non-Jews, if they wished to enjoy a blessed hereafter, to observe the Torah commandments." (17)

RESPONSE: In other words if the Gentiles don't observe 613 laws they can't be saved. In contemporary times the Jewish belief is that the Gentiles obey the 7 Noachide laws. The source of this Objection does not and cannot observe all of these laws. The law was to show that all these things must be done without fail to be perfect. No one lived up to that save one. After Messiah came one had to only place their faith in he who kept the law faithfully. How do the Jewish people who do not believe in Yeshua fulfill this flawlessly? They cannot. The Prophet Isaiah stated, "It is too light a thing that you should be my servant to raise up the tribes of Jacob and to restore the preserved of Israel; I will give you as a light to the nations, that my salvation may reach to the end of the earth." This was not fulfilled by Isaiah the prophet. This was brought about by the Jewish followers of Yeshua. The real problem is that neither Jews nor non-Jews can fully and completely observe all 613 laws and regulations in the Law of Moses IN THEIR HEARTS – and God judges not by what men see, but by what is in the heart. This is the fundamental teaching of the Sermon on the Mount, and Yeshua's' explanation to the disciples after it that bluntly says "for man, this is impossible; but with God, all things are possible." Especially since the destruction of the Temple, there is no way for any Jew to fulfill the Law. There is NO SUBSTITUTE for the Levitical sacrifice. A good Gentile is no better or worse than a good Jew – and neither one attains God's standard of being perfect, without blemish, in THOUGHT, word, or deed. (18)

SEGUE: Is it true that Paul did not require non-Jews to observe the Torah Commandments? Notice St. Paul's letter to the Romans, "Owe no one anything except to love one another: for he who loves his neighbor has fulfilled the law. The Commandments; you shall not commit adultery, you shall not murder, you shall not steal, you shall not covet, and any other commandment, are summed up in this sentence, you shall love your neighbor as yourself. Love does no wrong to a neighbor; therefore love is the fulfilling of the law." (19)

OBJECTION: It simply is not plausible that Jews who knew anything about Judaism could have been stirred up to persecute the apostle by the mere fact that he taught "the word of God" to non-Jews. (20)

RESPONSE: St. John and St. Paul speak specifically about the word of God. "In the beginning was the Word and the Word was with God and the Word was God. And the Word became flesh and dwelt among us, full of grace and truth; we have beheld his glory, glory as of the only Son from the Father. And take the helmet of salvation and the sword of the Spirit which is the Word of God. I write to you fathers because you know him who is from the beginning. I write to you young men because you are strong and the word of God abides in you and you have overcome the evil one. He is clothed in a robe dipped in blood and the name by which he is called is the Word of God." One explanation is that the Jews of that time were angry that Yeshua was being preached to them as the word of God not that the Gentiles were learning about the God of Abraham. In the Acts of the Apostles we see the Jewish people were not stirred up because the "word of God" was preached to non-Jews. It was when the Jews saw the multitudes they were filled with jealousy." Paul suddenly became more popular than they. They didn't care what Paul said to non-Jews, they were upset with his popularity and therefore became jealous. (21)

SEGUE: It seems as though the Objection fails to account for human emotions or weaknesses especially among the Jewish people. They didn't want Paul to succeed because they did not agree with his message. They could care less what the Gentiles believed. If the objection were valid, explain God-fearing kheredim in

Israel throwing stones at tour buses traveling near their neighborhoods on the Sabbath (as if throwing stones at Gentiles is Godly at all, much less doing work on the Sabbath). Explain God-fearing "anti-missionaries" attacking Messianic Jewish pastors, vandalizing their churches, and burning copies of the New Testament. Would they dare do this to Muslims, mosques or Qur'ans? Would the Jews have turned the utterly non-violent and harmless Yeshua over to the Romans to be crucified if they could not harbor ungodly hatred in their hearts? Jews are fallible humans just like their Gentile brothers.

OBJECTION: <u>What he really sought to do was undermine it from within...He otherwise wished to hollow out the accepted meaning of the Hebrew scriptures...This was internal subversion...The traitor is more dangerous since as a native son, .he knows the ways of his nation...When Jews turn away from God's commandments, the whole community will suffer</u>. (22)

RESPONSE: This Objection misses the mark. Paul wanted Jews to accept the Messiah. He did not want them to trash the Torah. He stated it wasn't necessary for gentiles to become Jews before coming to Messiah. Through the Pauline method Isa.49:6 was fulfilled. It was never fulfilled under the Old Covenant. The Objection then admits that Paul is an insider, meaning he was Jewish. Finally the Jews resist Paul because if they turn away from the commandments the whole community will suffer. Paul does not want the Jews to forsake the Torah. The issue is with the Gentiles; furthermore, the Jews do in fact reject Paul. Following this argument the Jews therefore did well. If they did well by rejecting Yeshua and St. Paul's message why did God permit

Jerusalem and the temple to be destroyed a few years later? See Luke 19:41-44. Also, there was no "accepted meaning" by Paul's time. Pharisees, Sadducees, and Essenes disagreed, sometimes violently, over the substance and meaning of the Tenakh. Today, there is huge dispute amongst non-Messianic Jews over the meaning and even the inspiration of nearly every aspect of the Tenakh. Further, just because the rabbis wanted to interpret the Torah in a certain way did not mean that any other interpretation was automatically not only false, but "subversive" or "traitorous." If one wishes to play the Objection's game, it must be the non-Messianic Jews who have misinterpreted the Torah, because there are far more well-educated people who agree with the Christian interpretation of the Tenakh than are those who agree with the rabbinical interpretation.

[SEGUE: Paul was devious, Paul was subversive, Paul was a traitor, and Paul was dangerous. Paul was successful in getting the Gentiles to know the God of Abraham. Most Jews living at that time did not lose sleep over the fact that the Gentiles did not know the God of Abraham. Today some Reform Jewish leaders applaud the early church for spreading an awareness of the Torah and of the God of Israel amongst the otherwise lost and debauched pagan masses of humanity.

OBJECTION: Worrisome rumors circulated about Paul that "you teach all the Jews who are among the Gentiles to forsake Moses, telling them not to circumcise their children or observe the customs". The Asian Jews who seized Paul in the Temple were acting on the belief that he sought to nullify the covenant. The rumors were perfectly true. (23)

RESPONSE: This argument like others before plays to a Jewish readership that is not learned in the New Covenant scriptures. In the Book of Acts Paul as a Hebrew fulfills the commandment of Moses. The rumors were not true as it related to Jews only to Gentiles. (24)

SEGUE: Gentiles are under a different dispensation because the original Covenant was not made with them but with the Israelites. The rumors were not all together accurate. Ultimately, what Yeshua taught was that the circumcision that mattered was the circumcision of the heart, not of the flesh; that what made a man "unclean" was not what he ate, but what he said and did towards God and his fellow man; and that the Sabbath was made (as a blessing) for man, not man for the Sabbath. The contemporary Jewish criticism of Paul and the other early Messianic Jewish Christians was valid at a superficial level, but missed the entire point of both the Tenakh and of the Gospel at a fundamental level. We cannot be saved by attempting to keep the Law in the flesh. We can only be saved by our faith in Yeshua, in His perfect sacrifice on the cross, and claiming that sacrifice for our redemption. Circumcision, keeping kosher, observing the feasts and fasts - all good, but none can redeem the soul of a single sinner (any more than any other external "sacrament" can). Faith, not works, redeem. Gentiles and Jews are under the same dispensation. The ancient covenants ensure the survival of a remnant of the descendants of the Patriarchs and of David, but they do not ensure the salvation unto eternal life of anyone, Jew or Gentile. Only the New Covenant in the blood of Yeshua, the New Covenant prophesied of in Jeremiah 31, can ensure salvation of the individual soul (Jew or Gentile) to eternal life in heaven.

OBJECTION: Where Paul departed from Jesus' thought process was in broadening the exception to include all of the Torah law. (25)

RESPONSE: In the Gospels of Matthew and John, Yeshua indicated that his mission was clearly to the house of Israel. These words tie into the words of St. James in the Book of Acts. In Chapter 15 he quotes from the 9th Chapter of the Prophet Amos. James' decision regarding St. Paul's earlier testimony brings the message of the Messiah to the Gentiles and they embrace it. Gentiles did not have to become Jews first in order to believe in Messiah. (26)

SEGUE: Paul's thought process was to bring the Gentiles to Messiah, then teach them all the rules, because he understood the cultural differences. The Objection advocates that the non-Jews first become grounded in the Tenakh and Oral tradition before they come to the God of Abraham. Since Yeshua was the fulfillment of the law, the Gentiles could come to him first and then learn about God's will for their lives in the scriptures. Jesus rejected the so-called Oral Law (Talmud), as did the Sadducees. Jesus stated that the Oral Law was an unnecessary and heavy burden that the rabbis created but did nothing to help the masses bear it. Yeshua often confronted the Pharisees with the superficiality and hollowness of the so-called Oral Law.

OBJECTION: Paul was playing games with words. If he personally sometimes obeyed the laws this was only for appearance sake. (27)

RESPONSE: In St. Paul's letters to the Romans and ICorinthians Paul was simply addressing what Yeshua had alluded to in the Gospel concerning what truly defiles a person. Although Yeshua and Paul kept the dietary laws, a spiritual point was being made. Eating with dirty hands, eating a Sausage and pepper sandwich, a pork chop, cooking ribs in Spaghetti sauce or eating a Maryland crab cake do not defile people. Evil intent and evil deeds defile people. The point being made that people can love God with all your heart soul mind and strength and love your neighbor as yourself without meticulously following 613 laws. (28)

SEGUE: The point of Rom. 14 is to not hinder folks coming to Messiah. Be culturally aware. A thing in itself is not unclean, but if something offends someone and prevents them from coming to Messiah it is unclean to them. In 1Cor. 9 Paul believes in meeting people where they are. For example if I greet someone and know for example that they are Jewish they usually appreciate it if I remember High Holy days, appropriately use a Hebrew word, or mention the Jewish roots or parallels to a Christian holiday. It would not make sense for me to speak to them about a Gentile Christian cultural practice unless they asked me.

OBJECTION: <u>Paul taught the dissolution of the terms of every Jew's relationship with God: The commandments. Paul taught...faith as opposed to works...he thought that his understanding of what God wants differed from that of the Jews. He was wrong about this too</u>. (29)

RESPONSE: The Objection makes no distinction between the law and the Commandments. It was not necessary to follow the law as defined by the oral tradition in order to gain salvation. There is freedom in Messiah but not freedom to do evil. The argument goes that Paul was wrong about everything and although he was wrong about everything Gentiles still came to know the God of Abraham and his messiah. Christians, like Jews, recognize the holiness of God as His most uniquely defining attribute. Christians SHOULD be loving – Yeshua ordered this as the means by which His followers would be known – but Christians in practice all too often lapse into sinful prejudices and hatreds. It is very hard to "love the sinner while condemning the sin" and very hard to treat those who despise you as brothers. As for the Objection, Christians are as much obliged to live by the Ten Commandments as Jews. The only commandment where there is even much difference in interpretation is on the meaning of "honoring the Sabbath."

SEGUE: To believe this Objection one must believe that Paul knowingly wanted to destroy the Jews relationship with God by teaching faith vice works. What is not stated is that Paul's change in heart is only explained by his Damascus road experience. There is no argument that Paul used to persecute Christians. The question then becomes what changed St. Paul's heart? We do know that his heart changed. We also know that he had the insight to bring the Gentiles to the God of Abraham. None of the Jewish people save Yeshua himself had the insight of how to reconcile the Gentiles to God. Reconciling Jews and Gentiles was not a major project for pre-Christian Jews.

OBJECTION: Paul had misunderstood the verse Deut. 27:26... the Hebrew word he took to mean "abide by" really means uphold...In other words ...there was no expectation of perfect conformity in his actions. The rabbis made this clear in B. Sanhedrin 8ia. (30)

RESPONSE: From the Hebrew Bible "Cursed be he who does not confirm to all the words of the law." Paul in Gal 3:10 uses the word abides. This means to endure, continue and stand firm. Confirm means to strengthen to ratify. Uphold means sustain, maintain, defend, encourage. Within these meanings are the words continue, ratify, and maintain. The meaning is plain. We are speaking of God's standards. His standards are perfection. The Rabbis realize that perfection cannot be attained so they gave their interpretation and thereby water down the intent of the scripture. The Hebrew Bible states the following from Deut 27:26 **"Cursed be he that confirms not the words of this law to do them...."** The point is that if one does not confirm the words of the Law in order to carry them out, one is cursed under the Law. Just confirming the words of the Law is insufficient. One must not only be a reader or speaker of the words, but a doer of them. Again, God judges by what is in one's heart, not by one's outward words and deeds alone.

SEGUE: God's standard is perfect adherence to the law. This was not possible since no one save Yeshua was able to do this. Therefore Paul made the case that righteousness came through faith in God and this righteousness came to the Gentiles not through the law but through faith.

OBJECTION: <u>Assuming that Paul was a Jew...raises disturbing questions about his truthfulness...I would like to suggest...he led Jews away from the commandments... He did this based on a reading of scripture distorted by his own predetermined conclusion...an outrageous character...they sensed him to be a deceiver...Any</u>

observant Jew...must have found it hard to believe he had ever been a Pharisee. (31)

RESPONSE: To be frank those who oppose reconciliation do not like St. Paul. One way to totally discredit St. Paul is to deny who he was. This line of argumentation suggests that he was Greek. The author of the third Gospel is a Greek physician named Luke. He is also the author of the Book of Acts. Luke was a contemporary of St. Paul. They knew one another. To believe this argument one also has to believe that Luke could not spot a fellow Greek after a long association. One would have to think that Luke knew that Paul was Greek but purposely changed the story. Why didn't Luke become a Hebrew? He didn't hide the fact that he wasn't Hebrew. The above argument omits that Paul's letters are directed at Gentile believers in Yeshua. If Paul were never a Pharisee this should have been an easy trace. Why would Paul return to Jerusalem? There they would know if he was not a Pharisee. This would have proved him false if this was discovered. He had no concern for this at all. He stood before his Jewish accusers. No one questioned his authenticity as a Hebrew. Now back to those who oppose reconciliation. The learned Jews were right to reject Yeshua (he was a fraud), they were right to reject Paul's message of salvation even to the Gentiles. Although the Judeans handed over Yeshua to the Romans and abused Paul many times, he never physically hurt anyone, Even though the Jews preserved Judaism from the "Yeshua distortion" and got this right still a few short years later the Temple and Jerusalem lay in waste and the Jews entered the dispensation of those who are disobedient to God via Lev. 26 and Deut. 28. Historically, the Jews, the Romans, and those in between (like Herod) all acknowledged that Saul of Tarsus, St. Paul, was both a Jew and a Roman citizen.

He had been well known in the Sanhedrin of his day, and had been an approving witness of the stoning of St. Stephen by members of the Sanhedrin for Stephen's forthright presentation of the Gospel from a foundation in the Tenakh. He was known as an enforcer of the most radical religious efforts to violently suppress "the followers of the Way." This was not the behavior of a Gentile. Neither was it the behavior of a Jewish peasant or workman unlearned in the Law. He was miraculously by grace transformed from Saul the Jewish rabbinical enforcer into Paul the Messianic Jewish evangelist and church founder. There is no historical reason to deny this, even if one rejects Paul's teachings about Yeshua and the Gospel.

SEGUE: St. Paul is guilty of one thing. He explained how both Jews and non-Jew fit within the framework of the New Covenant. The books of the Tenakh do not concern themselves with the theology that apples to non-Jews and non-Jewish salvation. St. Paul's work brings this theology to the world and explains how both believing Jews and Non-Jews belong to the family of God.

OBJECTION: <u>Jewish communities...take umbrage at him... whipping beating and stoning him...The contemporary scholars...are wrong. The Jews who Paul encountered... coming close to killing him, rejected his message... regarded him as a faker who didn't understand the faith...they were right</u>. (32)

RESPONSE: According to this reasoning the Jews who disagreed with Paul had every right to abuse him. Paul was a non Jewish faker who did not understand Judaism. Although he was wrong in every conceivable way he was still able to produce 1Cor. 13 and have a profoundly positive influence on Western civilization. Basically Paul could see the big picture. The Jewish people of yester year and sadly even today could not. They could only see their privileged position and reluctance to share it with the Goyim. St. Paul had an appeal to the Gentiles where his Jewish persecutors found it hard to compete. He was not confined by the stovepipe interpretations of Jewish tradition and in his conversion experience came to meet the risen Messiah. All his Jewish antagonists could say was that the accounts of his life are false and his teachings are purposely misguided while never looking at the big picture i.e. God's plan for Jew and Gentile alike.

SEGUE: To the majority of Jews in his own time, St. Paul is a blasphemer and a subversive advocate for a false prophet, and thus warranted stoning in accordance with the Mosaic Law. This was not a matter of a dispute over a point of view. This was a matter of blasphemy. Either one accepted Paul as speaking the truth, and accepted Yeshua as Messiah, Savior, and Lord, or one rejected Paul as a deceiving blasphemer and promoter of a false prophet, and would stone him, for such behavior was a capital offense under the Law.

OBJECTION: Paul said he was taking leave of his fellow Israelites giving up on them in favor of evangelizing the Gentiles. (33)

RESPONSE: In the Book of Acts St. Paul continues to reason with the Jews, but they once again revile him. "Your blood is upon your own heads. From now on I will go to the Gentiles." The Prophet Isaiah spoke about these events. Here Isaiah is speaking of his people. They hear but do not understand, they have a heavy heart, and they shut their eyes and ears and therefore refuse to be healed. The Prophet predicts that the Jews will accept it but not until much of Israel is made desolate, where the land is burnt and only 1/10 remains. If the Jewish people had it right concerning Yeshua why then was this prophesied against them? Paul declares that "I will go to the Gentiles." This doesn't mean that other Christians should not reason with the Jewish people concerning Yeshua. (34)

SEGUE: Paul ALWAYS, in every city he visited, went first to the Jew, then to the Gentile. He would preach Yeshua crucified and resurrected in the synagogue until he was thrown out, and only then preach to the Gentiles. Thus, in every city, he would reach the point of taking leave of his fellow Israelites to evangelize the Gentiles. But he preached to the Jews even when arrested and on trial, whenever he was able.

OBJECTION: <u>In Rom.7:6 Paul said "But now we are discharged from the law dead to that which held us captive so that we serve not under the old written code but on the new life of the Spirit</u>." (35)

RESPONSE: What was not quoted was Rom.7:12 "So the law is holy and the commandment is holy just and good." Rom.7:23 "For I delight in the law of God in my innermost self." Rom. 7 must be read in its entirety. Paul was simply saying that we know sin through the law but find life through the Spirit of God.

SEGUE: The Objection to the message of reconciliation with Messiah seems to be based on either Yeshua or Paul trashing Judaism. The case that Paul makes is that there is room for both the natural sons and daughters and the adopted sons and daughters in the Kingdom of God. The argument against reconciliation also tries to make the case that there is a deviousness if not with Yeshua then certainly with St. Paul. The main issue is reconciliation between Jews and GOD, a reconciliation that can only occur through confession, repentance, and acceptance of redemption in the sacrifice of Yeshua on the cross. Disharmony between unsaved Jews and Christians (Messianic Jews or Gentile Christians) is real, but secondary, to the problem between ALL people and God. It is important to be clear on this. But it is FAR more important to seek to bring about reconciliation of individual Jews with God through Yeshua. Jews are just as much in need of salvation in Yeshua as Gentiles.

OBJECTION: <u>Paul's substitution of Christ for the Torah as the focal point of religious experience colors everything a Christian sees in the Hebrew Bible. But it doesn't for a Jew at least not a Jew who absorbed the Hebrew Bible and its assumptions before evaluating the offer of Jesus as Messiah</u>. (36)

RESPONSE: This assumes that Jewish interpretation of the Tenakh is based on nothing else. This is not true. Jewish interpretation of the Tenakh is based on the opinions found in the Jewish oral Torah or tradition that can be found in the Talmud. This effort put forth in these pages has shown that the oral tradition has been incorrect more than a few times. The sages of the Jewish oral tradition are not Prophets. If they were without error or if scripture spoke of an oral tradition that was necessary to interpret the Tenakh this would give credence to that argument. The central issue is not what Paul said. Paul said we know sin through the Law. The central issue is what Yeshua said in Matthews

Gospel "Why do you transgress the commandment of God for the sake of your tradition?" After citing an example of this he quoted the Prophet Isaiah "The Lord said, Because this people draws near to me with their mouth and with their lips to honor me, but have removed their heart far from me and their fear toward me (worship) is taught by the precept (tradition) of men." What is the result of this? The Prophet continues, "Therefore I will proceed to do a marvelous work among this people...for the wisdom of their wise men (sages) shall perish and the understanding of their prudent (discerning) men shall be hidden." What other tradition is there? It does little to follow the drill but not have ones heart in it. Jewish preference is to follow the tradition as provided by sages, of which the Lord states that their wisdom will perish and the discerning in the oral tradition whose understanding will be hidden (occult). There are no scriptures that tell the Jewish people to follow the traditions of their sages and their discerning men of tradition. The Tenakh is the source book that is unlocked by the New Covenant. The Key is Yeshua of Nazareth. In Isaiah and in Matthew we have just read the Lord is not pleased that the Jewish people follow their tradition to the detriment of God's intent in the Commandments. (37)

SEGUE: The Response above reverses the core argument of the Objection. Jewish tradition colors everything that God's natural sons and daughters see in the Hebrew Bible.

OBJECTION: Unlike Paul, we do not say of this Providence that it knows neither Jews nor Greeks, for that implies an inadmissible level of differences, a suppression of nationality. (38)

RESPONSE: Let's address this in St. Paul's letter to the Romans. "There will be tribulation and distress for every human being who does evil, the Jew first and also the Greek, but glory and honor and peace for everyone who does well the Jew first and also the Greek. For God shows no partiality." There is no mention that Providence knows neither Jew nor Greek. The scripture states that God is certainly aware of their differences but will show no partiality when it comes to punishing sin "to the Jew first and then the Greek" and rewarding those who do well "to the Jew first and then to the Greek". (39)

SEGUE: As described in the response the Objection makes the point. After attacking Paul, none of the arguments establish Paul as anything but a committed Jew who has the gift to see the big picture, endure suffering, and presenting his case to the Jew first and then to the Greek.

Chapter 7 Notes

1. Klinghoffer, Why the Jews Rejected Jesus, P.7
2. Matt. 8:5-13; Acts 10, 11, 15
3. Klinghoffer, P.68
4. Rom.1:1-4; 8:32; IICor.4:4; Col 1:15; Col 1:3
5. Klinghoffer, P.89
6. Rom.1:1-6
7. Klinghoffer, P.93
8. Klinghoffer, P.94
9. Klinghoffer, P.95
10. Acts 22:3

11. Klinghoffer, P.96
12. 1King 12:21-24
13. Klinghoffer, P.97
14. Ibid, P.97
15. John 16, 21
16. Klinghoffer, P.104
17. Ibid, P.105
18. Isa. 49:6
19. Rom.13:6-10
20. Klinghoffer, P.106
21. John 1:1, 14; Eph 6:17; 1John 2:14; Rev. 19:13; Acts13: 44-51
22. Klinghoffer, PP.106, 107
23. Ibid, P.107
24. Acts 21:23-26
25. Klinghoffer, P.108
26. Matt. 10:6; John 10:16; Acts 15:16-18; Amos 9:11-12
27. Klinghoffer, P.108
28. Rom.14:14; ICor 9: 20, 22; Matt. 15:1-20
29. Klinghoffer, P.109
30. Ibid, PP.110-111
31. Ibid, PP.112-113
32. Ibid, P.115
33. Ibid, PP.119-120
34. Acts18:6; Isa. 6:9-13
35. Klinghoffer, P.195
36. Ibid, P.215

37. Matt.15:1-9; Isa.29:13-14
38. Klinghoffer, P.219
39. Rom.2:9-11

Chapter 8

Yeshua: Fraud, Misguided Jew, or Son of God—Messiah of Israel

OBJECTION: An anointed who will be cut off before the destruction of the Second Temple. This Messiah was a morally corrupt individual: (1)

RESPONSE: The Objection uses various scriptures to prove a point. Dan.9:26 states, "After 62 weeks shall the anointed be cut off and there shall be none to succeed him: and the people of the Prince that shall come shall destroy the city and the sanctuary" The Objection uses Gen.17:14. It states that any uncircumcised male shall be cut off. This could not apply to Yeshua; the Gospel of Luke (2:21) clearly states that Yeshua was circumcised. Ex.12:15 states if anyone eats leavened bread during the days of Passover he shall be cut off. Yeshua didn't do that. Ex.31:14 states everyone who profanes the Sabbath shall be put to death. Did Yeshua profane the Sabbath? Yeshua and the disciples plucked grain to eat. Deut.25:23 states that it is lawful to pluck grain from your neighbor's field. 1Sam.21:1-6 states David entered the House of God and did what was only permissible for the priests. See Lev.24:9. In Num.28:9-10 the priests profane the Sabbath and are considered guiltless. Yeshua also healed a man on the Sabbath. Did he deserve death for this? On another occasion he healed a man with an unclean spirit, St. Peter's mother-in-law, and many others with diseases. It is lawful to do good things on the Sabbath. Lev.7:20 states a person that eats the Lord's peace offering while in a state of being unclean shall be cut off. Where did Yeshua eat the Lord's peace offering while in a state of being unclean? Better yet what made Yeshua unclean? Lev.18:29 states whoever does an abomination shall be cut off. What are the abominations? Do not uncover the nakedness of a relative, approach a woman while she is menstruating, commit adultery, offer your children to Molech, perform a homosexual act, or commit bestiality. When did Yeshua commit any abomination? Lev.22:3 states that anyone in a state of being unclean who approaches holy things they shall be cut off. When did Yeshua approach anything holy in a state of being unclean? If one does work on the Day of Atonement that person shall be cut off. When did Yeshua profane the Day of Atonement? A person who approaches the sanctuary and is dirty shall be cut off. When was Yeshua not bathed when he approached? Dan.9:26 states the Messiah, the Anointed One, will be cut off. It does not say why the anointed would be cut off. Just because the words "cut off" are used does not mean that the person cut off was guilty of anything. Dan.9:26 gave no such reasoning. (2)

SEGUE: Why would God associate the word Anointed, meaning anointed by God, to one who was morally corrupt? A morally corrupt person is a degenerate never anointed by God. The Anointed who was cut off before the destruction of the Second temple was Yeshua. He was cut off in that he was killed and became a sin sacrifice for all of us. How did he behave in a morally corrupt manner? By claiming to be God's Son? There is no corruption here if it is true. Following the logic of this argument all the Old Covenant Prophets who were scorned and killed must have also been corrupt. As Yeshua asked, "I showed you many good works from the Father; for which of them are you stoning me?" (John 10:32) The truth is people who strive to obediently serve God are often hated, scorned and sometimes killed. This Objection is not true. It reflects a misreading of both the Tenakh and the Gospels.

OBJECTION: I present neither an ethical nor an apocalyptic but instead a foxy, ambiguous Jesus. It is this Jesus whom the Jews of his time rejected; to the extent they could understand him: (3)

RESPONSE: If Yeshua was ambiguous wouldn't he appear ambiguous to non-Jews as well? Are we to understand that only Jews can see what others cannot? The Objection to reconciliation presupposes that Jews will recognize the true Messiah, but then again Bar Kockbah, Sabbatai Zvi and The Brooklyn Rebbi suggest that the Jews get this wrong a lot. Any supposed ambiguity from Yeshua was not the reason the Jewish religious leadership handed him over to the Pagans for execution. They understood Yeshua's words very well -- but chose to reject them despite the miracles he performed in God's Name and seek his death.

SEGUE: The Jewish leaders' actions can be explained after the fact by modern post-Diaspora standards. But by the standards of the day, for the Jews to deliver another Jew, up to an alien government occupying the land, for crucifixion when he was not guilty of murder or insurrection was in itself criminal. The argument also assumes that the Jewish religious leadership of the day was not corrupted by Rome. After all surely no one could hold such positions if not approved by the Romans.

OBJECTION: By saying that the Jews rejected him we are speaking in Christian language...To speak of the Jews corporately taking any position vis-à-vis the Christian savior is then quite a stretch: (4)

RESPONSE: The Objection to reconciliation fails to explain some facts to the Jewish audience. The authors of three of the four gospels are Jews. In their writings they refer to the Jews or Jewish rejection of Yeshua. Who are these Jews? These Jews are specifically the Jewish religious leadership based in Jerusalem -- the priestly authorities in the Temple and the majority of the Sanhedrin -- under the influence of the Romans. The majority of the Jews of Judea had no say in the matter, and even of the Jews in Jerusalem, it was only some undefined portion that followed the Pharisees in the Sanhedrin and the Sadducee priestly leadership in condemning Yeshua and seeking his execution by the Romans. Most simply did not understand what was happening -- they were eager for Messiah, they knew that the time was ripe according to prophecy, but while Yeshua claimed to be Messiah and performed miracles in God's Name like Messiah, he confused them by not accepting the kingship or leading a revolution against Rome. Only the scholars would have been aware of the distinction between the "Suffering Servant" role of Messiah and the later "Conquering King" role, and many of them chose to overlook it or, then as now, claim that the Jews were the "Suffering Servant" -- even though the Jews had repeatedly been disloyal to God and evil towards their fellow man, and thus could not be the unblemished servant who was chastised for the past sins of Israel. How do we know this? The Apostles who practiced Judaism are never referred to as Jews. They are referred to as Galileans. However; it is inaccurate to make a distinction on the basis of the Judeans rejecting Yeshua and the Galilean Jews accepting Him. There were many in the north who did not accept Him, as well as some who did. The New Covenant authors simply described the people of Israel in terms of their geographic area not their faith. Today the term Jew refers either to one who has a Jewish mother or one who practices Judaism. A Jew in those days could also refer to one who is descendent of the tribe of Judah including Levites and the tribe of Benjamin.

SEGUE: This item is true enough. The Christian Church had misapplied this stigma upon generations of Jews. It was the Judeans, the leadership of the Jewish people influenced and possible corrupted by their Roman overlords that rejected Yeshua as Messiah. For Christians to be anything but helpful, truthful and supportive of our Jewish friends is wrong and sinful. The point of this work remains that characterizations of Yeshua, St. Paul, and other New Covenant authors have been tainted by the opinions of the sages in the Jewish oral tradition.

OBJECTION: In Jesus lifetime, if the Jews did reject him passively; their rejection of him arose not from a definite decision, but from a combination of simple unawareness of his activities and skepticism about the roles he was casting himself into. Among those who knew him it was...a turning away, a questioning of the authenticity or even the importance of the personas he adopted. (5)

RESPONSE: In the Gospel of Matthew, Pilate said to them, "Then what shall we do with Yeshua called Messiah? "They all said let him be crucified and he said, what evil has he done? But they shouted all the more Let him be crucified; Mark's Gospel continues; And the high Priest tore his garments and said, why do we still need witnesses? You have heard his blasphemy. What is your decision? And they all condemned him as deserving death. And some began to spit on him and to cover his face and to strike him saying to him Prophesy! And the guards received him with blows. Luke's Gospel states, The chief priests and the scribes stood by vehemently accusing him and Herod with his soldiers treated him with contempt and mocked him; then arraying him in gorgeous apparel he sent him back to Pilate, What evil has he done? I have found no crime deserving death: I will therefore chastise him and release him. But they were urgent demanding with loud voices that he should be crucified and their voices prevailed, The people stood by watching but the rulers scoffed at him saying, He saved others let him save himself if he is the messiah of God, his Chosen one! From the Gospel of John, Pilate answered, your own nation and the chief priests have handed you over to me. What have you done? The Judeans answered him, We have a law and by that law he should die because he has made himself the Son of God, Pilate said Behold your King! They cried out Away with him, Crucify him, Pilate said Shall I crucify your king? The Chief Priests answered we have no King but Caesar. St. Luke wrote in the Book of Acts, The God of Abraham. Isaac, and Jacob, the God of our fathers, glorified his servant Yeshua whom you delivered up and denied in the presence of Pilate when he had decided to release him. But you denied the Holy and righteous one and asked for a murderer to be granted to you and killed the Author of Life whom God raised from the dead. To this we are witnesses... Brothers, I know that you acted in ignorance as did also your rulers. Many of the Jews neither committed themselves to Yeshua nor joined the priestly leaders and the Pharisees in the Sanhedrin to condemn Him and demand His death before Pilate. This should not be surprising for relatively uneducated people who don't understand what is happening -- they have seen or heard of the miracles and the teachings, but the Messiah isn't "following through" the way they expected, while their leaders, whom they believe to be godly, are calling for his crucifixion, and the Romans are hesitant. (6)

SEGUE: These scriptures and others contradict the assertions stated in the argument. Those contradicting this Objection claim to be eye witnesses. They also state that the Judeans did this out of ignorance. The Jewish people rejected a Yeshua who was not born of a virgin, was not the Messiah, was not the Son of God, did not die for their sins, did not resurrect, and did not ascend. The majority of the two power elites among the Jews and some of their ardent supporters wanted Yeshua killed because they saw him as a blaspheming false prophet DESPITE his words and miraculous and benevolent deeds.

OBJECTION: <u>There is reason to doubt that in historical reality he presented himself as Messiah and divinity</u>: (7)

RESPONSE: Basically, the Objection asserts that the four evangelists, the apostles, and other disciples who like Stephen and Philip are recorded as attesting to the Messiahship of Yeshua are liars for they would/should have known better. They not only publicly attested to these things despite ostracism and threats, but most died martyr's deaths for doing so. None acquired any worldly power or wealth for proclaiming their witness to Yeshua's Messiahship, crucifixion, and resurrection. According to the Revised Standard Version Bible, Jamisson Faucett & Brown Commentary and the William MacDonald Bible commentary The Gospel of Matthew was written around 60-70 C.E., Mark between 58-66 C.E., Luke between 63-75, John between 85-95. These gospels were written from 28 to 65 years after the time of Yeshua. Matthew, Mark, and John were eyewitnesses to the events described. We read about the divinity of Yeshua in Matthew chapter 1, Mark chapter 1, Luke chapter 1, and John chapter 1. Actually, throughout the entirety of the Gospels it comes up repeatedly. The argument is written for a Jewish audience that may not take the time to read the New Covenant. The argument is false. (8)

SEGUE: According to Luke 2:41-52 Yeshua was 13 years old and knew that he was God's son.

OBJECTION: <u>Jesus healed a blind man by making a salve on the Sabbath. The Pharisees objected stating this man is not from God for he does not keep the Sabbath. The written Torah says nothing about using medical salve, the oral Torah rules it out except for an emergency which this clearly was not</u>: (9)

RESPONSE: The fifth Chapter of the Gospel of John seems to distinguish more than anything else the difference between Judaism and Christianity. Yeshua heals (Where does a fraud, claiming that God is his Father get this power?) meaning he did a good thing for a man who was ill for 38 years. The Objection states that this violated the Oral Torah (rabbinic commentary). Using this reasoning Yeshua should have waited one more day to heal the man. Leave him suffering in that state another day as to not violate the rabbinic commentary. The Objection continues that the state of the man did not qualify as an emergency. I'm sure the man who was in that state thought it was an emergency. With this thought process the commentary of the rabbi's is elevated to the will of God. Not to heal a man when the opportunity presents itself can never be considered God's will, literally a prohibition against doing good to one's fellow man. With the Oral Torah compassion is lost because the opinions of the rabbis become more important than loving one's neighbor as you love yourself. (10)

SEGUE: According to the Objection, Yeshua did wrong to heal a man on the Sabbath. The written Torah says nothing about medical salve. The written Torah also says nothing about blood transfusions, brain surgery, or heart transplants. Is it valid to assume "that which is not allowed is prohibited?" If so, then whence do the rabbis gain their authority to establish "oral Torah?" There is no establishment of rabbis in the written Torah, only called and inspired prophets, Kohanim (priests), Levites (holy workers and musicians), and tribal and clan elders whose authority is secular. Is observing the letter of the law more important than doing well to our fellow man? This would seem to contradict the teachings of the Prophets in the Tenakh (Isaiah 1:17, Micah 2:7, etc.) This means God would be displeased by a merciful healing of a suffering member of Israel, and is not at all reasonable towards people who do well? If the Oral Torah has any valid authority, then its authority would be greater than that of an individual thankful for being healed. This is a poor argument.

OBJECTION: Jesus did not see himself as a link in the chain of tradition. This was a repudiation of the very heart of rabbinic faith. Without tradition, either the cryptic text of the Torah was locked forever and rendered indiscernible or a free for all of scriptural interpretation where the Torah means whatever the reader wants it to mean. (11)

RESPONSE: The key to understanding the Torah is Messiah. A Tradition written by ancient rabbis was/is not the key. Where do the Rabbi's claim in their tradition "Thus says the Lord" as if they were receiving a divine revelation that equaled the written Torah? It becomes clear in this context that the rabbinic commentary prohibits the Jewish people from following their spiritual thought process to find their Messiah since it prejudices them against one who healed, did great works, raised the dead, predicted his own rejection and death and stated that "You will not see me again until you say blessed is he who comes in the name of the Lord." (12)

SEGUE: A repudiation of the very heart of rabbinic faith? True faith comes from and is a gift from God. The opinions of rabbis, after the destruction of the Temple, changed to account for the destroyed Temple and the new Christian faith. Tradition is fine but should not be elevated to the status of God's word. It is opinion i.e. commentary, it is not the word of the Lord. This dependence on the oral tradition over the clear, straightforward meaning of the Tenakh and the witnessed testimony of one who performed miracles in God's Name and prophesied rightly is what prejudices Jewish opinion concerning Yeshua.

OBJECTION: To reject Jesus in his lifetime or after was to condemn oneself as an unbeliever. This hardly seems fair. You were supposed to acknowledge Jesus in a role he refused to publicly claim? (13)

RESPONSE: Yeshua clearly proclaimed his Messiahship and his Sonship in relation to God the Father. He was so clear that he was on the verge of being stoned on more than one occasion. Further, any who approached Yeshua in person, or after the Ascension in prayer, and sincerely asked for help to believe was so helped. If the Gospel writers are harsh with anyone it is with the Jewish religious leadership in Jerusalem, not other Jews as the Objection suggested. It is entirely possible that the Jewish religious leadership had been corrupted by the Romans. In the Gospel of Matthew Yeshua tells the Pharisees they ARE condemned AS hypocrites -- a most severe condemnation that implies they knew the truth but denied it and misled others away from the truth. The Pharisees tell Yeshua, "Rabbi we know that you are true and teach the way of God truthfully". If they were lying they were violating the law, if they were telling the truth then why conspire against Yeshua? The Objection fails to realize that Yeshua made them look bad in public. Instead, they wanted this same public to look up to them. What we see from them is false pride, jealousy, and envy. The Objection has no problem subtly casting doubt on the motives of Yeshua and the New Covenant authors yet it finds no such fault in those who would reject Yeshua and lead other Jews to do the same. If Yeshua was a fraud they did well but if Yeshua was Lord then they bear responsibility for keeping the People of the Covenant from their Messiah. (14)

SEGUE: The Lord's first Love is forever the people of Israel. The non-Jewish believers of Yeshua are God's adopted. St. Paul wrote in his letter to the Romans "Lest you be wise in your own conceits, I want you to understand this mystery brothers, a hardening has come upon part of Israel until the full number of the Gentiles come in and so all Israel will be saved, as it is written (Isa. 59:20-21) The Deliverer will come from Zion and will banish ungodliness from Jacob, (Isa. 27:9). This will be my covenant with them when I take away their sins." (15)

OBJECTION: Jesus never told them who he was. Probably he entertained the possibility that Peter was right, that his messiahship would be revealed clearly to him, by God at a later date that never came; Henceforth, the foxiness and the reluctance to go public. He was pleased by the idea, but not entirely confident that it was true: (16)

RESPONSE: These statements are directed at Jewish people who are not learned about Yeshua. Yeshua played down the term messiah because of its political significance but he never played down that he was the Lord. It is clear from Zech.14 that Messiah and the Lord are one and the same. By saying "Probably he entertained" the Objection to reconciliation admittedly does not know. What it infers is that Yeshua cannot be the Messiah and Jews must not believe in him. The Gospel of Matthew recalls how Yeshua predicted his own death. When Yeshua predicted his death this did not display a lack of confidence but proper insight into the events that would occur. The Objection also stated "A later date that never came", but in fact it did. It is the burden of those who object to reconciliation to explain the Resurrection, New Covenant dialogue after the Resurrection, behavior of the modestly educated Galileans after the Resurrection, and the steadfastness of Yeshua's message. (17)

SEGUE: Arguments concerning Yeshua should be confined to scripture both Tenakh and New Covenant for those who refuse reconciliation. The question still remains what did Yeshua do wrong? Why did the Gentiles accept him? The Gentiles certainly were not looking for a Jewish Deity. It has always been the message and the sacrificial love that denied self. He sought blessings for others even those who reject the message.

OBJECTION: The Gospel writers faced the challenge that Jesus never raised an army, fought the Romans, returned any Jewish exiles, ruled over any population, or did anything else a king Messiah would do. His kingdom was not on any earthly stage but in the human heart. This is not what the Hebrew Bible had promised for the messianic future. (18)

RESPONSE: The distinctions in the Prophets between the "Suffering Servant" (viz Ps.22:1-21, Ps.110:1-3, Isa.53) and the "Conquering King" (viz Ps.22:22-31, 110:4-7) are quite clear. The former must redeem sinners from Adam on down who put their faith in God and His promises for a Redeemer who would cleanse them of sin. The latter would come subsequently to establish the Messianic Kingdom on earth. As Yeshua admitted to Pilate, "My Kingdom is not of this world." In Pilate's day, Yeshua's kingdom was supernatural and heavenly; it would not become an earthly kingdom until after crucifixion, resurrection, ascension, and a Second Coming. (19)

SEGUE: What the Bible promised was not necessarily what the oral tradition said it was. The choice is clearly between reading the Tenakh and accompanying Talmudic opinions and reading the Tenakh in the light of the New Covenant.

OBJECTION: Truly, I say to you this generation will not pass away till all these things take place. That didn't happen. (20)

RESPONSE: This verse is viewed as a proof that Yeshua got a prediction wrong. The context of Matt 24, like Mark 13 and Luke 21 concerns the end of the age, when the world as we know it will change. "This generation" does not apply to the generation of 2000 years ago but the generation that witnesses all these things taking place, a future generation. The "generation" that would see all of these events occur was not a generation of a human lifespan, but the "generation" of the church, or the "church age." Yeshua emphasized that no one on earth knew when the end would come or when he would return, but that the believers must be prepared for it at any time. As with many prophesies, especially Messianic ones, there is a partial fulfillment in the near future, to validate the prophet and the prophesy as true, and then a complete fulfillment in the distant future -- usually in the End Times or the Millennial kingdom.

SEGUE: The context of all three chapters in Matthew Mark and Luke speak of a future time. Although the Jerusalem that these first century Jews knew certainly came to an end in 70 C.E., the scope of the woe that is described deals with events that are approaching but have not as of yet occurred.

OBJECTION: Jesus' miracles are magical feats. If faith healings are to be considered valid what is the concern? He revived two "thought" to have died. The Messiah must rule as a monarch, rule over the earth, return the exiles, rebuild the Temple, defeat the oppressors and establishes universal peace. (21)

RESPONSE: Yeshua may have performed miracles and healed people and he may have revived the dead, but there is no mention of where he got the power and why he used this power to do good things. The argument disregards these feats claiming that he did not rule as a physical monarch. According to the Prophet Zechariah the Messiah is the Lord. All that was foretold by the prophets will be fulfilled. Yeshua's kingdom is not of this earth, but of the world to come. It is an eternal kingdom. He is truly a king by descent, by right, and by authority -- but he is dealing with a demonic rebellion led by Satan. The earth is rightly His, but under enemy occupation. Yeshua's people are His -- He knows them, they know Him, and He assures them of eternal life, resurrection, and joy in His presence in heaven and on the reclaimed earth when all of the promises will be fulfilled in earthly terms in His Second Coming. (22)

SEGUE: Are we to dismiss everything Yeshua said and did according to the Talmudic tradition? The first century Jewish leaders were permitted by Rome to assume their religious authority because they didn't oppose Rome. Pilate didn't care whom the Jews believed in or what religious directions they followed, so long as there was order in the city and taxes were paid in full and on time. He was a "moderate pragmatist," who could sincerely ask "What is truth?" The Jewish leaders were desperate to retain their socio-religious and economic power over the Jews and the very profitable system surrounding the Temple and the quarterly pilgrimages (The Sh'losh Reglaim of Pesakh, Shavuous, and Sukkos plus the High Holy Days of Yom T'ruah [Day of Trumpets =Rosh Hashonnah] and Yom Kippur [Day of Atonement]). The Romans were the inventors of federalism -- unlike the Greeks and Egyptians, and more comprehensively than the Persians, they tried to minimize the intrusiveness of their rule by allowing for a high degree of self-governance by conquered peoples. Judea originally had a Jewish political ruling elite (lost due to rebellions), and its social, commercial, and civil law were administered by the Sanhedrin, not Roman courts. The Romans only enforced law pertaining to payment of taxes, proper respect to the Emperor (worship wasn't required until later), not impeding Roman troop movements, and not conspiring against the Roman conquest, etc. The Romans put the Latin Pilate in charge after the Jews repeatedly revolted against the increasingly corrupt and dissolute Herodian line. The Romans were being manipulated by the collaborating Jewish leaders as the Jews were being manipulated by Rome. The Jewish leaders had long ago fallen out of step with God's plan for the Jewish people, and were "doing their own thing." God judged them accordingly -- He set them aside as His ministers, and established the church to do His work. But His promises to the Patriarchs remained -- the Land remained covenanted to the Children of Israel. Jewish people today and for the past 2000 years have denied Yeshua based on their decision. If their decisions were based on Roman corruption and protection of their appointed status then Jewish people have based their decision on the Sanhedrin's less than perfect conclusion. According to John's Gospel "Many of the Judeans therefore who had come with Mary and had seen what he did, believed in him; but some of them went to the Pharisees and told them what Yeshua had done. So the Chief Priests and the Pharisees gathered the council and said what are we to do? For this man performs many signs. If we let him go on then everyone will believe in him and the Romans will come and destroy both our holy places and our nation. But one of them Caiaphas who was High Priest that year, said to them, You know nothing at all; you do not understand that it is expedient for you that one man should die for the people and that the whole nation should not perish. He did not say this of his own accord, but being High Priest that year he prophesied that Yeshua should die for the nation and not for the nation only, but to gather into one the children of God who are scattered abroad. So from that day on they took counsel how to put him to death." These leaders convinced their contemporaries and those who would come after to reject Yeshua, yet Jerusalem, the Temple and the nation were still destroyed 40 years later. (23)

OBJECTION: Let Jesus come up with the real messianic goods, visible to all rather than requiring us to accept someone's assurance that for example, he was born in Bethlehem and then we'll take him seriously: (24)

RESPONSE: According to this objection the assurances of some 2000 years ago are to be dismissed, even with a historical explanation provided in the New Covenant text. However, this argument has no problem accepting the historical records of the first Passover that occurred 3400 years ago with miracles and all. The only way that the Objection to reconciliation can deny Christianity is to attack its text. Basically, Yeshua, who came in God's name, cannot be the Messiah but this argument will accept one who comes in his own name. (25)

SEGUE: The Objection wished to remove faith. These are the messianic goods. Read the scripture, free of rabbinical commentary, study the New Covenant to determine if Yeshua is worthy of such a designation then seek God in prayer. Those who truly seek will find, and those who find will never have to deny who they are; Jews if Jewish and Gentile if of the nations.

OBJECTION: <u>But on the days leading up to Passover in the year 30, his movement suddenly exploded in numbers and enthusiasm. It spun out of Jesus' control:</u> (26)

RESPONSE: The Gospel writers all give an account of Yeshua's entry into Jerusalem on Palm Sunday. The crowd shouted "Hosanna to the Son of David, Hosanna in the highest." How is any of this spinning out of control? An argument can be made when Yeshua alone drove out the money lenders from the Temple. This account can be found in Matt.21:12-13; Mark 11:15-17; and Luke 19: 45-46. Those following Yeshua do nothing wrong to anyone. How is this spinning out of Yeshua's control? It goes back to the envy of the Temple priests and religious leaders because they were not only losing the popularity contest, but were appointed by the Romans to have the positions that they held and maintain order. The Yeshua phenomenon was a perceived threat to that Roman order. (27)

SEGUE: This argument acknowledges that Yeshua had a following, yet his actions at the Temple prove that he was not trying to win a popularity contest. Those who followed him did not cause a riot or harm anyone. In another instance those who rejected Yeshua caused such a commotion that Pilate himself feared that a riot was beginning. Pilate, especially after hearing Herodia's dream (the Romans were very superstitious and took dreams and portents seriously), did all he could (short of putting his own position and liberty at risk) NOT to imprison or execute Yeshua. He repeatedly tried to get Yeshua off his hands, but the leaders among the Kohanim (priesthood) and the Pharisees in the Sanhedrin finally forced Pilate into action by insisting that since Yeshua claimed to be king of the Jews, He was denying the authority of Caesar, and that anyone in authority who tolerated such treason against Rome was no friend of Caesar (and hence worthy of being relieved and brought back to Rome in chains). With this thinly veiled threat (and the Jewish leaders had contacts back in Rome who could bring these charges before Caesar, and Pilate knew it), Pilate caved in and did what was personally and politically expedient. (28)

OBJECTION: <u>If contemporaries believed that Jesus worked his miracles by the misapplication of the power of God's name, by blasphemy -- we can imagine why they would not object to seeing him killed</u>: (29)

RESPONSE: What miracles did Yeshua perform? He healed people, raised the dead, fed people, calmed a storm, and walked on water to save Peter. Where did Yeshua get this power a power that he only used for good? Many of those who he came to save hated him because they were jealous of him and were corrupted by the Roman imperial power that bestowed their position.

SEGUE: In the Book of Numbers Moses states," He who blasphemes the name of the Lord shall be put to death; all of the congregation shall stone him." This term defined meant Blasphemy-Impious, profane or mocking speech concerning God or sacred things. Also, expressing contempt or scorn for the authority of God and being Impious-Irreligious; Profane-irreverent. By definition the blasphemy charge was inaccurate. He was not impious, profane, mocking, contemptible or scornful. By these definitions he was never a blasphemer. Furthermore; the prescribed mode of death was stoning not Roman crucifixion. (30)

OBJECTION: <u>We possess no reliable record of how Jews who had not become followers of Jesus reacted to such tales</u>: (31)

RESPONSE: The post-resurrection account in the Gospel of Matthew contradicts this argument. These folks who did not object to seeing Yeshua killed had no objection to giving/taking a bribe when they had no explanation for what just happened? In other words if the testimony of the New Covenant authors agreed with the Talmud it was true and where it did not agree with the Talmud then that account given by the New Covenant was false. (32)

SEGUE: The reason that Jewish sources other than those who wrote the New Covenant were silent was because they had no explanation for post resurrection events nor did the Jews or the Romans ever locate a Yeshua corpse. This is true and beyond dispute.

OBJECTION: <u>Perhaps the tomb wasn't sealed; perhaps wild dogs ate the body; perhaps the resurrected Jesus was really his brother James. We don't know</u>. (33)

RESPONSE: This is the definitive argument against the resurrection. According to St. Matthew's account the Pharisees got permission from Pilate to make the tomb especially secure by sealing the stone and setting a guard. The litany of "Perhaps" takes none of this into account let alone all of the Post-Resurrection dialogue found in all the Gospels, the Acts of the Apostles and the Epistles of St. Paul. According to Matt.27:62-66, the guard on Yeshua's tomb was a Jewish Temple guard, but placed with Pilate's approval -- they would have been pretty hard to bribe into allowing Yeshua's body to be taken away, and in the aftermath, they would probably have been tortured in response to claims that the seal had been broken and stone had been removed by divine powers. Yet, apparently, no one was able to get evidence from the guard to disprove the Christian claim -- and I'm sure they'd have tried pretty hard to get such evidence to silence the "Yeshua movement" once and for all. The priests and Pharisees wanted that tomb sealed and occupied, not unsealed and empty. Wild dogs would not have approached an armed guard, and even if the guards had been derelict and were sleeping somewhere, the dogs would not have eaten large bones, nor would they have folded the death cloths. There's no indication of a Roman guard. (34)

SEGUE: This event is problematic for those who oppose reconciliation. The wild dogs would not have eaten the cloth nor would they have left no trail only three days after the crucifixion. The guards told a different story and beyond the inability to locate the "Corpus Mortem" undeniably lives were changed.

OBJECTION: Maybe the notion of a messiah who dies was known; they must have understood the verse from Zechariah in some other way. (35)

RESPONSE: This argument once again proves that the Objection to reconciliation does not know. There must be some explanation but the resurrection of Yeshua cannot be one of those options it must be anything except Yeshua as Messiah therefore conjectures as to what occurred reigns with those who refuse to accept the saving claim of Yeshua.

SEGUE: As one goes through these arguments it becomes clear that there are no rock solid alternate explanations to the resurrection of Yeshua.

OBJECTION: If Jesus set himself up as an authority independent of Jewish tradition this-rather than the fact that he died-would have definitely ruled him out as a claimant to the exalted messianic role. (36)

RESPONSE: Where in the Torah does it state that the oral tradition is on par with Yahveh's revelation to Moses? None of this answers the question why Paul and the Apostles suffered as they did to bring this message to the world. The heart felt reason why the Judeans rejected Paul's message is the same reason as today. Jews assume that they will recognize their Messiah. From Yeshua through Bar Kochbah to Sabbatai Zvi they have always been wrong. How can a people psychologically deal with or entertain the notion that their religious leaders handed over the Holy One of Israel to the Pagans who brutalized him to death? Only by declaring him a fraud and stating that he got what he deserved. To admit otherwise would place culpability on the Jewish leaders of that day and place the oral tradition of the rabbis as nothing more than a rendering of men. Neither the Sadducees nor the Essenes agreed with the Pharisees that "Jewish tradition" or "rabbinical tradition" held sway. The former rejected everything beyond the Torah (including the rest of the Tenakh) as being the writing of men, not the Word of God. The Essenes held to the entirety of the Tenakh but viewed the Pharisees as corrupters and false teachers. The Sadducees and Essenes disappeared no later than the end of Bar Kochbah's Rebellion (135 C.E.), and as a result, Orthodox rabbinical Judaism (and offshoots like Khasidism) is the direct descendant of Pharisaical Judaism. Yeshua extensively quoted the Tenakh and in God the Father's name performed literal "good works" -- miracles that could only be seen as praiseworthy such as healings. It would seem that it is the rabbis, not Yeshua, who were blasphemous and rebellious against the Word of God, preferring their own rules and rituals.

SEGUE: If Yeshua pointed to the Tenakh to prove that he was the Messiah then those who point to the Jewish tradition must also point to the Tenakh and prove their point that the Tenakh foretells the importance of the oral tradition and that it is needed to interpret the Tenakh.

OBJECTION: <u>It is not clear what the phrase Son of God actually meant. Jesus likely did not think of himself as divine</u>. (37)

RESPONSE: The Apostle Paul and the Jewish Gospel writers were not conflicted when it came to how Yeshua viewed himself. Yeshua was not conflicted. He knew who he was with certainty. This argument again wants a Jewish audience to know that those who oppose reconciliation have everything figured out and the gospel writers are a bunch of self-serving liars. The Jews of the day had no doubt that Yeshua meant the phrase Son of God to mean that He was a part of the very nature and presence of God, along with the Father and the Ruakh HaKodesh. That is why they tried to stone Him on more than one occasion. He acknowledged that He had been declared "king of the Jews," but clarified this to Pilate by saying "My Kingdom is not of this world." He knew exactly what He was saying, and so did those listening to Him. (38)

SEGUE: Trying to place doubt in the historical Yeshua with the Gospels as a resource is a losing proposition. To insinuate that Yeshua was conflicted has no basis in fact only conjecture of those who refuse to believe.

OBJECTION: <u>The fact that Jesus had planted seeds of a religion whose overall message abrogated Torah observance was enough to condemn all Jews who counted themselves as his followers</u>. (39)

RESPONSE: The Gospel account in Matthew makes the objection, as stated above, look opportunistic. Just as other arguments fail to distinguish between Gentile and Jewish believers in Yeshua, the Objection to reconciliation claims that Yeshua sought to abrogate the Torah and thus his followers are condemned. This Objection refuses to distinguish between The Talmud and the Torah. These views are contradicted by Yeshua's actions during his ministry. He clearly placed more emphasis on doing well than being perceived as doing many religious rituals. Yeshua was more interested in internal piety vice external piety. The issue again is with the Talmud not the Torah. (40)

SEGUE: The fact that Yeshua was an observant Jew is borne out in the Scriptures. Matthew's Gospel makes it clear that Yeshua never abrogated the Law of Moses.

OBJECTION: The True Messiah would not have found a religion that presumed to abolish the commandments. (41)

RESPONSE: In the Gospel of Matthew Yeshua states, "Think not that I have come to abolish the law and the prophets. I have come not to abolish them but to fulfill them." Rather, Yeshua states the following to the Pharisees and Scribes, "Why do you break the commandment of God for the sake of your tradition. For God commanded. Honor your father and mother and he who speaks evil of father and mother let him surely die. But you say If anyone tells his father or mother what you would have gained from me is given to God he need not honor his father. So for the sake of your tradition you have made void the word of God." When asked by a Jewish lawyer which is the greatest commandment in the law Yeshua quotes Deut.6:5 and Lev.19:18. In the Gospel of Mark Yeshua lists the commandments to be followed by quoting. Ex.20 and Deut.5 St. Paul reaffirms the Commandments in his Letter to the Romans. In the Gospel of Luke Yeshua while affirming the Commandments also speaks of the heart and the Gospel. "The heart is what matters; the law and Prophets were until John, the Good News of the Kingdom is now preached. It is easier for heaven and earth pass away than for one dot of the law to become void. "St. Paul recognized the commandments but stated they are summed up by Lev.19:18. "Love does no wrong to a neighbor therefore love is the fulfilling of the law." St. John states in his Epistle "By this we know that we love the children of God when we love God and obey his Commandments. For this is the love of God that we keep his Commandments." (42)

SEGUE: For believers in Yeshua what is listed above is not optional. It must be followed. There never was an abrogation of the law by Yeshua. There is a repudiation of Rabbinical Judaism as detailed by the Oral Torah/ Talmud, but the Commandments given by God were never abrogated by Yeshua or any of the New Covenant Authors.

OBJECTION: <u>Luther believed that the Catholic Church promoted the worship of idols. If Luther was right Jesus could not be the Messiah because according to Isa.2:18 the coming of the true Messiah would abolish the idols</u>. (43)

RESPONSE: The precondition for Isa. 2 is the latter days when the word of the Lord goes forth from Jerusalem. It's a time when there will be no more war, when the Lord is exalted. The idols are explained in verse 20 "In that day men will cast forth their idols of silver and gold which they made for them to worship. Catholics have statues that are 3 dimensional representations of Bible Characters. The veneration of saints bothered Luther and there were Biblically illiterate Catholics who over did it with the statues. The Church however did not make silver and gold idols and tell people to worship them. Reconcile the child born in Bethlehem with one coming on the clouds in power and to the Ancient of Days (Dan.7:13-14). Isa.2 is speaking of this future time.

However, Messiah is also a son of David and therefore had to be born in Bethlehem. Isa.2:18 does not prove that Yeshua was not the Messiah. Just as Jewish people can make a distinction between Moses and Jewish people who fall short of keeping the law blamelessly, so there must also be a distinction between Yeshua and Christians who fall short of Yeshua's teachings. The rabbinical traditions that equated aspects of the Temple and its rituals as equal to the holiness of God Himself were as much a matter of idolatry as any graven image. Sadly, the Orthodox and Roman Catholic Churches lapsed into a dangerous situation where it became easy for the ignorant and/or confused and/or misled to begin praying to the saints, to "holy relics," and to images of Christ, Mary, and the saints as if they had saving or beneficent power in themselves. This did not happen until centuries after the founding of the church 35 C.E. The Roman Catholic Church also lapsed into the errors of the late Aaronic Temple priesthood by acting as if they could forgive sin by their own authority (granting of indulgences) and by arrogating and sometimes abusing the application of apostolic authority unto themselves (such authority was placed upon the chosen disciples who had been in the physical presence of Christ and upon Paul, nee Saul of Tarsus, who had clearly and inarguably been touched and transformed by the presence of Yeshua). The Roman Catholic Church has subsequently recanted the granting of indulgences as identified by Luther and other medieval reformers. The Catechism of the Roman Catholic Church clearly states that one can pray to the departed saints, including Mary, for intercessory prayer on their behalf to the Son and the Father, but that the departed saints now in heaven have no power in themselves to influence events on earth. Errors in belief and practice among the faithful do not in themselves prove error in belief or doctrine in any faith.

SEGUE: St Paul spoke of stumbling blocks. Certainly ritualistic Christians can unwittingly do this through prayers in front of statues or icons. These creations should be viewed for what they are works of art. No believing Christian would ever tell a Jewish person that an icon, painting or statue that represents the sanctified can of itself answer prayer or receive prayer. That is reserved for God alone.

A FINAL WORD CONCERNING YESHUA AS PRESENTED IN THIS CHAPTER

For those believing that Yeshua is the Messiah, Son of God, those who are not sure, and those who are still opposed to reconciliation, kindly consider the following. History, both Jewish and non-Jewish, is full of examples of humanity's sinfulness. How can we who are imperfect stand justified before a Holy and Just God? We cannot do enough good deeds to cancel our sins in order to be blameless before a Holy and Just God. Therefore God sent what was Holy and sinless into the world to bear our sin and guilt. By exercising our free will those who accept this vicarious sacrifice for sin are deemed acceptable to God for we have accepted God's perfect sacrifice and are redeemed. In order to give us hope Yeshua the Messiah not only died for all who accept him but also overcame death by rising from the dead and ascending to heaven according to the Scriptures. Since he rose and ascended he will come again to establish his Kingdom and bring true peace as foretold by the Prophets. Yeshua is the Son of God and Messiah because he came from God, fulfilled the scriptures concerning the suffering servant, told the truth, resurrected and ascended into heaven. If this is true Yeshua is the Messiah the Son of God and thus deserves Lordship over our lives. This book makes the case that Yeshua is the Son of God, the Messiah and reconciliation is a good thing for not only the Jewish people but the world. The "reconciliation" described here is reconciliation between Jews AND all other people with a Holy, Pure God into whose presence no one impure in thought, word, or deed can enter. However, if we are to conclude that Yeshua is not the Son of God, the Messiah we must conclude that he is either a liar, delusional, or the New Covenant Authors fabricated the texts.

Was Yeshua a liar?

If Yeshua was a pathologic liar then he was a bad person. Selfish people lie to knowingly cover the truth or profit and pursue money, fame, pleasure or power. The evidence suggests if Yeshua was a pathological liar he was not a good one because in his pursuit of worldly gain he received hatred, rejection, persecution, torture and death. If Yeshua were a pathological liar none of these earthly pursuits were realized, therefore he was a bad liar. But wait! His Apostles and Disciples were convinced that he was not only sinless during his life but actually the Son of God. What we know about Yeshua states that he was unselfish, loving, caring compassionate, gave examples and taught about truth, he also healed and always helped others. The accounts that we have of Yeshua has him continually predicting his rejection, suffering, and execution. Folks, these are not the traits of a pathological liar. (44)

Was Yeshua delusional?

If Yeshua was delusional then he really believed he was the Messiah and the Son of God when he was not. Since these statements would also be untrue it would prove that Yeshua was mentally ill and a liar because his statements were not true. It is true that many people have had a "messianic" complex and modern science has had the opportunity to study them in asylums. Delusional lunatics suffer from psychopathology. They are mentally ill. The traits of these psychopathological suffers are egoism, narcissism, inflexibility, dullness, predictability, unable to really understand and love other people, and the inability to creatively relate to other people. What we know of Yeshua is that he was concerned about the welfare of others. He lived modestly and followed his convictions to a public execution. If he were consumed this self love his motivations and actions towards others would not have been that profound. Yeshua enjoyed discourse with those close to him and the masses. He taught people to love, but ultimately left the decision to listen and follow him up to the individual. Yeshua was never dull. No believer or non-believer ever accused him of this for Yeshua's words challenge us. Yeshua was never predictable. No one knew what he was going to say next. He had insights into the behaviors of others and telling them how to get right with God. He did and continues to move and motivate his followers to a holy life and communion with the God of Abraham. Yeshua's words and actions as recorded in the New Covenant are not those of a person who was delusional. The selflessness and caring for others unto death do not fit the profile of a delusional personality. (45)

Was the story of Yeshua as written by the four Evangelists in the 1st Century C.E. fabricated?

If the four Evangelists fabricated this lie, what was their selfish motivation? We know what they ultimately gained from their testimony persecution and execution. If they all knew this was a hoax why could history not produce one insider who could pull the plug on the grandest deception ever perpetrated on humankind? Thousands who knew them and followed afterward also suffered persecution torture and death. Not one of them knew this was a hoax? How could this lie eventually win the hearts of the Romans? The sanctity of these saints and martyrs converted the Romans. Why would the early Jewish believers in Yeshua invent a story where God becomes a Jew, who is rejected by his own people and then this Jew who is the real messiah gets nailed to a tree by the conquerors of the Jewish people, the Romans? Why would these Jews invent and agree on this story? 25 of 27 books written in the New Covenant were written by Jews and no one deviates from this story. Since three of the four Gospel accounts were written within 40 years of Yeshua's life wouldn't some people be alive and know that the accounts of Yeshua's life were a hoax? Could these Evangelists invent the most compelling story of human history if they were liars or delusional men? We know the Yeshua story was not invented by later generations because we have five hundred consistent different manuscripts of the New Covenant that date prior to 500 C.E. Most of St. Paul's letters to the early churches predate the Gospels and his testimony is most certainly consistent with the Gospel accounts. The details contained in the Gospels are also consistent with what we know of first century life in Judea and the Galilee. Why would these mythmakers risk crucifixion, stoning and decapitation for their fabricated belief in the Lordship of Yeshua including His resurrection from the dead and post-resurrection dialogue that included Yeshua and his disciples? (46)

Did Yeshua rise from the dead?

When it comes to the resurrection of Yeshua we have a few more options. We can believe that he rose from the dead. This proves beyond doubt that Yeshua is the Messiah the Son of God. We can believe that all of Yeshua's followers thought that they experienced Yeshua after the crucifixion. We can believe that the Apostles conspired to make up the story including stealing his body, and we can believe that Yeshua resuscitated in the grave, meaning he never died on the cross.

Did Yeshua resuscitate from a supposed death?

Let's tackle the swoon theory first. What we know is that Yeshua was shredded with a Roman flagellum perhaps 50 to 100 times. He was further beaten and crowned with a cap of 1-2 inch thorns which were driven into his head as his Roman torturers continued to beat Yeshua on the head. He carried a 75-125 pound crossbeam (patibulum) on his back where he fell many times to his final destination outside of Jerusalem. At the place called Golgotha 7 inch iron spikes ½ inch wide were driven though his wrists. Then another larger spike was driven through His feet. When the cross was lifted and dropped into its base dug into the ground his shoulder and elbow joints were dislocated. Breathing became a painful ordeal of pulling himself up against the spike in his pierced feet and letting gravity pull him down which caused further pain in his wrists. The agony would not cease. Yeshua, hardly recognizable from this torment exists 6 hours on the cross and then he died. To make sure Yeshua was dead a Roman soldier drove his spear through the right side of Yeshua towards his heart and the spear exited out of Yeshua's back. Yeshua was eventually taken from the cross and wrapped according to Jewish custom with linen and spices before being placed in the tomb of Joseph of Arimathea where a two ton stone was rolled to secure the tomb entrance. Then based on Jewish insistence Pilate granted that a guard was posted at the tomb to ensure that the body could not be taken by one of his followers. (47)

For anyone to believe that Yeshua resuscitated in the tomb three days after enduring the most horrible torture and execution one must believe that he unwrapped himself, somehow found clean cloths, moved a two ton stone, walked on mutilated feet and sometime later really died. If this happened where were the posted guards? To entertain the notion that Yeshua resuscitated one must also believe that the accounts of the Apostles are all lies. What one must answer is if any person endured this horror could anyone escape death and resuscitate three days later with no medical treatment? (48)

Did the Apostles deceive us by embellishing the facts or stealing Yeshua's body?

According to the gospel accounts the Apostles never thought that Yeshua was going to resurrect. When these events occurred they all ran for cover except for John who witnessed the crucifixion. The Apostles would have had to quickly gain courage, over power a Roman-approved Temple guard; let's just say they would have had to have neutralized the Temple guard, whether by force, by guile, or by bribery and there is no indication that they had or would have been able to do so, move the Stone, take the body and then dispose of it in such a way that it could never be located. Then all must conspire to write false accounts and go to eventual painful deaths knowing that they were all dieing for this lie. In addition not one of them or those who followed would ever capitulate and tell the real truth. What could any of them gain in this world by perpetuating this hoax? Can living a known lie sustain one through eventual torture and death? Those who would have been knowledgeable of this hoax were eventually hated, scorned, persecuted, forbidden from synagogue observance, imprisoned, tortured, exiled, crucified, boiled alive, roasted, beheaded, disemboweled, and fed to lions. In the book of Acts the Apostles boldly proclaim Yeshua rose from the dead weeks after the events of the passion in Jerusalem in front of the Jews and Romans casts doubt on this theory. (49)

Did the Apostles and disciples only imagine that they saw Yeshua resurrected?

If this is true then the following people imagined that they saw the risen Messiah: The Women who returned from the empty tomb and reported that an angel told them that Yeshua had risen Matt. 28:1-10; to Mary Magdalene John 20:10-18, Mark 16:9-11; to Peter Luke 24:34, 1Cor. 15:5; to Cleopas and another disciple on the road to Emmaus Luke 24:13-35, Mark 16:12-13; to 10 Apostles minus Thomas on resurrection Sunday Luke 24:36-40, John 20:19-23, 1Cor:15-5, Mark 16:14-18; to 11 Apostles including Thomas John 20:26-28; to some of the disciples at the sea of Galilee John

21:1-23; to the Apostles in the Galilee Matt. 28:16-20; to James 1Cor. 15:7; to the Apostles at the Ascension Luke 24:50-52, Acts 1:3-8, Mark 16-19; to 500 believers 1Cor 15:6; and to Saul of Tarsus on the Damascus road 1Cor 15:8, Acts 9:1-9. To believe that all of these people imagined seeing Yeshua resurrected at different times meant that the tomb had to have been empty. This mass appearing would have been meaningless if Yeshua's body was still in the tomb. If the body was still in the tomb, easy to verify, the stories of his appearing would have been dismissed. If the appearances were only imagined by many different people at different times then how do we explain the empty tomb, the rolled stone, and the missing corpse? The Romans and Jews would have had no reason to disturb the corpse. (50)

How therefore can we conclude this chapter?

For those who opposed reconciliation as they began to read this book one must ask; what is the likelihood that Yeshua was a pathological liar? What is the likelihood that Yeshua was delusional? What is the likelihood that all of the Authors of the New Covenant fabricated the life of Yeshua? What is the likelihood that Yeshua resuscitated after being beaten, scourged, carrying a cross in a weakened state, crucified for 6 hours, pierced through the heart with a spear, then laid in a tomb for three days with no food or medical attention? What is the likelihood that the Apostles stole the body of Yeshua from a guarded tomb and or fabricated the entire account of the resurrection while never disclosing their fraud and kept this all secret even to their own painful deaths? What is the likelihood that many people in many different places only imagined that they experienced the resurrected Messiah? If you find yourself running out of excuses then kindly consider reconciliation with Yeshua. In doing so he will become your Atonement, he will become your Savior, He will become your Messiah and he will become your Lord in unity with the God of Abraham, Isaac and Jacob in fulfillment of the promises that God made through the Patriarchs, Moses, the Judges, The House of David , the Psalmists, and the Prophets.

Chapter 8 Notes

1. Klinghoffer, P.33; Dan.9:26; Gen.17:14; Ex.12:15; 31:14; Lev.7:20; 18: 29; 22:3; Num. 19:20
2. Luke 2:21-24; Matt.26:14-19; Mark 14:12; Luke 22:7-8, 14-16; John 13:1; Matt.12: 1-8, 9-14; Luke 4:31-44
3. Klinghoffer, P.43
4. Ibid, P.47
5. Ibid, P.48
6. Matt.27:22-23; Mark 14:63-65; Luke 23:10-11, 22-23, 35; John 18:35; 19:7, 15; Acts 3: 13-15, 17
7. Klinghoffer, P.48
8. Revised Standard Version Bible, Dictionary of the Bible PP.37-39; Jamisson Faucett & Brown Commentary, PP.879, 952, 987, 1025; William MacDonald Bible Commentary, PP.1202, 1318, 1367-1368, 1464; Matt.1:18-25; Mark 1:1; Luke 1:26-35; John 1:1-5

9. 9. Klinghoffer, P.57; M. Shabbat 7:2; 14:3; Yoma 8:6
10. 10. John 5:6-18
11. 11. Klinghoffer, P.59
12. 12. Matt.23:37-39
13. Klinghoffer, P.61
14. Matt. 22:15-16; 21:23-32, 41-46
15. Rom. 11:25-27
16. Klinghoffer, P.62
17. Matt. 12: 38-42
18. Klinghoffer, P.63
19. Isa.61:1-2 (Luke 4:18-19), Isa.6:9-10 (Matt.13:14-15), and Isa.29:13 (Matt.15:8-9)
20. Klinghoffer, P.70; Matt. 24:34
21. Ibid, P.71
22. Zech.14:1-5
23. John 11:45-53
24. Klinghoffer, P.71
25. John 5:39-47
26. Klinghoffer, P.74
27. Matt.21:1-9; Mark 11:1-10; Luke 19:29-38; John 12:12-18
28. Matt: 27:23-24
29. Klinghoffer, P.77
30. Num. 24:16
31. Klinghoffer, P.77
32. Matt. 28:11-15
33. Klinghoffer, P.77

34. Matt 27:62-66
35. Klinghoffer, P.85
36. Ibid, PP.101-103
37. Ibid, P 103
38. 1Cor 8:6; Matt.12:40-41; 25:31-34; 26:39; Mark 14:36; John 5:17, 14:9, 17:11
39. Klinghoffer, P.117
40. Matt. 5:17-20
41. Klinghoffer, P.138
42. Matt.5:17; Matt.15:3-6; Matt.22:35-40; Mark 10:19; Rom.13:8-10; Luke 16:15-17; 1John5:2-3
43. Klinghoffer, P.202
44. Kreeft & Tacelli, PP.158,160
45. Ibid, P.159
46. Ibid, PP.156-157, 160-165
47. Ankerberg & Weldon, PP.17-27
48. Ibid, PP.185; Kreeft & Tacelli, PP.183-184
49. Ibid, P.186; Ibid, PP.185-186
50. Ibid, PP.64-71, 187; Ibid, PP.187-188

CONCLUSION:

To all who have endured through this journey, thank you. For those of you who are now convinced that Yeshua is the heir, the Holy One sent by God, Welcome. For those of you who want to be adopted by the Father there are numerous Churches that will welcome you into the family. For members of the Mishpocah who are now convinced that Yeshua is the messiah, welcome to you also. As I stated in the Foreword, there is no reason for you to give up or compromise your Jewishness. The church has finally come to recognize that one can, and always has been, able to accept the Messiahship of Yeshua and the redemption from sin He purchased for mankind on the cross while remaining culturally Jewish and observing the feasts and fasts of Israel as prescribed by Scripture. Some of you still may not be sure. By all means continue in prayer and study the scriptures further to settle the issue in your mind. The God of Abraham alone will tend to our hearts, because all who seek Him will find Him, for He is near at hand, and not distant.

BIBLIOGRAPHY

Ankerberg, John & Weldon, John; The Passion and the Empty Tomb. Eugene Oregon: Harvest House, 2005

Berger, David, translator and editor. The Jewish-Christian Debate in the High Middle Ages. Philadelphia: Jewish Publication Society, 1979

Bruce, F.F. The New Covenant Documents: Are They Reliable? Downers Grove, IL: Inter Varsity Press, 1971

Chevallier, Temple. The Apologies of Justin Martyr and Tertullian, London: Rivington, 1851

Eusebius. The History of the Church, Translated by G.A. Williamson, London: Penguin, 1965

Falk, Harvey. Journal of Ecumenical Studies, PP 105-111, 1982

Flannery, Austin. Vatican Council II, Northport, N.Y: Costello Publishing Company, Inc., 1987

Harkavy, Alexander. Holy Scriptures. New York: Hebrew Publishing Company, 1936

Hereford, R. Travers. Christianity in Talmud and Midrash, New York: Ktav Publishing House, 1975

Jamieson, Fausset, and Brown. Commentary on the Whole Bible. Grand Rapids: Zondervan, 1976

Jaynes, Julian. The Origin of Consciousness in the Breakdown of the Bicameral Mind, Boston: Houghton Mifflin, 1976

Katz, Jacob. Exclusiveness and Tolerance: Studies in Jewish-Gentile Relations in Medieval & Modern Times. West Orange, N.J.: Berhman House, 1961

Kee/Young/Froehlich. Understanding the New Covenant. Englewood Cliffs, New Jersey: Prentice-Hall Inc., 1973

Kennedy, D. James. What if Jesus had never been born? Nashville: Thomas Nelson Inc, 1994

Kimchi, Joseph. The Book of the Covenant. Toronto: Pontifical Institute of Medieval Studies. Translated by Frank Talmage, 1972

Klinghoffer, David. Why the Jews rejected Jesus. New York: Doubleday, 2005

Kreeft, Peter &Tacelli, Ronald K. Handbook of Christian Apologetics, Downers Grove, Illinois: Intervarsity Press, 1994

Lindsay, Hal. The Messiah. Eugene: Harvest House, 1982

Lockyer, Herbert. All the Messianic Prophecies of the Bible. Grand Rapids: Zondervan, 1973

Maccoby, Hyam. The Mythmaker: Paul and the Invention of Christianity. San Francisco: Harper, 1986

MacDonald, William. Believers Bible Commentary. Nashville: Thomas Nelson Inc, 1995

Maimonides, Moses. The Guide of the Perplexed. Translated by M. Friedlander. Reprint. New York: Dover, 1956

Maimonides, Moses. Mishneh Torah

Peters, F.E. Muhammad and the Origins of Islam. Albany: State University of New York Press, 1994

Revised Standard Version Bible. New York: Thomas Nelson Inc, 1972

Schoeman, Roy. Salvation is from the Jews. San Francisco: Ignatius Press, 2003

Shereshevsky, Ezra. "Rashi's and Christian Interpretation" Jewish Quarterly Review 61:76-86, 1970

Spencer, Robert. The Myth of Islamic Tolerance. Amherst: Prometheus, 2005

Spencer, Robert. The Truth about Muhammad. Washington D.C.: Regnery Publishing, 2006

Stein, Robert H. Difficult Passages in the New Covenant. Grand Rapids: Baker Book House, 1990

Strobel, Lee. Finding the Real Jesus. Grand Rapids: Zondervan, 2008

Talmage, Frank. Disputation and Dialogue: Readings in the Jewish-Christian Encounter. New York: Ktav Publishing House, 1975

Talmud, Babylonian

Talmud, Jerusalem

Twersky, Isadore. A Maimonides Reader. New York: Behrman House, 1972

Vermes, Geza. Jesus the Jew: A Historian's Reading of the Gospels. Philadelphia: Fortress Press. 1981

Whiston, William. The Works of Flavius Josephus. Grand Rapids: Baker Book House, 1980

Warraq, Ibn. Why I am not a Muslim. Amherst: Prometheus Books, 1995